Writing in the Computer Age

 A Headlands Press Book

Writing in the Computer Age

Word Processing Skills and Style for Every Writer

Andrew Fluegelman and Jeremy Joan Hewes

ANCHOR BOOKS
Anchor Press/Doubleday
Garden City, New York
1983

Produced by The Headlands Press, Inc.,
Tiburon, California

Design: Howard Jacobsen
Copy editor: Pat McClelland
Proofreader and consulting editor:
 Linda Gunnarson
Composition: Design & Type/TypeLine,
 San Francisco, California
Illustrations: Michael Fennelly
Mechanical production: Craig DuMonte

Library of Congress Cataloging in
Publication Data
Fluegelman, Andrew, 1943–
Writing in the Computer Age.
Bibliography: p. 249
Includes index.
1. Authorship—Data processing.
2. Word processing (Office practice)
I. Hewes, Jeremy Joan. II. Title
PN171.D37F58   1983   808'.02'072
81-43852
ISBN 0-385-18124-8
ISBN 0-385-18125-6 (pbk.)

First edition

To our parents,
who encouraged our appreciation for words
and our sense of adventure.

Contents

Part I: Skills

Chapter 1
New Tools of the Trade:
Hardware for Word Processing   27

The Parts of a System / The Computer / The Keyboard / Keyboard
Ergonomics / The Screen / Disk Drives / The Printer / Cords, Cables,
and Plugs

Chapter 2
Up and Running: Software for the System   43

Programs and Languages / Word Processors / Operating Systems /
Formatting and Booting / Getting Started

Part II: Style

List of Figures and Tables

Figures

Tables

Acknowledgments

We had a great deal of help from friends and professional colleagues as we did the research and prepared the manuscript for this book. Among the people who contributed to our understanding of both word processing and writing and offered suggestions for our text are Mike Young, Jim Edlin, Baron Wolman, David Bunnell, Barbara Dean, Larry Magid, Camilo Wilson, Cheryl Woodard, Larry Press, Melba Beals, Barbara Elman, Harvard C. Pennington, Candice Jacobson, Susan Mauk, Laurie McCann, David Burton, Kay Glowes, Stuart R. Schwartz, Linda Williams, Elizabeth Fishel, Mollie Katzen, and Carolly Erickson.

We also extend our grateful thanks to Jeannette Maher of International Business Machines Corporation in Boca Raton, Florida; Wendy Mitchell of MicroPro International in San Rafael, California; Paul Goldmacher, Dennis Abbott, and Chuck Kinch of Computer-Land in San Francisco; Larry Van Valkenburgh of Sunset Computers in San Francisco; and W.R. Kales for their cooperation and technical assistance.

We received generous advice and assistance from many computer manufacturers and software distributors, who provided us with copies of their word processing programs and manuals for evaluation. We wish to thank Artsci, Inc. (N. Hollywood, CA) for Magic Window and Basic Mailer; Digital Equipment Corporation (Marlboro, MA) for information on word processing software; International Business Machines Corporation for Displaywriter manuals; IJG Computer Services (Upland, CA) for Electric Pencil; Information Unlimited Software (Sausalito, CA) for EasyWriter and EasyWriter II; InfoSoft Systems (Westport, CT) for WpDaisy; Lexisoft, Inc. (Davis, CA) for Spellbinder; Lifetree Software (Monterey, CA) for Volkswriter; MicroPro International (San Rafael, CA) for WordStar, Mail-Merge, and SpellStar; Muse Software (Baltimore, MD) for Super Text II; Perfect Software (Berkeley, CA) for PerfectWriter; Radio Shack (Fort Worth, TX) for Scripsit; Select Information Systems (Kentfield, CA) for Select; Vector Graphic (Thousand Oaks, CA) for Memorite III; and Xerox Corporation for a demonstration of the 860 word processor and the Star work station.

Finally, we wish to thank the publishing colleagues who contributed their talents and expertise to this book: editors Lindy Hess and Laura Van Wormer of Doubleday and Company; literary agent Meredith Bernstein; designer Howard Jacobsen; copy editor Pat McClelland; proofreader and consulting editor Linda Gunnarson; and typesetting coordinator Lori Small.

Writing in the Computer Age

Introduction

For Every Writer

Above all, this book is about writing, for writers. Because its pages focus on a technology that is relatively new to most of us, some of the ideas and many of the terms here will be new also. But our work hasn't changed: we still must discover the words, invent the phrases, and fill the pages. What has changed is our tools.

Word processing is a catch-all term for the work these new tools can do. In fact, this work is "computing"—but with letters and punctuation marks instead of numbers. The tools are a keyboard with a few more keys than a typewriter, a screen that displays the words as you write or revise them, a printer that automatically types your work when you give the signal, a set of disks or cassettes to store the work, and a quiet box of electronics that runs the whole show.

Myths and Rewards

To use these tools you'll have to learn a few techniques, but the rewards are well worth the effort. The keyboard lets you type as fast as you can go, and your words appear instantly on the screen in front of you. If you decide to add a sentence, you can put it in any-where, and the words after it will move over to make room. If you see a misspelled word, you can go to that spot and type in the correction, wiping out the wrong letters in the process. If you want to see whether a paragraph works better at the beginning or in the middle of your text, you can move it or make a copy in both places and take your choice. In short, word processing is the power to manipulate your work at will and the liberation from the most tedious parts of writing. No more cutting and pasting, no more "white out" to correct typing errors, no more retyping at all.

There are some common myths about using computers, though, and we'd like to acknowledge them. Lots of writers have read or heard about the mishaps of word processing—the sudden loss of power that wiped out an hour's work, a push of the wrong magic button that erased a whole chapter, or a disk that somehow self-destructed. Yes, these disasters can and do happen, but rarely in proportion to the amount of time that work goes smoothly for word processing writers. Wiping out your work, even by mistake, is like dropping your wedding ring down the sink or throwing a manuscript in the fireplace with the trash—it tends to happen only once.

Other writers protest that the screen-and-keyboard method of writing just won't suit their style of working. They could be right, of course; but most people who make that assumption haven't actually sat down with a word processor for an hour or two and given themselves and this technology a chance. Certainly some writers will not feel comfortable with an electronic writing system, and they'll pass it up. But for the vast majority of working writers, these tools offer ease, productivity, and new insights into creating worlds with words that far outweigh the nuisance of learning a slightly different way to work.

The main lesson we've learned as word processing writers is that these machines do exactly what we ask of them. When we give them an instruction, they carry it out instantly and obediently. (This total responsiveness is just what many people find intimidating at first.) When they do foul up, it's usually because we've given them the wrong message—not because of some mysterious event or electronic foible. Word processors are as reliable as television sets, use less electricity than many light bulbs, and don't smoke, drink, or sass back.

For us, the rewards have indeed been worth the effort of applying this new technology. We've doubled or tripled our writing production; been able to design and dress up our manuscripts; stayed away from pastepots and copying machines; and—most exciting—

have become better writers because we can easily and painlessly revise and reprint until we're truly satisfied with our work.

Using This Book

As we've used this set of tools, we've also discovered many techniques to improve both our writing and our mastery of word processing skills. Our experience, along with the contributions of a number of other writers who've shared their knowledge with us, is the foundation for this book.

The first group of chapters—Skills—provides a thorough grounding in the technology of word processing and the fundamental skills in using it. The second part—Style—concentrates on the work of writing, by presenting word processing techniques and applications for a number of writing styles and approaches. The concluding section of our text—Writing Reborn—postulates where this technology can take us and how it is changing our lives and our work.

Throughout the book you'll find special "tips," which are designated with a ▶ symbol. Each of these tips can be used by every writer who works with word processing or is thinking about taking advantage of this new technology. The tips in the beginning chapters may be most useful to writers who have not yet acquired systems, though they may also give experienced word processing writers a new understanding of the technology they're using. In the later chapters, the tips are more complex and oriented toward applications of this technology to specific writing styles and tasks. Regardless of your level of experience with word processing, these hints will help you make the most of your writing time and tools.

The chapters are likewise arranged in an order of increasing complexity. Writers who are new to word processing probably will want to study the first ten chapters (Part I) for a general orientation to the technology, whereas writers who are familiar with a word processing system may turn immediately to the chapters in Part II, which emphasize the practical applications of word processing to the work of writing. If you are most interested in learning about the fundamentals of word processing, you may want to skip over Chapters 1 and 2, which focus on computer terms and technology, and begin with Chapter 3, "The Silent Screen." Chapters 3 and 4 introduce the basic writing and editing features of word processing, and the remaining chapters in Part I expand this discussion to include printing, filing, advanced features and techniques, and caring for a word processing system.

All of the information in Parts I and II is intended to be supplemental to the manuals that are specific to each word processing system. Because our focus is on writing and we can't anticipate all the variations among systems, you will be able to use our tips and explanations most profitably if you are thoroughly familiar with your system's manuals.

In addition to the technological vocabulary you'll encounter in these pages, we have adopted several general terms for our lexicon of word processing. The first is an abbreviation, "w/p," which takes up a lot less space than "word processing" and is easier to read with a slash between the letters. On occasion we've also used only "processor" to signify "word processor"—just for the sake of variation. When we use "system," we mean the whole set of equipment and programs for the equipment that a writer uses for word processing; when we use "machine," we're referring to the computer that is at the heart of every system. Occasionally, we've used the term "word processor" to describe the program that contains the instructions for manipulating words, rather than the entire system. Both the w/p program and the system as a whole are commonly called "word processors" in the computer world, and we've gone along.

Because the text contains many references to words or letters that you would type on the w/p keyboard or see on the screen, we've distinguished these passages by enclosing them in single quotation marks. In addition, we've introduced the specialized vocabulary of word processing and computer technology in capital letters, providing a definition of each term at its first occurrence in the text. You can easily locate these terms and definitions by consulting the Index. In some instances, we've introduced key terms more than once— either to present them in a new context or simply to offer a reminder of their meanings.

As you page through this book, you may notice that there are no pictures of brand-name products and no comparisons or discussions of specific programs or systems. In other words, we have not written a buying guide to word processors; several other books cover that territory amply, and no others speak to writers directly and comprehensively. Instead of charts that name the top ten word processors, we've presented all the functions of word processing in the context of your needs and uses for them as writers.

The hardware and software are likely to change in the coming months and years; the process of writing will not. You will be able to make the best use of today's technology and tomorrow's improvements if you know what they can do for your work and how to use them—and that's what we've presented here. We don't want to make any decisions for you, including the one to use a word processor for writing. But we've loaded our text with tips and techniques so that you can make the most informed analysis and decision possible about every part of this process—from the moment of wondering what it's like and if you can understand how it works to the choice of a system that suits your work style precisely. (In the Appendix, we do offer some advice, though; our "Biased Guide to Word Processors" names the w/p features that we consider most useful for satisfying and productive writing.)

Be Curious—Be Fearless

Finally, we'd like to offer a bit of advice that has helped us as both writers and computer users. That advice is: Be curious— be fearless.

As writers, all of us have faced an empty page and dared to fill it with our ideas, told in phrases of our own invention. That same spirit of wanting to learn and daring to try almost anything is an ideal way to approach working with these new tools. Yes, we will make mistakes—but we've been taking that risk for years as writers and signing our names to boot.

In the chapters that follow, we've tried to alert you to all the things that can go wrong or require your careful attention when working with a word processor—such as saving your work often on disk, handling disks prudently, and paying close attention when moving or deleting parts of a manuscript. But even though a w/p system is not immune to problems, you can't blow up your computer—or your house—in the course of experimenting with the program, keyboard, and screen.

Perhaps most important, when you try to find the limits of this set of writing tools, you'll learn as much from your mistakes as from any operations manual. Very often, by doing something wrong the first time, you will discover better ways of organizing your work or using your word processing program. So plunge in—and expect some glories to come with your gaffes.

Part I

Skills

Chapter 1

New Tools of the Trade

Hardware for Word Processing

The Computer Age has a vocabulary of its own. Some of the terms are highly esoteric; others have found their way into common parlance. But even the oft-heard expressions, such as "interface" or "programmed," have precise meanings in the computer world. We will introduce some of these specific computer terms as we discuss the skills and style of working with this versatile new technology for writing.

If you are already working on a word processing system, you're likely to know many of the details in these first two chapters. If word processing and all its verbiage are new to you, don't worry—there won't be a quiz in the morning. The vocabulary of computing is here when you need it, and you won't have to master all of these terms and concepts just to write with this set of tools. But becoming familiar with the way your system works—and with the words that inhabit your manuals and all computer literature—will help you go about the business of writing with a clear knowledge of how these machines get the job done and how best to match their talents to your own.

Three of the biggest buzz words of this era—computer, hardware, and software—are both confused and abused. Here's a brief explanation of each.

• At its simplest level, a COMPUTER is any machine that has two fundamental abilities: to accept instructions and to take in and manipulate information.

• In the vocabulary of computers, HARDWARE is all of the physical parts that make up a computer and any other components in its system.

• SOFTWARE is a collective term for the sets of instructions that tell the hardware what to do. Individual sets of instructions are called PROGRAMS.

One more definition is in order here, of a term that's central to this book—WORD PROCESSING. For many people who haven't worked with this technology, word processors suggest the gadgets that have replaced typewriters in lots of offices, or the infernal machines that spit out endless junk mail pitches and send them our way. Those impressions are correct, of course, but when reduced to its simplest description, word processing is a way of creating, revising, printing, and storing text, using a system of components that contains a computer, other hardware, and software specifically designed to manipulate words.

This particular collection of equipment is often called a WORD PROCESSOR. Some manufacturers offer DEDICATED word processors, which actually consist of computers with software and hardware; these systems are essentially limited to word processing and seldom are able to perform other common computer functions, such as accounting. To add to the confusion about the definition of a word processor, the makers of software that manipulates words also label their programs word processors. Both connotations are widely accepted, and both are strictly correct.

Of course these definitions are minimal, but it's important to begin with an understanding that a "computer" is not necessarily some room-sized phalanx of blinking lights and whirring reels or some little gray box with typewriter keys on it. In fact, a computer can be a calculator, electronic game, microwave oven, video tape recorder, or any other device that's "programmable"—that accepts instructions and manipulates information.

From their earliest beginnings, computers were conceived and designed for speed. They take in data, convert it to signals that their electrical circuits can read, perform their assigned tasks, and send the data out in human-readable form at a lightning pace that is measured in milliseconds. A set of intricate calculations that would take a person with a slide rule and a blackboard several days—or years— to work out can be performed by a computer in minutes or even seconds.

We often think of "computing" as those mathematical tasks that once required slide rules, but a computer can handle words just as readily as it crunches numbers. For writers, its power means almost unbelievable speed in writing and moving text around and almost painless revising and copying of our work.

The Parts of a System

Writing with a computer involves a system of components. The particulars can vary, but each system must contain the computer itself, a device to transmit information and commands to the computer (most often a keyboard), a device to display the product of the computer's work (a screen or printer, or both), and some means of storing the information that the computer has manipulated (usually a disk or cassette tape). All of these components except the computer are called PERIPHERALS. Figure 1-1 shows a typical system.

These systems can fill whole buildings, as in banks or corporate headquarters, or they can fit in your pocket. The type of system that is most useful for word processing—and most affordable for

Fig. 1-1: Typical microcomputer system

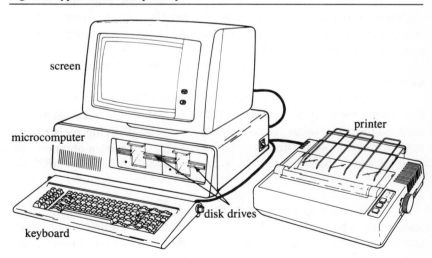

writers—is a MICROCOMPUTER system. This is a small-scale outfit that usually costs between $3,000 and $10,000 for the computer and components. There are ways to spend less—or lots more—and still be writing with a computer, but the systems most widely used by writers seem to fall in the price range of a reasonable, dependable car.

The Computer

The guts of this writing system is obviously the computer, and its engine is the MICROPROCESSOR, a power-packed half-inch of silicon circuitry. Although it's literally the size of your thumbnail, this device does all of the computing work. Its construction also indicates the "size" of a computer; that is, the amount of information a microprocessor can handle at once determines how fast a computer can function and how much internal storage that machine can have.

The microprocessor (also called the CENTRAL PROCESSING UNIT or CPU) handles information in tiny computer-readable units. Although there are two sizes of these units, the most relevant to a writer's work is the BYTE, which represents one character—a letter, number, symbol, or space. The computer's internal memory capacity is measured in bytes, and so is your writing whenever it's being processed by the computer system. (The other unit of measure used by a microprocessor is a BIT, which is an abbreviation of BINARY DIGIT. Each bit is one unit of the binary number system—either 0 or 1; in most microcomputers, eight bits together make up one byte.)

Because a byte represents only one character, however, the computer's memory and computer-generated manuscripts are commonly expressed in KILOBYTES, units that are just over a thousand bytes each (1024 to be exact). Kilobyte can be abbreviated with a lowercase or capital 'K', so you're likely to see references to 64k of memory or a letter that is 4K long.

In addition to the microprocessor, a microcomputer contains an internal memory and some means of transmitting information back and forth to other parts of the system. The transmission processes are called INPUT and OUTPUT, often abbreviated as I/O. Any point at which different signals or parts of a system meet is called an INTERFACE, another of the computer terms that has crept into general use.

A microcomputer has two kinds of memory—permanent and temporary. The fairly small permanent memory contains "read-only" sets of instructions that are essential to the computer's operation and that can't be changed without major effort. The memory area where your writing and programs are held is called RANDOM-ACCESS MEM-ORY, or RAM.

The amount of RAM in a computer is important, for it deter-mines how much information the machine can work with at any one time. The writing you do goes into this memory before being sent to any storage device outside the computer, and some or all of the pro-grams that direct the computer's activity also are stored here as you're using them. So the random-access memory area must be ade-quate to hold programs and still accommodate a reasonable amount of your work.

In the case of word processing, the programs that allow highly sophisticated operations, such as moving blocks of text or searching for a word or phrase, may occupy 30K (30,000 bytes) or more of the computer's memory. Some w/p programs won't even operate in a computer without a certain amount of RAM; the common minimum for such programs is 48K or 64K. A few computer manufacturers offer word processing programs that are written into the permanent memory, thus leaving all of RAM for work or other programs.

The advantage of random-access memory is that it lets you move around quickly in the text you're writing or editing and add new text as rapidly as you can strike the keys on a keyboard. The dis-advantage of this memory is its temporary condition; if you turn off the computer or accidentally pull the plug, the contents of RAM are wiped out. Of course your work is protected if you've copied it from memory to your storage system—disk or cassette—outside the com-puter, but any work that hasn't been SAVED, as it's called, will be lost. Your programs are safe, though; they reside on disks or cassettes and are copied (commonly called LOADED) into memory but are not erased from their original source.

All of these basic elements of a computer—the microprocessor that computes and controls, the memory that holds data, and the input-output pathways—are made up of electronic parts, circuit boards, and signal-carrying wires. And although the microprocessor is a tiny chip, many similar chips must keep it company to hold and move the information it manipulates. If you take the cover off a com-puter (check the warranty restrictions first!) or see one open in a dis-play, you'll find several circuit boards, each of which is loaded with little black chips and even smaller colored parts soldered into the holes on the board. Wires of various sizes link the boards to one another and to plugs at the back of the cabinet. When you see the intricate layout of this machine, you can begin to understand how it tackles jobs in millisecond rhythms, and you'll probably marvel that it misfires as seldom as it does.

The Keyboard

Some of the wires inside the computer carry signals from the KEYBOARD, which is the standard input device in a word processing system. The location and packaging of the keyboard differ among systems: in some it's part of the computer cabinet; in others it's built into a separate cabinet that also contains a screen; or it may be a separate unit with a cable linking it to the screen's cabinet or to the computer itself. The keyboard-screen units—in one cabinet or in separate boxes connected by a cable—are called TERMINALS.

Whatever its configuration, the keyboard is much like that of a typewriter. All the familiar keys are there—in the standard office-machine format or in a condensed version similar to that of a portable typewriter. (Many keyboards also include a numeric keypad to the right of the regular key set; this group of number keys is especially useful for entering numerical data.) Depending on how much you use the touch typing system and how accustomed you are to a certain arrangement of keys, the keyboard format could be rather critical.

▶ If you will be continuing to use a typewriter for some tasks even though you work mostly on a w/p system, you may want to be certain that both keyboards have the same arrangement of standard keys for letters, numbers, and punctuation marks.

A computer keyboard has additional keys, as well. Most systems have extra rows of FUNCTION KEYS, which are labeled with short words or abbreviations indicating their purposes. The locations of these special function keys vary among systems; Figure 1-2 illustrates a typical keyboard layout that includes such function keys. The keys to the left of the main keyboard, labeled 'F1' through 'F10', can be used to perform special word processing functions, based on the word processing program in use.

Fig. 1-2: Typical keyboard layout

function keys | typewriter keyboard | cursor keys and numeric keypad

In most dedicated word processing systems and some micro-computer systems, the function keys identify the tasks they control. On the right side of the keyboard illustrated, for example, the keys identify some common functions used in word processing, such as Insert, Delete, and moving a Page Up and Down. When one of these keys is pressed, a signal is sent to the computer that registers the appropriate COMMAND—that is, the program's instruction to perform that function.

In some word processing programs and on all keyboards that don't have special function keys, commands are sent by typing some combination of regular keys, usually with the CONTROL KEY held down. The Control key in the keyboard illustrated is labeled 'Ctrl'. This key appears on all computer keyboards, even in systems that have many special function keys, because it effectively doubles the number of signals that can be sent to the computer from the keyboard. Without the Control key pressed, each letter or symbol is sent as it appears on the key; if the Control key is held down and then one or more letter or symbol keys are pressed, a completely different electronic signal goes to the computer. A sophisticated word processing program will take advantage of these many extra keystroke possibilities by designating a considerable library of commands. (The keyboard illustrated has another supplemental key, labeled 'Alt', for 'alternate', which also operates in conjunction with other keys to produce additional command possibilities.)

One set of function keys that is usually found on a computer keyboard consists of four arrows, one to a key, pointing up, down, right, and left (to the right of the keyboard in the illustration). These keys move the CURSOR, a symbol that appears on the system's screen to show you where you are in a section of writing or a program. Some of the other keys may have arrows on them as well, including the BACKSPACE key (to the right of the equal sign key in the illustration) and possibly the key for entering commands or marking paragraphs, the RETURN key (to the right of the brackets key). All of these keys will be discussed in detail in the chapters that follow.

Keyboard Ergonomics

As screen-and-keyboard combinations have replaced typewriters in thousands of offices, specialists in ergonomics—the study of the human body's relationship to tools and work—have turned their attention to these devices. Some ergonomic studies have already influenced the design of keyboards and terminals, but as yet there has been no clear consensus among experts regarding the correct placement of special keys on a keyboard or the keyboard's positioning with the screen. So the best guide for evaluating a keyboard is still your own comfort and preferences, and the best way to make that evaluation, if you are not already using a system, is to test the keyboard thoroughly before buying the equipment.

▶ Because the Control key is used extensively by most word processing programs, its location on the keyboard is important. It should be easy to reach but at the periphery of the "home" position for touch typing so that you won't hit it inadvertently (although nothing awful will happen if you do). Because this key must be held down as you strike other keys for certain commands, its location should also allow your hand to be comfortable as you press it and reach elsewhere on the keyboard.

Similarly, the function keys should be easy to reach but not too close to regular keys that you use often. On most keyboards that have such function keys, these special keys are separated from the main keyboard by a small divider between the sections of the keyboard or by the visual distinction of different-colored key tops for the main keys and function keys.

▶ Whatever the format of your keyboard, get to know the locations of special keys by using them with practice text (rather than when you're writing an article that's due in an hour). If you haven't acquired a system yet, be sure to test each keyboard thoroughly before choosing one.

Another consideration in using a system's keyboard is the physical shape of the keys, their positions on the machine, and the feel of the keys as you strike them. Like typewriters, computer keyboards vary widely in their ease and comfort of use. A keyboard—typewriter or computer—designed for heavy use by a touch typist will have "sculptured" keys; that is, the key tops are all slightly concave and the keys for letters at the center of the keyboard, where your hands rest in the home position, are slightly more concave than the others. Similarly, the rows of keys on a well-designed keyboard are "stepped" at a distance that is easy to reach from the home position; this keyboard arrangement is likely to make even poor typists or "hunt-and-peck" specialists faster and more accurate.

The feel of the keyboard is also important in a word processing system—for two reasons. First, the keys' tactile response should be at least tolerable and preferably enjoyable in a machine that's so intimately a part of your work. Some writers prefer keyboards that are "soft," while others like "stiff" keys; the touch doesn't matter as long as you don't pound the keyboard with more force than it is meant to absorb.

And that's the second consideration about touch: because the keys are mechanical devices that send electronic signals, they are more likely than typewriter keys to cause errors. This is not a common problem, but if you've gone from using a stiff old manual typewriter to a soft word processing keyboard, you'll have to retrain your hands to go gently. The consequence of too much pounding on an electronic keyboard may be an "echo" or "bounce"—getting two or more repetitions of the letter you intended to strike once. Or if your system's keys have a built-in repeat capacity (the character keeps repeating when you hold down the key), you may see many more letters on the screen than you intended.

One final note on keyboards and ergonomics. As computer systems have become commonplace in offices and homes, they have undergone scrutiny by various health experts. One of the chief areas of concern is the position of the person using the machine in relation to the keyboard and screen. Most studies have shown that a detached keyboard, which can be moved in relation to the screen's position, is preferable to one that is at a fixed distance and angle to the screen.

► This keyboard-screen positioning should be one of the principal considerations in using or buying a word processing system. You're going to be living with it, and if you can move the keyboard (or change the screen's position) you won't have to move yourself as often to stay comfortable. Besides, we've all seen those ads with the person writing away with the keyboard on his lap—and it works. (Try putting a pillow on your lap to hold the keyboard—it's even more comfortable.)

The Screen

The video screen of a w/p system is essentially a temporary piece of paper. It displays everything you write, shows the typos and corrections, and gives you the feedback provided by the program you're using. Everything you enter from the keyboard is also stored in the computer's memory, but having the screen in front of you offers a chance (all the chances you want, actually) to study and revise your work before saving it on a disk or cassette or printing it out on paper.

Often the screen is built into the cabinet with the computer and keyboard, but some systems have the computer as a separate component, requiring use of a keyboard-screen terminal, and some have the keyboard in the computer cabinet but require a separate video screen. This self-contained video display is called a MONITOR. The vast majority of these display screens are powered by a cathode ray tube (CRT) like that in a television, although the newer and more compact "flat-screen" technology has been used for the monitors in some computer systems. In fact, you can connect a computer to a TV set with only minor modifications, but the quality of its display of text is poor by comparison to that of a specially designed computer display screen. Use of a television as the display unit is not a good idea if you're doing extensive writing and reading of work on the screen.

Some manufacturers offer true COLOR MONITORS (also called RGB MONITORS—for red, green, blue), which display text more readably than a television can, and a few w/p programs are designed to work with color monitors. As different types of programs—graphics, calculations, and word processing, for example—become integrated into single packages, color monitors will undoubtedly achieve wider general use. For writers, however, the main requirement of any system that utilizes a color display must be the ease and comfort of working with text on the screen.

Most systems have screens that measure about 12 inches diagonally—the size of an average portable television—though some monitors have 9-inch screens and some portable computers have built-in 5-inch screens, which display rather tiny characters. Regardless of their size, most of the screens display 24 or 25 lines of text at one time. A few deluxe word processing systems have large screens that display a full page (about 55 lines) or even two full pages side-by-side. These outfits are beyond the price range of most writers, however, and their extra features are designed for heavy-duty office work, such as comparing legal documents or complex correspondence.

The standard-sized screen is just about right for most writers' work, because 24 lines is a good chunk of material to view at one time, and most people's eyes can't really make use of the larger screen display. If you're writing something that's single-spaced, the screen's 24 text lines hold approximately half a page; if your text is going to be printed double-spaced but you display it as single-spaced on the screen, you'll see a full page or nearly a full page in one screenful. (Many programs allow you to display double-spaced text on the screen, but then you see only 12 lines of your work at a time.)

The width of the screen's line is usually 80 characters (or COLUMNS, in computer parlance), though some popular microcomputers limit the screen display to 64 or 40 characters unless extra hardware is added to the machine. The least expensive microcomputers also display only capital letters, although lowercase adapters can be added to the computer to solve this problem. If you're working with a computer that displays only capital letters, the screen will indicate when you've used the uppercase shift by HIGHLIGHTING the character. Highlighting is often done in "reverse video"—if the characters are normally displayed in a light color on a dark background, the highlighting reverses this to show dark letters on a light background. Some word processing programs take advantage of highlighting for other special functions, such as marking a section of text that will be copied, moved, or erased. A few common terminals are not capable of displaying highlighted text, which may be a limitation if you're using a program that highlights many of its features.

Like the keyboard, the screen is something you live with, and you will be a lot closer to it than to your television. So the size and resolution of the characters, the color of the display, and your ability to control the screen's brightness and protect it from glare all are important considerations. The distance and angle of your position in relation to the screen also are important: although comfort at the screen is an individual matter, in general you should sit at arm's length or farther from the screen; you should avoid staring at it constantly; and you should move away from the keyboard and screen for as much as ten minutes of every hour that you work with the system.

The letters and symbols on the screen should be easy to read. The primary ingredient in this readability is the resolution of the characters—that is, the number of tiny dots (called PIXELS—a great word for Scrabble) that make up each one. The smaller they are and the greater their number, the more each character looks as if it's a solid line, even though a video image is not made up of solid lines.

▶ The quality of resolution differs among various brands of monitors and terminals; one good way to compare them is by looking carefully at letters that have curved parts, such as the "s," and at the letter "v," which is the hardest to make look solid with a series of vertical dots on the video screen's matrix of horizontal lines.

The shapes of characters also contribute to their readability. The most limited (for which read "inexpensive") screens show large characters with fairly poor resolution, and if they display lowercase letters at all, these are faked. That is, the cheapest way to make an uppercase screen show lowercase letters is to eliminate the "descenders"—the little tails of such letters as "p" and "y" that go below the line on which the body of the letter sits. This imperfect attempt to show lowercase letters makes the text a good deal harder to read than text with true descenders on the screen. Figure 1-3 shows a printout of text with and without true descenders.

Screens that display descending characters and everything else still can vary in the shape of letters, and thus in the readability of their text. In effect, each manufacturer chooses a type style that can be presented well on the video screen; these type styles differ principally in their height or width. Some screens show characters that are quite vertical in appearance, while others have letters that are quite wide in proportion to the height of their ascending parts. A writer's preference for one style or another is purely personal.

▶ If you don't yet have a system and are looking at different screen displays and sizes, be sure to ask the person demonstrating each monitor or terminal to show you the screen when it's full of text. When all 24 lines are filled with characters (not just a chart with widely separated columns), you'll get a far better idea of the readability of that screen's text.

If you've worked with a system already or have been shopping for one, you know that the color of the characters on the screen can also vary. The predominant display colors are black-and-white or black-and-green, though screens that show amber characters are also offered by some manufacturers. The color of a display is certainly a matter of preference, but some studies have shown that green or amber is more restful to the eyes than white characters on a black background or black on white.

▶ The best way to test your own comfort level with a color is to spend several hours working at that screen, in the same way that you'd test a keyboard for comfort.

Placement of the screen likewise can affect the comfort with which you work. Natural or artificial light can cause glare that may be distracting or even cause eyestrain or headaches. Some screens have built-in or detachable covers to reduce glare, and accessory suppliers sell similar covers for most screens that don't have such protection. Another useful feature that many screens offer is a brightness and contrast control, which can be changed to compensate for changing room light. If bright lights or reflections are a problem as you use the screen, experiment with different positions and locations of the screen and keyboard to find the arrangement that is most comfortable.

▶ The options for changing the screen's position in relation to the keyboard are severely limited by the all-in-one cabinets that contain the keyboard and screen (and often the computer as well). These units can be moved around to avoid or reduce glare on the screen, but the keyboard's position is less flexible—so the best screen location may be less convenient for sitting at the keyboard. All of the considerations of screen comfort and position, as well as similar aspects of keyboard use, suggest that the keyboard and screen should be in separate cabinets for the greatest versatility.

Disk Drives

Once you've written some text on the keyboard (concurrently entering it in the computer's memory) and checked it on the screen, your work must be stored in a more permanent place than the machine's RAM. Most word processing systems use DISK DRIVES—preferably two—and magnetic DISKS for this purpose. The drive is a mechanical device that spins the disk and uses electronic controls to copy information onto the disk and read information from it. The disk is a flat, round plastic object that fits into the drive and stores data on its specially coated surface.

Disk drives can be built into the computer cabinet or contained in separate small boxes; in either case, they are connected by cables to the main portion of the computer. Magnetic disks are inserted in the drives, and when the appropriate command is entered from the keyboard, the computer—in a process called SAVING or WRITING TO DISK—sends the contents of its memory to the disk. (Detailed discussions of disk anatomy, storage methods, and care of disks and drives are presented in Chapters 7 and 10.)

In addition to storing your work, disks and drives are the method used by most systems to store and load the word processing program and any other programs you use. Having two disk drives in your system is very handy for a number of reasons. You can use the word processing program in one drive and reserve the other for your writing, and you can easily copy or transfer work from one disk to another with two drives.

Disk drives are among the few mechanical parts of a w/p system, and they announce their presence with clicking and whirring noises whenever they're active. They are not always in motion, though; generally they only move into gear when you load a program or file into the computer's memory, give the signal to save your work on the disk, or when the computer's holding area—called a BUFFER—becomes full and your program signals you to slow down for a few seconds while it writes information on the disk. While the disk drives are spinning, a red light on the front of the one in use at the moment will be lit; you should never open the small gate on either drive or try to remove a disk when a light is on.

One other type of disk storage has become increasingly accessible to microcomputer users. This is the HARD DISK, a high-capacity disk that is sealed into a cabinet and thus is not interchangeable as regular disks are. Hard disks offer two clear advantages over conventional disks; they have far greater storage capacity (typically ten to twenty times as much), and they work much faster. A hard disk is considerably more costly than a conventional disk-and-drive unit, however; the least expensive hard disks are more than $1,000.

The most workable hard disk configuration for any system is in combination with at least one conventional disk drive. Typically, all working files and programs would be stored on the hard disk and copied to individual disks in the conventional disk drive for backup purposes. This backup capability is essential with a hard disk, because if anything goes wrong with it (and there is no conventional disk drive and set of duplicate disks), you won't be able to use your system until the hard disk is repaired.

Cassette tapes can be used instead of disks for storing your text and programs, but tapes are slower and less efficient than disks, and sophisticated word processing programs cannot be put into the cassette format. Still, many of the low-cost microcomputers have built-in hookups for cassette recorders, and there are simple w/p programs on cassette too. A tape system may be a necessity if you must begin your system on a shoestring budget, but it's a good idea to make certain that any such computer will also handle disk drives so that you can add them later. Computers that use tapes generally can accommodate disk drives as well, and all of your work stored on cassettes can be transferred to disks by loading it into the computer's memory from a tape and then saving it onto a disk.

The Printer

The biggest and noisiest component of many w/p systems is the printer. The type of printer used by most writers produces copy like that of a typewriter; it's called a LETTER-QUALITY PRINTER and uses a printing element that spins and prints each character in solid type. Letter-quality printers are relatively expensive; they generally cost between $1,000 and $3,500—as much as the computer and disk drives combined in some systems.

Less expensive printers are available, of course; these are DOT-MATRIX PRINTERS, which form characters as a series of dots much the way that the video screen does. (The examples in Figure 1-3 were actually produced with a dot-matrix printer.) Dot-matrix printers work much faster than letter-quality ones, but their output is far less

```
in response to your inquiry concerning
in response to your inquiry concerning
```

Fig. 1-3: Printout of characters with and without true descenders

professional-looking, because the matrix of dots they create for each character is obvious to any reader. As the quality of dot-matrix-printer images improves (and this is inevitable), and as computer printouts become an increasingly common form of manuscript, dot-matrix printers may gain wider acceptance than they now have among writers.

Like the disk drives, the printer has mechanical parts as well as electronic ones. Considering its speed and ability to work continuously, a letter-quality printer is quite amazing. The most widely used versions can print from 15 to 55 characters per second (cps), far faster than even the most skilled typist. At an average of 6 characters per word, 15 cps would equal 150 words per minute, and the top-line 55 cps model does an astounding 550 words per minute.

Some office typewriters also can be converted to serve as w/p printers by attaching special keyboard covers or electronic drivers; these mechanisms usually aren't as durable as printers built for computer systems, and their top speed is about 15 cps. For relatively light use, however, such conversion packages may provide a low-cost entry into word processing for some writers.

The most popular letter-quality printers use one of two kinds of printing elements to form characters on the paper. One of these elements is a THIMBLE, which looks like an inverted type ball for an office typewriter. It spins until the desired letter is facing the appropriate spot on the paper, and then a tiny hammer strikes it, pushing that character and the ribbon in front of it against the paper.

The second common printing element is a DAISY WHEEL, which looks somewhat like a daisy with tiny raised characters at the end of each petal. This element works in the same way as the thimble in that the character is struck from behind by a hammer, which pushes the letter and the ribbon against the paper. Of course, all of this happens in a fraction of a second, so it's quite difficult to see the hammer striking the spinning element. Both of these printers use cartridge ribbons that can be cloth or the sharper-imaged carbon ribbon.

Various printer accessories make working with long manuscripts or individual sheets of bond or letterhead easier. A TRACTOR can be attached to the top of the printer to guide the special CONTINUOUS-FORM or FAN-FOLD paper (which is perforated along the sides and between sheets) through the machine. This allows accurate printing of many pages without the paper's sliding sideways or becoming wrinkled, as it may be carried by the printer's normal FRICTION FEED mechanism. You don't need a tractor to print single pages or even to use continuous-form paper, although the friction feed may occasionally cause a line to be crooked or a sheet to become creased.

For high-volume work with single sheets, an expensive sheet feeder can be added to most printers so that someone doesn't have to hand feed the pages. Some dedicated word processing systems are equipped with a simple type of sheet feeder, so that you simply put each page in a plastic holder and pull a lever to load the paper into the printer. These mechanisms generally can hold only one sheet at a time, but they're easier to use and faster than the insert-and-roll-up method that's standard for single sheets in a printer or typewriter.

Cords, Cables, and Plugs

The only other standard feature of a basic word processing system is what may seem like a quarter-mile of cords and cables and a plethora of plugs. That's an exaggeration, of course, but one of the chief logistical problems for writers who set up a system at home or in a small office is where to plug everything in and how to make it all fit together so that someone doesn't trip over the cords and cables (and perhaps destroy the work you were about to save on disk).

If you're new to computers and word processing, this collection of equipment may seem imposing. But these components are really just a sophisticated typewriter and filing system built into two or three boxes. Once you've arranged your work space, assembled the pieces, and plugged in the cords and cables, you will have a fantastic tool at your fingertips. And you'll probably forget about input and output or bits and bytes, because you'll be learning the intricacies of your word processing program and turning out phrases and pages.

Chapter 2

Up and Running

Software for the System

One observer of the microcomputer industry has suggested that software is the tail that wags the dog. He's right—the machines won't work without instructions, and the usefulness of a system is directly proportional to the programs available for it. Even the dedicated word processors made by the office equipment giants depend on software to make them easy to learn and able to print or insert text with just the push of a button.

Still, software may be a bit underrated. Certainly the developments in hardware have been astounding in recent years: half-inch microprocessors do more work faster than their room-sized predecessors; disk drives pack eight times as much data on a disk as they did five years ago; and printers whiz back and forth depositing letters five times as fast as a crack typist. But the programs and languages for computer software—word processing among them—have come just as far, just as quickly.

Programs and Languages

All software is designed to make the computer perform specific tasks, such as handling text, maintaining a ledger, or converting human language into computer-readable form. In most systems the software is stored on disks, from which it is copied into the computer's RAM for use. In a few instances, though, a program may be stored permanently in the machine's read-only memory. Even these programs, though they are built into the hardware, are considered "soft"—because the term "software" refers to their being sets of instructions for use in the computer, not to the electronic circuit or the disk that stores them.

Software that does word processing or accounting is known as an APPLICATIONS PROGRAM, because each set of instructions applies computer power to clearly defined problems and tasks. The program itself is invisible; the only things you see are the messages that are printed on the screen and the information that you supply, such as your writing or the entries for your ledger.

Other programs are designed to write more programs. The most widely used of these are HIGH-LEVEL LANGUAGES, such as BASIC, Pascal, or COBOL; these languages consist of limited series of English words that can tell the computer what to do, but mastering the correct form for creating and executing a program takes study and practice. A few computers have the simplest language, BASIC, built into the permanent part of their memory, although most systems require that you use separate software on a disk to write a program in any language.

Still other program-writing software can be used to convert a program written in a high-level language to computer-readable form, which is called MACHINE LANGUAGE. Machine-language programs generally work faster and more efficiently than ones written in BASIC, for example, but they are harder to write because the steps and codes for machine language are specific to each type of microprocessor and you don't write these programs in English. In other words, machine-language programming—and most programming, for that matter—is a lot farther down the computer road than we have to get to become accomplished w/p writers.

Word Processors

But it was the programmers who really started word processing for us. The earliest word processing software for microcomputers consisted of a simple program, called an EDITOR, that was designed mainly for writing programs. An editor is "line-oriented"—that is, it handles and stores text one line at a time, which is the way programs are created and executed. Editors are still used extensively for this purpose and for creating relatively simple, short documents; they are inexpensive (routinely under $100) but far more limited in capabilities than a full-blown word processor.

Editors can perform some functions of standard word processors, such as deleting a line or searching for a series of characters. As program designers and manufacturers of office systems saw the potential for handling words with the versatility that computers had always brought to numbers, full-screen editing and formatting of text was developed.

From these beginnings, word processing programs have become increasingly sophisticated, and in the process they have also become—to borrow from the purest computer jargon—"user-friendly." A user-friendly program contains an extravagant amount of help for the person operating it, usually in the form of messages or PROMPTS on the screen. Some programs also make use of a bell (more like a beep, actually) in most keyboards to signal that you've hit a forbidden key or given an unrecognized command.

The on-screen HELP MESSAGES, as they're often called, may take the form of rather lengthy explanations of each program feature, which you call to the screen with a one- or two-letter command, or they may be simple MENUS, which give a digest of common commands and stay on the screen most of the time. Usually you can "suppress" the help messages or menus once you've become familiar with the program, but they are still available for viewing if you send for them.

Some word processors also include a teaching section or tutorial as part of the program, which gives you a hands-on demonstration of the program's features. All w/p programs come with manuals (or "documentation," in computer terminology) that generally give more detail than menus or on-screen messages. Occasionally, though, the manuals are less user-friendly than the screen help; given more room to write and presumably to explain, some program developers have resorted to vocabulary and concepts that are challenging for readers who haven't previously worked with computers.

For the most part, however, word processors are well documented and easy to use. The more sophisticated programs may be confusing at first, because of their large selection of features, but you can sort out most of these possibilities simply by experimenting with them.

▶ If you do not yet have a system and are looking at various word processing programs, try to spend an hour or two using each one with the hardware that you're considering. There is enough variation in the amount of on-screen help and the actual working segments of a program—called MODES—that you may find some you enjoy using and some you definitely dislike. And a salesperson's facile demonstration of a program is not likely to tell you how you'll respond to using it.

Operating Systems

In addition to the word processing program, any computer system that uses disk drives must have another important software component. This is the DISK OPERATING SYSTEM, or DOS, which determines the way information is routed through the computer and stored on the disks. In essence, the DOS is a file manager. It consists of a group of small programs, called UTILITIES, that are stored together on a disk. These programs let you name files, look at them, copy them, and list the contents of your electronic filing system. (These programs are discussed further in Chapter 7.)

Although the DOS may be included on the same disk with the w/p program in a dedicated word processor, every computer-and-disk combination must have an operating system to function. All applications programs, such as word processors, must be designed to work in conjunction with a specific operating system. Several of the widely used personal computers have their own disk operating systems; other computer manufacturers have chosen operating systems made by independent software developers.

Formatting and Booting

For the most part, you don't see the operating system at work, but it performs one critical function that you couldn't do without— getting the software and hardware to work together. Specifically, the DOS is what you use to prepare blank disks for storing your work (or copies of your programs), and to load the software's contents—the programs already on disks—into the computer's memory.

Because the precise method of storing information on disks varies among microcomputer systems, you must register your system's instructions for storing data on each new disk before you can use it. This process is called FORMATTING, and it is accomplished by one of the utility programs (which is usually named Format). The formatting program establishes a pattern of circular TRACKS and straight-sided SECTORS that are perpendicular to the tracks on the disk's surface; each track and sector is numbered, providing accurate reference points for all the information on the disk. (A detailed discussion of disk anatomy is presented in Chapter 7.) Once you've formatted a new disk, you may use that disk to store your work or programs, add new data, or erase old files without ever having to repeat the formatting process.

▶ Because formatting a disk erases any data that was stored on it, you must be certain that the disk in question is blank and that you specify the correct disk drive when using the Format program. You can verify that the disk is blank with the DOS utility that lists the DISK DIRECTORY (the contents of a disk, sometimes called the CATALOG); if you get no response when you initiate this program, the disk has not been formatted.

The other major step in preparing to use software in the system is being able to BOOT a disk. The term "boot" derives from the DOS utility called the BOOTSTRAP PROGRAM, which actually loads the essential DOS information into the computer so that you can begin using the word processing program or whatever other programs you have available. Although the physical maneuver for doing this varies among systems, booting is usually done by inserting a disk and hitting the Reset button on the computer or simply by turning on the machine.

Getting Started

Up to this point in our text, we've introduced a lot of computer terminology and presented the fundamentals of a word processing system. Now we're going to put all this hardware and software together and concentrate on writing. Whether you are new to word processing or an old hand at the computer keyboard, you're certain to find some new ways of going about your work in the pages that follow.

Because we don't want to limit our examples to one or two popular word processing programs—and there's no way to anticipate what might be invented next month or next year—we've created a mythical, universal word processor, along with a computer and two disk drives to use it. This imaginary system contains all the standard functions of word processing and most of the sophisticated and exotic features as well. Of course our program's commands will probably differ from those of your system, but the particular keystrokes don't matter. What does matter is that you can sample the variety of tasks a w/p system will do for you, and that you see this power in action.

In fact, you now know everything you need to know to begin using the imaginary word processing system we've divined. But figuring out how to proceed once all the hardware has been assembled and the program disks are ready and waiting can be the most mystifying time in anyone's computer life. So we'd like to take a quick tour of the operations that will get you from the silence of contemplating those boxes to the efficient clicking—or silence—of using the system to write.

For this example we'll assume that you are working with two specific disks; one contains the word processing program and the DOS utilities, and the other will store your work but is currently blank. You may not need to use all of the following steps, depending on your system's way of working. But we'll cover all the territory and let you choose what you need.

First, you'll turn on the power to the computer and to the terminal or monitor if it's a separate component. After waiting for the disk drive light to go out, you'll insert the program disk in the main drive and the blank disk in the second drive, then close the drives' "doors."

Then you'll boot the disk in the main drive by pushing the reset button, turning the power off and on again, or following the procedure specified in your system's manual. (The system always "assumes" that you are using the main disk drive—called 'A' or '1'—unless you specify otherwise; in this situation, you must begin with the main drive, because the disk in the second drive is blank.)

After some routine disk whirring and rattling, the DOS prompt (its identification symbol) will appear on the screen. The CURSOR—a little rectangle or bar of light on the screen—will be next to the prompt and will move to the right each time you type a character.

Next you'll give the command to list the directory of the disk in the second drive. (We may be a little ahead of our explanations here, but we want to establish that the blank disk is truly blank. File contents and directories are discussed in Chapter 7.)

Assuming that no directory appeared for the second disk, you'll next use the Format program to prepare that disk for use. When formatting is complete, the program will return you to the DOS prompt for the main drive.

Now you're ready to load and use the word processing program. Enter the program name (or the short form used to designate it on the disk) and in a few seconds the program's SIGN-ON MESSAGE will appear on the screen.

This is where programs diverge—the sign-on message for each one is unique to it. But what you're likely to see first is a message that disappears after a few seconds; it usually shows the name of the program and its publisher. That message yields to a list of the basic options your system offers. Your program probably calls this some kind of menu—the COMMAND MENU, MAIN MENU, or something similar. (A typical command menu is illustrated in Figure 2-1.)

```
===================================================================
:              <<< C O M M A N D   M E N U   >>>                 :
: R - Retrieve a file    E - Edit a file   F - Format selection :
: S - Save file on disk  P - Print a file  X - eXit to system   :
: Z - delete a file                        H - Help             :
===================================================================
  Please enter your choice:▷
```

Fig. 2-1: Typical command menu

The final step in getting started is to choose the command to
begin writing. This command—like most menu commands—is usually one letter or number, which is paired on the menu with its function. Depending on the program's terminology, you might give the
command to 'Edit', 'Create a File', 'Open a File', or 'Insert Text'.
Even when no file or text exists yet, some programs have you create
one by "inserting" or "editing"—a logic that seems to be peculiar to
the computer world. Whatever the terminology for your system,
you'll readily get used to it and you probably won't give this odd
vocabulary a second thought when you see a blank screen. After all,
that's where every writer starts.

Chapter 3

The Silent Screen

Writing with the System

You're ready now to start writing. When working on a typewriter or a yellow pad, this was the point at which you said, "I've got to get it down on paper." Now you're working in a new medium. There's no paper before you—just a display screen—and the creative act is going to involve "sending it in" rather than getting it down.

Writing on a word processor involves using the keyboard to send text into your system's memory, while seeing it displayed on the screen. Though this new medium may take some getting used to, you'll find that it affords you speed, flexibility, and continuity in your writing that was never before possible. In subsequent chapters, we'll be looking at the powerful revising and printing capabilities of your word processor, but first we're simply going to experience what it's like to write on the silent screen.

First Words

The last chapter left off with your "booting" the word processing program and giving the appropriate command to begin writing. Once the command menu has cleared, you'll be in what is commonly called the EDIT MODE. (In w/p parlance, working with text in any way, whether revising or creating it, is usually considered "editing" it.)

Depending on your system, you might see a blank screen—the Computer Age equivalent of the blank page—or you might see some information displayed at the top of the screen. This is the STATUS LINE, which usually includes:

- The name of the file you're working on (if you've already named it)
- The length (size in characters) of the file
- Where in the file you are (by page number)
- Where on the screen you are (by line and column number)
- Whether the Insert Mode is in effect

You might also see a RULER LINE, which indicates where the left and right margins and any tab stops are set, and you might be provided with a HELP MENU, describing some of the most frequently used commands.

As you'll see, all this can be useful information. If you're just beginning to write on a word processor, however, it may be an over-whelming introduction. Don't worry about it for now. Instead, look below this information and spot the cursor.

The cursor may appear in different forms. Depending on your system, it might be a block, square, or triangle about the size of a screen character, or it might be a simple underline. It might flash on and off or remain as a steady image. Regardless, the cursor marks "where" in the word processing program you are at the moment and indicates that the machine is ready to accept some information from you. And, true to the Latin word *currere* ("to run") from which it derives its name, the cursor is going to run wherever your words take you. Figure 3-1 illustrates a typical status and ruler line display, with the cursor positioned in the upper left corner of the screen (line 1, column 1).

Type a character on the keyboard. The character appears on the screen, in the position where the cursor was, and the cursor moves one space to the right. Continue typing. Each time you strike a key, the corresponding character appears on the screen and the cur-sor moves over (see Figure 3-2).

Fig. 3-1: Typical status and ruler line display

```
        B:FIG3-1  PAGE 1 LINE 1 COL 01              INSERT ON
L——!————#————!————#————!————#————!————#————!————#————!———#——R
☐
```

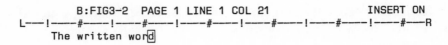

```
        B:FIG3-2  PAGE 1 LINE 1 COL 21              INSERT ON
L—--!---—#----—!---—#----—!---—#----—!---—#----—!---—#----—!---—#---R
      The written word
```

Fig. 3-2: Text entry and cursor movement

This process functions like the movement of the type ball on an office typewriter, but the experience is totally different. The characters simply appear—there's no hammer strike, no ink laid down on paper, no mechanical connection evident between the keys and the image on the screen, and no sound. The keys might make a click as they're struck, or the keyboard may function in complete silence. For a first-time user, the whole process may seem illusory, remote, or "soft," as though nothing is really happening.

Something really is happening, though, and it shouldn't take long for you to adjust to the feel of this new writing tool. In fact, you'll probably quickly discover that the minimal physical intrusions of the processor make writing a more pleasant experience and help make your writing flow more easily. Many writers even prefer to turn off the key clicks if they have that option.

▶ Explore the keyboard/screen as a writing medium in itself. You'll fall into this naturally, over time, but you'll get off to a more comfortable start if you don't try to think of the word processor as a substitute for a typewriter. It's quite a different tool—and a much more powerful one, to be sure. In terms of the physical act of writing or editing, however, the processor is actually simpler and less intrusive.

Word Wrap

An even more dramatic difference between a typewriter and a word processor becomes apparent with the writing of your very first sentence. In Figure 3-3, you have typed 62 characters, as indicated by the status line: line 1, column 62. (COLUMN is the term used for the horizontal positions on each line.) If your right margin was set for 65 characters and your next word was 'surely', it wouldn't fit on line 1.

You don't have to concern yourself about this, however; just continue typing. When text becomes longer than the available space

Fig. 3-3: Text before Word Wrap

```
        B:FIG3-3  PAGE 1 LINE 1 COL 62              INSERT ON
L—--!---—#----—!---—#----—!---—#----—!---—#----—!---—#----—!---—#---R
      The written word is in the grip of a revolution that will
```

on a line, the computer automatically sends the excess down to the next line, as illustrated in Figure 3-4.

Notice that you don't have to listen for a prompting bell or remember to hit a carriage return (commonly called the RETURN key in w/p systems). The machine keeps track of this for you and lets you concentrate on writing. That means twenty-five or more times per page that you're not going to be distracted from your flow of thoughts—one thousand eliminated interruptions in the course of writing a forty-page report.

The most common term for this word processing feature is WORD WRAP, and every writer instantly loves it. It works simply. The system is programmed with margins for the screen display, much like the margins on a typewriter. (More on margins in Chapter 5.) The program interprets a WORD as consecutive letters, numbers, or characters that are not separated by spaces. If such a "word" extends beyond the right margin, the text is "wrapped" around the margin and the whole word is sent to the beginning of the next line.

Different programs may keep track of "words" according to different rules. If you're already writing on a processor, take some time to experiment with the way the Word Wrap feature of your program works. See whether there is any limit to the length of words with which it will function. Make sure that all consecutive characters, including numerals and other non-alphabetic characters, dashes, and ellipses, are treated alike in following the Word Wrap rules. See how two consecutive spaces in your text are treated. If you do discover any unusual results, you should keep them in mind as you rely on your Word Wrap feature to keep your writing flowing from line to line. We'll be making this point again and again throughout this book, but we'll state it here as a general tip:

▶ Test every feature of your program to the extreme. Learn what your word processor will do, and how and when it will do it.

Actually, the Word Wrap features of some programs do operate differently. The simpler programs assiduously follow the rules, regardless of whether they might leave rather large holes in your text. Some of the more elaborate programs attempt to compensate for such occurrences by alerting you if a word would extend into a "hot zone"

Fig. 3-4: Result of Word Wrap

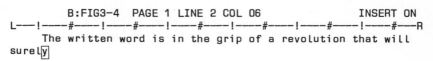

```
          B:FIG3-4  PAGE 1 LINE 2 COL 06              INSERT ON
L--!----#----!----#----!----#----!----#----!----#----!----#---R
     The written word is in the grip of a revolution that will
surely[y]
```

at the right margin and giving you the option of hyphenating that word. In some programs, the computer might even suggest where the hyphens should be placed (based on internally stored hyphenation rules).

For a number of reasons (which we'll cover in detail in Chapter 5), we recommend that you make sparing use of this hyphenation feature. The point to bear in mind now is that if you were intentionally to hyphenate a word at the end of a line and continue it onto the next line, your program would probably treat the hyphenated parts as two separate words, and that might lead to problems later on.

▶ When doing your initial writing, it's best to rely on Word Wrap. Don't try to hyphenate or anticipate the ends of lines.

Returns

As you continue writing and reach the end of a paragraph, you've got to send an appropriate signal to the computer. You do this by hitting the Return key. The program indicates the termination of the paragraph, usually by placing a marker of some sort after the last word or in the right margin (in our illustration, a '<' symbol). The cursor, which has been keeping a character ahead of your text, jumps to the next line, as illustrated in Figure 3-5.

Depending on your system, the Return key might be called the Carriage Return (which is really an anachronism, since there's no typewriter-style carriage) or it might be called ENTER (since this key is also used to enter information into the computer in non word processing applications). In this book, we'll always call it the Return key.

At the text-entry stage, the Return key sends the cursor back to the left margin and down a line automatically with a single stroke;

Fig. 3-5: Paragraph terminated with Return

```
        B:FIG3-5   PAGE 1 LINE 12 COL 01              INSERT ON
L--!----#----!----#----!----#----!----#----!----#----!----#---R
      The written word is in the grip of a revolution that will
surely change the writing arts as dramatically as the invention
of moveable type.  If you are one of the thousands of people who
write on a word processor, you've already discovered the new ease
with which you can record your thoughts, revise your text,
produce copy on demand, and streamline your research and filing.
And if you're a writer for whom the notion of word processing
still seems a mysterious tangle of hardware, software, and
jargon, you should count on being thrust into the word processing
era much sooner than you expect—or find yourself still working
with the technological equivalent of a stone tablet.<
□
```

you can think of it as functioning exactly as the carriage return on an electric typewriter. The difference is that you don't have to hit it at the end of every line—just at the end of each paragraph.

If you want to insert an extra line between your paragraphs, you can hit Return once again before continuing with your text.

Scrolling

As noted in Chapter 1, the screen is able to display only a limited number of lines. (The most common standard today is 24.) In Figure 3-6, the first two lines of the screen are displaying the status and ruler lines and you have filled the screen with 22 lines of text, with the cursor poised at the end of the last line.

If the next word you type would extend beyond the right margin, it gets wrapped onto the next line, according to the regular Word Wrap rules. But the text on the screen has to SCROLL to make room for the new line.

Figure 3-7 shows the result of scrolling. What had been the first line of text in Figure 3-6 has disappeared, all the rest of the lines have moved up, and your new line of text has appeared at the bottom.

Fig. 3-6: Screen filled with text

```
        B:FIG3-6   PAGE 1 LINE 22 COL 59              INSERT ON
L——!————#————!————#————!————#————!————#————!————#————!————#———R
     The written word is in the grip of a revolution that will
surely change the writing arts as dramatically as the invention
of moveable type.  If you are one of the thousands of people who
write on a word processor, you've already discovered the new ease
with which you can record your thoughts, revise your text,
produce copy on demand, and streamline your research and filing.
And if you're a writer for whom the notion of word processing
still seems a mysterious tangle of hardware, software, and
jargon, you should count on being thrust into the word processing
era much sooner than you expect—or find yourself still working
with the technological equivalent of a stone tablet.<
     The most striking innovation of word processing is speed—a
capacity that is vital to writers.  The word processor has the
ability to record notes, ideas, and paragraphs as fast as you can
hit the keys, without distracting clatter, carriage returns, or
changes of pages.  Consequently, this speed can improve both your
writing and your thinking processes.<
     Even more important than speed is the word processor's
ability to let you revise your writing thoroughly and almost
painlessly.  With a word processor, you can move phrases,
sentences, and blocks of text from one place to another within a
manuscript, copy sections at various places in your text or
```

L──!────#────!────#────!────#────!────#────!────#────!────#───R
surely change the writing arts as dramatically as the invention
of moveable type. If you are one of the thousands of people who
write on a word processor, you've already discovered the new ease
with which you can record your thoughts, revise your text,
produce copy on demand, and streamline your research and filing.
And if you're a writer for whom the notion of word processing
still seems a mysterious tangle of hardware, software, and
jargon, you should count on being thrust into the word processing
era much sooner than you expect—or find yourself still working
with the technological equivalent of a stone tablet.<
    The most striking innovation of word processing is speed—a
capacity that is vital to writers. The word processor has the
ability to record notes, ideas, and paragraphs as fast as you can
hit the keys, without distracting clatter, carriage returns, or
changes of pages. Consequently, this speed can improve both your
writing and your thinking processes.<
    Even more important than speed is the word processor's
ability to let you revise your writing thoroughly and almost
painlessly. With a word processor, you can move phrases,
sentences, and blocks of text from one place to another within a
manuscript, copy sections at various places in your text or
duplicate them in another

Fig. 3-7: Text scrolled down 1 line

This scrolling process occurs automatically as you continue typing; when you get to the end of the new line, the screen will scroll again.

By the time you have typed 22 more lines, the screen will have kept scrolling so that none of your first 22 lines are displayed. To be able to go back and view those first lines—now out of sight—you use the various scrolling commands on your processor.

Before exploring some of these commands, it's helpful to think of your text as actually residing on a long scroll that is passing through your screen display. Figure 3-8 illustrates this concept. It represents in graphic form about 70 lines of text on such a scroll. The screen outline marked A indicates what you would be able to see if you scrolled to the beginning of your text. Position C shows the screen scrolled to the end of the text. And position B shows the screen scrolled to display roughly lines 30 through 54.

▶ Learn to visualize your text as extending above and below what you can see on the screen. For some people, this notion of scrolling is a natural one. For others, it might take some getting used to. It's important, though, that you get a feel for the extent of all your text, rather than thinking of isolated fragments of your writing being flashed on the screen.

A   **B**   **C**

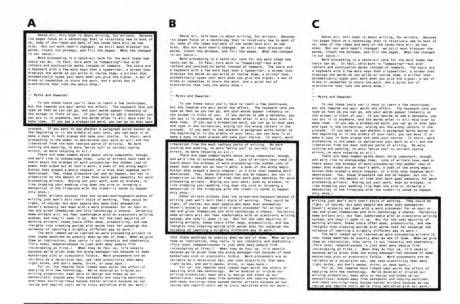

Fig. 3-8: A text "scroll" and "windows"

If you're just starting to work on a processor, it will be helpful to type in several screenfuls of text and then experiment with your w/p program's scrolling commands. Most word processors have commands for Scrolling to the Beginning of the Text and Scrolling to the End, as illustrated above. All processors have a way of Scrolling by Screenfuls, in either direction. (Usually, the text jumps one or more lines less than a whole screenful, so that some text from the bottom of the previous display is retained at the top of the new display for reference.)

Some processors include commands that allow you to Scroll a Specified Number of Lines, or to Scroll to a Specific Line (identified by line number). Some programs permit Continuous Scrolling, at various speeds.

There is a bit of confusing terminology surrounding the notion of scrolling and how to apply the terms "up" and "down." If you start with the beginning of the text and scroll to the end, the lines of text will move up on the screen. The manuals for some w/p programs call this "scrolling up," because the words are moving up.

Other systems' manuals take the opposite view. They visualize in terms of which direction the "window" moves and reason that if you're trying to see what's "down" below the bottom edge of your screen, "scrolling (your gaze) down" more accurately describes the process.

We think that this latter viewpoint is the more useful one, and so will use "scrolling down" to mean moving from the first words in your text to the last. You should probably just adapt to your manual's terminology or devise whatever semantic convention makes the most sense to you. What is important is that you develop a perception of all your text and how to get to it, beyond what you see on the screen.

The Cursor

Every word processor has four main cursor control keys (or keystroke combinations) that move the cursor in each of the four directions. The Cursor Right key will move the cursor one character (letter or space) to the right for each time struck. If the cursor is at the far right position on the screen, moving it one position to the right will usually make it appear at the far left of the next line. If you wanted to, you could move the cursor from the beginning of your text all the way to the end just by repeatedly pressing the Cursor Right key.

As you would expect, the Cursor Left key operates by the same rules, in the opposite direction. When it is moved to the leftmost position of a line, another Cursor Left keystroke will make the cursor appear at the far right position of the previous line.

Figure 3-9 shows one paragraph of text, (double spaced here for clarity). The arrows indicate the way in which the Cursor Right and Cursor Left commands "wrap" the cursor from one line to the next.

Cursor Down moves the cursor from the top line of the screen to the bottom while maintaining the same column position. (On some systems, if the cursor is moved down to a blank line, it will jump to

Fig. 3-9: Cursor wrapping

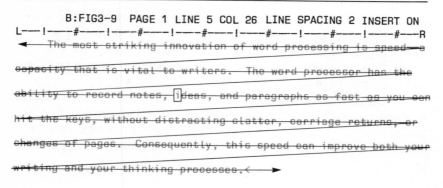

the leftmost position on that line.) Cursor Up operates like Cursor Down, in reverse.

An almost universal rule of word processing is that "The cursor cannot go where it has never been." This means that on most systems, you are not able to move the cursor past the last portion of text by striking the cursor keys. You must add characters or spaces or hit the Return key to advance the cursor into new territory.

On some systems, holding down any of the cursor keys will keep the cursor moving continuously. Other systems permit continuous movement of the cursor by pressing it in combination with a separate REPEAT key.

Most systems also provide a number of rapid movement commands for the cursor. The Home command moves the cursor instantly to the upper left of the screen. Some systems have an End of Screen command, which moves the cursor to the last line (left- or rightmost position, depending on the system). Many processors provide a command for moving the cursor to the far left or right of whichever line the cursor is on, or for moving it to the top or bottom line, maintaining its column position. Figure 3-10 shows some of these rapid cursor movement possibilities.

Many systems have a command for jumping the cursor a word at a time (following the same rules used in Word Wrap), either to the left or right. Some permit jumping a sentence at a time, or to the beginning of the next paragraph. And there may be some more exotic cursor movement commands on specialized w/p systems, as well.

▶ If you are working on a processor, you should learn your system's cursor commands and experiment with them thoroughly. The cursor is your vehicle for moving within your text. Moving it quickly and efficiently should become as close to second nature as driving your car.

Regardless of which cursor movement commands you have at your disposal, there is one technique that will help you get from place to place on the screen with greater speed and accuracy. We call this technique "verbalizing keystrokes." In Figure 3-10, imagine that the cursor is at the word 'text' and that you want to move it to the beginning of the word 'another', using the command for jumping a word at a time. If you rely on just your eyes to guide your hand, you'll have to look closely at the screen to see how far to go. And if the movement of the cursor on your system lags a bit behind the keystroke entry of the command, this task can become even more difficult.

▶ An excellent strategy for moving the cursor is to quietly verbalize the word jumps for each keystroke. If you say to yourself

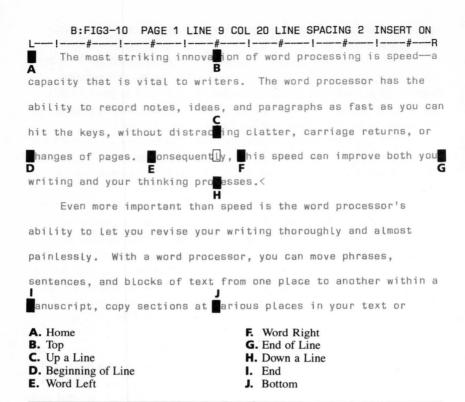

```
B:FIG3-10   PAGE 1 LINE 9 COL 20 LINE SPACING 2  INSERT ON
L——!——#——!——#——!——#——!——#——!——#——!——#——R
```

The most striking innovation of word processing is speed—a

capacity that is vital to writers. The word processor has the

ability to record notes, ideas, and paragraphs as fast as you can

hit the keys, without distracting clatter, carriage returns, or

hanges of pages. onsequently, his speed can improve both you

writing and your thinking processes.<

Even more important than speed is the word processor's

ability to let you revise your writing thoroughly and almost

painlessly. With a word processor, you can move phrases,

sentences, and blocks of text from one place to another within a

anuscript, copy sections at arious places in your text or

A. Home
B. Top
C. Up a Line
D. Beginning of Line
E. Word Left

F. Word Right
G. End of Line
H. Down a Line
I. End
J. Bottom

Fig. 3-10: Rapid cursor movement examples

"from one place to another" as you hit the Cursor Word Right key, the cursor should come to rest in exactly the spot you want. The same technique works well for moving up or down lines. Even though there's a stigma attached to moving one's lips when reading, try verbalizing your keystroke commands and see whether you don't become a better cursor "driver."

Cursor Movement and Scrolling

Scrolling is your method for moving from one place in your text to another, much like shuffling through the pages of a manuscript, while the cursor is used primarily to move around within a screenful of text. The two functions are related, however. If the cursor is on the last line of the screen, pressing the Cursor Down key will scroll the text down one line on most systems. The Cursor Up command does the same in the other direction. Moving the cursor can thus serve as another (though usually less efficient) method of scrolling.

On some systems, the method for scrolling to the beginning or end of the text is to send the cursor to those positions. This is much faster than scrolling through all the lines of text, and the screen usually shows only the text at the beginning and end of the process, rather than everything in between.

▶ You might want to experiment on your system and see what happens to the position of the cursor when the Scroll Screen (up or down) command is given. The cursor might remain in the same relative position (line and column), it might jump to the Home or End spot on the screen, or in some cases it might stay at its spot in the text (it would be unusual for the cursor to leave the screen entirely). This is another example of our general encouragement to test all the features of your system. Knowing how cursor movement works in conjunction with the scrolling commands on your word processor can help you devise the most efficient methods for manipulating text.

Chapter 4

Wordplay

Editing Text

In the previous chapter, we looked at the scrolling and cursor movement commands that permit you to locate any spot in your text. There's a reason for being able to do that, of course. Once a paragraph, word, or character is pinpointed by the cursor, it can be modified instantly. The nature and extent of revisions possible with a word processor are limited only by your editorial fervor.

In this chapter we'll look at some of the basic editing and revising tools that are the heart of most word processors. As we've noted, the precise operation of these functions varies from system to system. If you are shopping for a processor, the ease of operation of these functions (as well as the scrolling and cursor movement commands already described) should be important factors in your choice of a system. If you're already using a word processor, you'll want to be sure that you've developed comfortable and reliable routines for all of these methods of processing your words.

Overtyping

The most elemental form of revision is really more of a writing technique than an editing tool. Assume that you've written the sentence in Figure 4-1 and then decide that you'd rather start the sentence with 'The ability to revise'. If you move the cursor back to the first character of 'Even' and type 'The ability', your correction will be made as you type, as shown in Figure 4-2. As you continue typing, you would replace all of the old characters with new ones.

The most common term for this feature is OVERTYPING. Quite simply, any character typed at the cursor position will substitute for the existing character. You could keep typing over your previous text, and overtyping would destroy and replace everything in its path. (This is one way of making a wholesale revision, but other w/p features, such as inserting and deleting text, provide more effective alternatives.)

▶ Overtyping is most useful for correcting a word that you've just typed or for making a "spot" revision. As we'll see later in this chapter, Overtyping is not a particularly useful tool for elaborate revisions.

When you experiment with Overtyping, you'll realize quickly that word processors treat spaces (hitting the space bar) just like any other character. If you've written 'well-being' and hit the space bar with the cursor positioned at the hyphen, you'll substitute a space for the hyphen and thereby create two words.

▶ A common oversight for writers who are converting from a typewriter to a word processor is failing to remember that the space bar does not simply advance the cursor; rather, it inserts a "blank" character. So you can't move to a spot in your text by tapping the space bar, as you would on a typewriter. After the first couple of times you wipe out several letters by hitting the space bar, you'll quickly and easily make the adjustment.

Fig. 4-1: Text prior to Overtyping

```
        B:FIG4-1   PAGE 1  LINE 3  COL 11              INSERT ON
L——!————#————!————#————!————#————!————#————!————#————!————#———R
        Even more important than speed is the word processor's
ability to let you revise your writing thoroughly and almost
painlessly.
```

Fig. 4-2: Result of Overtyping

```
        B:FIG4-2   PAGE 1  LINE 1  COL 17              INSERT ON
L——!————#————!————#————!————#————!————#————!————#————!————#———R
        The abilitymportant than speed is the word processor's
ability to let you revise your writing thoroughly and almost
painlessly.
```

The (Sometimes) Destructive Backspace

On most systems, the keyboard will feature a BACKSPACE key, located in approximately the same position as on a typewriter keyboard. The very existence of this key is somewhat of an anachronistic carry-over from the age of typewriters, since the backspace key usually duplicates functions provided by other keys on the word processor. Typists converting to word processing will likely stay in the habit of using this key, however, and it can be handy.

The effect of the Backspace key varies from system to system. On some word processors, it merely moves the cursor to the left. Thus, it duplicates the Cursor Left function key, but it may be more accessible and therefore the better key to use when going back for Overtype corrections.

On some systems, this key operates as a DESTRUCTIVE BACK-SPACE (also sometimes called RUBOUT). It too moves the cursor back, but deletes characters as it does so, much like the correction key on a correcting typewriter, except that it's a one-key operation. If the Backspace key has this function, it's particularly useful for making corrections while writing, because it clears text from the screen in the process. If it operates as a Repeating key as well, it's even handier for corrections-in-progress.

Insert Mode

Most word processors provide a command for sending the system into what is called INSERT MODE. Once that happens, the normal Overtyping rules are no longer in effect. Instead, all characters typed are inserted into the text, at the position of the cursor. Two methods are generally used to accomplish this inserting of text, and we'll illustrate both.

On some systems, the newly typed character appears at the present cursor position; the character that had previously been at the cursor position moves one position to the right, as do all the characters following it. This process continues as long as characters are typed in Insert mode. For example, your text might appear as in Figure 4-3, with the cursor on the first letter of 'fast'.

If you type 'very', your text would now read as in Figure 4-4, with the cursor still poised at the beginning of 'fast'. If you wanted to insert just this word, you would type a space, then give the command to leave Insert mode. Or you could continue inserting additional words.

```
        B:FIG4-3  PAGE 1 LINE 1 COL 45                    INSERT ON
L---!----#----!----#----!----#----!----#----!----#----!----#---R
      Because writing on a word processor is ⌐fast, simple, and
   extremely flexible, writers have the unparalleled opportunity to
   improve their work significantly and still meet their deadlines.
```

Fig. 4-3: Text prior to Insert

```
        B:FIG4-4  PAGE 1 LINE 1 COL 49                    INSERT ON
L---!----#----!----#----!----#----!----#----!----#----!----#---R
      Because writing on a word processor is very⌐fast, simple, and
   extremely flexible, writers have the unparalleled opportunity to
   improve their work significantly and still meet their deadlines.
```

Fig. 4-4: Result of "squeeze-in" Insert

▶ The basic rule for this Insert mode routine is "Squeeze in Character at Cursor—Text Moves Right."

In this approach, the program might exit from Insert mode automatically upon movement of the cursor, or it might stay in Insert mode, ready for more insertions, until an Exit Insert command is given. Programs that use this insertion method will indicate somehow that Insert mode is in effect, either with an appropriate notice on the status line or by changing the appearance of the cursor.

The second approach to insertions creates blank space on the screen for the characters to be inserted. Using the same text as in the previous example, if the cursor were at 'fast' and the Insert mode command were given, all the text from the cursor position on would be pushed down one or more lines, as shown in Figure 4-5.

The cursor would remain at the beginning of the newly created blank space and would advance in the normal fashion as additional characters are typed, as Figure 4-6 illustrates.

Fig. 4-5: Text ready for "drop-in" Insert

```
        B:FIG4-5  PAGE 1 LINE 1 COL 45                    INSERT ON
L---!----#----!----#----!----#----!----#----!----#----!----#---R
      Because writing on a word processor is []



                                      fast, simple, and
   extremely flexible, writers have the unparalleled opportunity to
   improve their work significantly and still meet their deadlines.
```

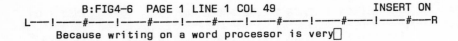

L—!——#——!——#——!——#——!——#——!——#——!——#——R
    Because writing on a word processor is very▯

                              fast, simple, and
extremely flexible, writers have the unparalleled opportunity to
improve their work significantly and still meet their deadlines.

Fig. 4-6: During "drop-in" Insert

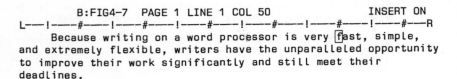

B:FIG4-7   PAGE 1 LINE 1 COL 50   INSERT ON
L—!——#——!——#——!——#——!——#——!——#——!——#——R
    Because writing on a word processor is very ▯ast, simple,
and extremely flexible, writers have the unparalleled opportunity
to improve their work significantly and still meet their
deadlines.

Fig. 4-7: After Close Up command

The final step in the insertion routine would be to give a CLOSE
UP (or Exit Insert) command, which would move the sections of text
back together (Figure 4-7).

▶ The alternate type of Insert mode routine is "Create
Space—Drop in Characters—Close Up Text." In this approach, the
Close Up command usually causes the program to exit from Insert
mode and establishes the Overtyping convention once again.

It's difficult to say which approach is better. The "squeeze-in-
character" method is probably a bit more convenient for making spot
corrections, while the "drop-in" system works better for adding substantial amounts of text. (The drop-in systems vary widely in their
operation, and we'll see shortly that most programs provide additional means of creating blank spaces within the text.)

Regardless of the way your system's Insert feature works,
using it will become an established routine once you've done some
writing and editing. We've explained this feature in detail for a reason, however.

▶ The Insert mode is one of the most useful and most used
functions on a word processor. You should feel completely comfortable with the way Insert works on your system: how to enter it, how
and where it adds characters, and how to exit from it. If you are
shopping for a word processor, investigate the Insert function closely
and make sure that it operates logically, reliably, and with a minimum of commands.

Delete

Hand in hand with the Insert mode go two functions that delete characters and words from the text.

DELETE CHARACTER (frequently simply called DELETE) does just what its name indicates: it deletes the character at the cursor position, while pulling the remaining characters to the left to close up the hole. This feature is obviously handy for getting rid of a spurious letter within a word that was the result of overanxious typing or faulty spelling. Just as often, however, it's used in conjunction with Insert to make substantive corrections.

In Figure 4-8, the word 'improve' is being replaced with 'revise'. The cursor was placed on the 'i', Insert mode was entered, and the replacement characters were squeezed in. Hitting the Delete key seven times is all that's necessary to complete the correction.

The DELETE WORD function provides a short-cut to the same revision. It will generally delete all consecutive characters from the cursor position to the next word (with one important wrinkle).

In the example shown in Figure 4-8, after typing in the new word, giving the Delete Word command would produce the desired result, as illustrated in Figure 4-9.

In the example shown in Figure 4-9, the rule followed by the Delete Word command was to delete all consecutive characters *up to but not including* the next space. But some systems follow a different rule, deleting the space as well. In such a case, the insertion of the new word would have to include an extra space, as illustrated in Figure 4-10, before giving the Delete Word command. The subsequent

Fig. 4-8: Text prior to Delete

```
        B:FIG4-8   PAGE 1 LINE 3 COL 10              INSERT ON
L——!————#———!————#————!———#————!————#————!————#————!———#——R
        Because writing on a word processor is very fast, simple,
and extremely flexible, writers have the unparalleled opportunity
to reviseimprove their work significantly and still meet their
deadlines.
```

Fig. 4-9: Result of Delete Word

```
        B:FIG4-9   PAGE 1 LINE 3 COL 10              INSERT ON
L——!————#———!————#————!———#————!———#————!————#————!———#——R
        Because writing on a word processor is very fast, simple,
and extremely flexible, writers have the unparalleled opportunity
to revise their work significantly and still meet their
deadlines.
```

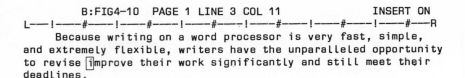

L———!————#————!————#————!————#————!————#————!————#————!————#————R
      Because writing on a word processor is very fast, simple,
and extremely flexible, writers have the unparalleled opportunity
to revise improve their work significantly and still meet their
deadlines.

Fig. 4-10: Text prior to Delete Word Plus Trailing Space

Delete Word command would then yield the correct spacing between words.

▶ Know thoroughly the rules of your system's Delete Word command, namely, whether the deletion includes the space following the deleted word. This distinction is particularly important, because the combination of Insert/Delete Word constitutes the most reliable and efficient routine for making revisions. It's an essential operation at which to become adept and a critical one to evaluate if you're choosing a system. (Chapter 12 presents detailed revision techniques and describes how you can develop the best editing routines for your word processor.)

More Deletions and Insertions

Most systems provide a variety of additional Delete commands to make large-scale alterations.

A common function is DELETE TO END OF LINE. All text is deleted from the position of the cursor to the end of the line. This command can be used to delete entire lines if the cursor is placed at the beginning of the line. Some systems provide a separate DELETE LINE command, which will delete an entire line of text regardless of where on that line the cursor is placed. An obscure feature found on some systems is DELETE TO BEGINNING OF LINE, which deletes a line from the left margin up to the cursor position.

We have already described the Delete Character and Delete Word functions. You may also be provided with DELETE SENTENCE and DELETE PARAGRAPH features, which identify the sentence or paragraph within which the cursor is placed and then delete it. A variation is DELETE TO END OF SENTENCE and DELETE TO END OF PARAGRAPH, which delete from the cursor position to a terminal punctuation mark or paragraph-end marker. Needless to say, before relying on these features, you should carefully investigate the syntax assumptions upon which they operate (such as how question marks, exclamation points, and quotation marks are treated).

► As our catalog of editing features swells, we'll make note here of a view to be developed further in Part II: It is preferable to have at your command a few editing functions with which you are thoroughly conversant, rather than to fumble with a multitude of functions whose effects constantly need to be double-checked.

Two other deletion features are handy if your w/p program provides them. DELETE TO CURSOR deletes everything from the beginning of your text up to the cursor position. DELETE FROM CURSOR deletes everything from the cursor to the end. These are useful for stripping away unwanted portions of text for various reasons. If your system does not have these functions, you can accomplish the same result slightly less efficiently by making repeated use of the Delete Line command.

A final related function found on most processors is INSERT LINE. This command simply creates blank lines between existing lines of text. It's useful for creating special text formats, and using it can also improve the efficiency or the legibility of large-scale insertions if your system has the "squeeze-in" type of Insert mode.

Block Moves

We now come to one of the word processor's most powerful editing tools—the feature that permits you to move blocks of text from one position to another. Although the operation of the BLOCK MOVE function varies widely from system to system, it invariably involves three steps: identifying the block, locating the position to which it is to be moved, and inserting the block at that position.

To identify the block of text, you insert two BLOCK MARKERS, at the beginning and the end of the segment to be moved. In most systems, you place the cursor at the first character of the block and give the command to insert a special character in the displayed text. You then perform a similar routine after the last character of the block. In some systems, the marked block may be highlighted on the screen or the block markers themselves may serve as delimiters. Figure 4-11 shows a screenful of text in which the last paragraph has been marked as a block with beginning and end symbols (<B> and <K>).

To move the paragraph, you move the cursor to the location in the text at which you want to insert the marked block (in our example, to the top of the screen). You give the BLOCK INSERT (or BLOCK MOVE) command, and *Voila!* the text disappears from its former location, appearing at the cursor position as illustrated in Figure 4-12.

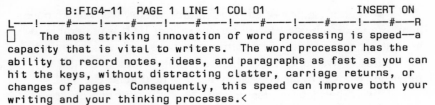

```
        B:FIG4-11  PAGE 1 LINE 1 COL 01              INSERT ON
L——!————#————!————#————!————#————!————#————!————#————!————#———R
☐    The most striking innovation of word processing is speed—a
capacity that is vital to writers.  The word processor has the
ability to record notes, ideas, and paragraphs as fast as you can
hit the keys, without distracting clatter, carriage returns, or
changes of pages.  Consequently, this speed can improve both your
writing and your thinking processes.<
     Even more important than speed is the word processor's
ability to let you revise your writing thoroughly and almost
painlessly.  With a word processor, you can move phrases,
sentences, and blocks of text from one place to another within a
manuscript, copy sections at various places in your text or
duplicate them in another manuscript, and study each successive
stage of revision in a clean printed copy as well as on the
word processor's screen.  Because writing on a word processor is
fast, simple and extremely flexible, writers have the
unparalleled opportunity to improve their work significantly and
still meet their deadlines.<
<B>     Many observers have expressed fear that the burgeoning use
of electronic tools such as word processors will severly damage
the literary process.  Just the opposite is true.  Because
writers can record their thoughts easily and then revise their
work extensively, writing has effectively been reborn through the
use of word processing.<<K>
```

Fig. 4-11: Text with paragraph marked as block

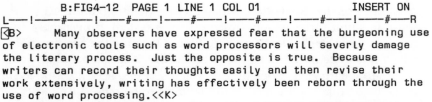

```
        B:FIG4-12  PAGE 1 LINE 1 COL 01              INSERT ON
L——!————#————!————#————!————#————!————#————!————#————!————#———R
◁B>     Many observers have expressed fear that the burgeoning use
of electronic tools such as word processors will severly damage
the literary process.  Just the opposite is true.  Because
writers can record their thoughts easily and then revise their
work extensively, writing has effectively been reborn through the
use of word processing.<<K>
     The most striking innovation of word processing is speed—a
capacity that is vital to writers.  The word processor has the
ability to record notes, ideas, and paragraphs as fast as you can
hit the keys, without distracting clatter, carriage returns, or
changes of pages.  Consequently, this speed can improve both your
writing and your thinking processes.<
     Even more important than speed is the word processor's
ability to let you revise your writing thoroughly and almost
painlessly.  With a word processor, you can move phrases,
sentences, and blocks of text from one place to another within a
manuscript, copy sections at various places in your text or
duplicate them in another manuscript, and study each successive
stage of revision in a clean printed copy as well as on the
word processor's screen.  Because writing on a word processor is
fast, simple and extremely flexible, writers have the
```

Fig. 4-12: After Block Move

Witnessing a block move for the first time invariably elicits a comment about "the magic of word processing."

Some systems provide a related function, BLOCK COPY. It works just like Block Move, except that the marked block is duplicated at the cursor position without disturbing the block at its original position. This is a useful feature for creating forms, as a small portion of text can be duplicated many times without retyping. (It will also come in handy if you ever write an epic poem with a repeating stanza.)

On some systems the Block Move feature works as simply as described above; on others, there are limitations. Some programs limit the size of a block or the distance it can be moved. Some programs require that the block markers be deleted after the move (rather than clearing them automatically). Some programs restrict block moves to sections of text constituting complete lines (rather than permitting a block to begin and end in the middle of a line).

▶ The Block Move is an important, powerful tool. You will have occasion to use it often if it works reliably for you, and it really should work as if by magic. Establish a set routine for making the best use of your program's Block Move function. And if you're choosing a word processor, don't make a final decision until you have investigated and tested this feature.

Search and Replace

We've saved the most spectacular and delightful w/p features for last. Generally collected under the name SEARCH AND REPLACE or FIND AND REPLACE are several functions which permit you to zip through your text at microprocessor speed and locate and change words to your specifications.

The basic operator of these is the SEARCH function. Generally, you give the Search command and a prompt appears on the screen, asking for the item to be located. You then type in the characters exactly as you wish to find them in the text, which is the signal for the computer to flex its muscles. The microprocessor at the heart of your machine then commences to "read" all of your text, from the beginning or from the cursor position, looking for a string of consecutive characters that matches your entered item. (The computer terminology for such groups of characters is in fact STRING.)

While the machine is searching, you'll usually see your text scrolling at a rapid clip until the first occurrence of the string is found. The scrolling will then stop, the cursor will poise at the beginning or end of the string, and the status line may even gleefully invite you to 'Continue'. At this point, you'll usually have the option of making some revision to what you have written or proceeding through the text.

Following the appropriate Continue command, the computer picks up the hunt until it locates the next place your chosen word or phrase appears, once more letting you make changes or perhaps simply take notes. When the computer reaches the end of your text, it will often respond with 'Search Completed'.

Word processors take these Search commands quite literally. For example, many systems distinguish between upper- and lowercase letters, so that the word 'Computer' at the beginning of a sentence would not be found if you were searching for 'computer'. To locate all instances of that word, you might therefore request a search for 'omputer'. (Some systems do give you the option of ignoring upper- and lowercase in searches or do that automatically.)

As with other w/p functions, Search treats blank spaces the same as any other character. For example, if you wanted to search for the word 'not' and typed your request as just the letters 'n o t' (without a trailing space), the Search function would probably pause at 'notice', 'notary', 'nothing', and 'notturno' as well, since those words all contain the specified string. If you really wanted to search for just the word 'not', you might want to request '(space) n o t (space)', and thus avoid getting tied up with 'knot'. (Some systems may automatically insert leading or trailing spaces.) Half the fun of the Search function is being creative in specifying your subject word.

▶ When using the Search function, try to specify the shortest possible string that is likely to be unique to your word or phrase.

The Search function has a multitude of uses. If you want to find the episode in your detective novel where the key evidence is discovered, you can search for 'rutabaga' and locate the reference instantly. Or you might want to see whether you spelled the word correctly each time, or determine just how many times you used 'rutabaga'. Unlike some of the other w/p functions, which are designed to do one specific job, Search is a greatly adaptable feature for which you can devise many creative uses. (In Part II we'll explore a number of specific editing applications of the Search function.)

What if, in the middle of your detective novel, your tastes suddenly become more sophisticated and you decide to change 'rutabaga' to 'pomegranate'? The tool for you is the REPLACE function. Actually, Replace usually can be used with two options. In GLOBAL REPLACE, you are asked for a Search word and then a Replace word to substitute for it. The program then automatically scans the entire text and makes the revision wherever the Search word occurs.

Needless to say, you must give some forethought to what might result from such a sweeping revision. If you command the computer to replace globally every instance of 'I' with 'we', you'll undoubtedly discover that your joint communique speaks in terms of 'we am'.

▶ Global Replace must be used very prudently to avoid unsuspected errors.

A more useful feature is SELECTIVE REPLACE, which combines the Search and Replace functions but leaves the decisions to you. Once the Search and Replace words are specified, the program proceeds through your text and stops at each occurrence of the Search word. You then have the option to substitute the Replace word (automatically, with the push of a key), make other editorial changes, or leave the Search word in the text and continue the search for the next occurrence.

Refinements of these Search and Replace features permit you to search either from the beginning of the text, from the present cursor position to the end of the text, or from the cursor position to the beginning of the text. These features are especially useful for spot checks as you are writing or editing.

▶ Some programs provide PLACE MARKERS, which can be inserted in the text in much the way Block Markers are inserted and then used as reference pointers to be located with the Search command. If your program does not include this feature, you can accomplish much the same thing by introducing seldom-used characters (such as '@' and '#') into the text to mark key passages and searching for them later. (Special Place Markers, like Block Markers, generally are not interpreted as actual characters when the text is printed; if you use regular keyboard symbols as markers, however, you'll have to remember to delete them before printing your work.)

The Electronic Pencil Case

The features described in this and the previous chapter make up the Computer Age tools for creating and revising text. As we'll see shortly, these writing and editing functions comprise only a part of the total word processing program. They are, however, the tools that you'll be using most extensively to "get your thoughts down."

Throughout these two chapters, we've repeatedly emphasized two points: If you're writing on a processor now, you should develop reliable routines that make the best use of your machine's capabilities. If you're about to choose a word processor, make sure that these basic tools function logically and conveniently.

We've risked being repetitious for a reason. If you have to struggle with these basics, writing on a word processor can be a crippling chore, making you wish you had the old typewriter back again. If, on the other hand, you transform these electronic functions into extensions of your own skills, you will experience unprecedented freedom, power, and creativity in your writing.

Chapter 5

Getting in Shape

Screen Formatting

Our discussion so far has dealt solely with creating and revising text. We've concentrated on getting the message across but haven't been concerned at all about the form the message takes. Up to this point, we've accepted the screen display at "face value"; in fact, we've stressed that proficiency as a w/p writer depends on recognizing the screen as a "real" medium.

The screen is not the final medium, however. In most cases, you will be printing your text as the end product, and at that point, the form your writing takes will be of major importance. So this chapter is a transition: we will still be talking in terms of what you can see on the screen, but now the screen will be serving as a preview of what will be printed.

In other words, designing your pages can be a two-step process. The first step is establishing the measurements of the text so that you can work with it easily on the screen. The second step concerns the printed pages, which you may wish to design differently from the on-screen text.

Although formatting your text can be done in two different steps, this entire chapter deals with only the on-screen part of the process. And formatting text on the screen involves but a single word processing concept—the length that each line of text will be when you print your writing. (All the other variables you can imagine about a printed page will be covered in the chapter that follows.) If you keep in mind that we're only talking about this one element—line length—all the shuffling, squeezing, reforming, and shaping up that's about to take place will be much easier to follow.

The Text String

In the last two chapters, we described how text is created and revised on the word processor. We saw letters appear and shift on the screen, but what does the text look like to the computer?

Within the machine's memory is stored what amounts to a "super string" of characters, each one in the form of one byte. (You'll recall from Chapter 1 that a byte is a collection of eight bits, each consisting of a 1 or a 0. There are 256 eight-bit combinations possible.)

Some of these byte values represent the letters of the alphabet according to a standard convention known as ASCII (the American Standard Code for Information Interchange). The ASCII (pronounced "ass-key") code for the letter "A" is 65; "B" is 66, and so on up to 90 for "Z." A lowercase "a" is ASCII 97; "z" is 122. (The value for each lowercase letter is 32 greater than its uppercase counterpart.) All the punctuation marks have ASCII values too: a comma is 44; a hyphen is 45; a period is 46. The numerals 0 through 9 are represented by ASCII 48 through 57. A blank space, which we've noted is treated just like any other character, is ASCII 32. There's no need for you to learn these values, or even to think of them while you're writing, but you might find it interesting to look at the ASCII chart in Table 5-1, just to see how the letters and other characters are assigned their values.

For each character you type at the keyboard, the byte for the corresponding ASCII code is stored in the computer's memory. Although the actual storage scheme within the computer may be complex, you could think of your text as a succession of byte values—each representing one character—as though they were in a long chain or string. If you later insert one or more characters within your text, their ASCII codes are inserted in the existing text string. If you delete characters, the bytes representing them are deleted from the string.

Table 5-1: ASCII Character Set

Value	Character	Value	Character	Value	Character
0	(NUL)	43	+	86	V
1	(SOH)	44	,	87	W
2	(STX)	45	-	88	X
3	(ETX)	46	.	89	Y
4	(EOT)	47	/	90	Z
5	(ENQ)	48	0	91	[
6	(ACK)	49	1	92	\
7	(BEL)	50	2	93	]
8	(BS)	51	3	94	^
9	(HT)	52	4	95	_
10	(LF)	53	5	96	`
11	(VT)	54	6	97	a
12	(FF)	55	7	98	b
13	(CR)	56	8	99	c
14	(SO)	57	9	100	d
15	(SI)	58	:	101	e
16	(DLE)	59	;	102	f
17	(DC1)	60	<	103	g
18	(DC2)	61	=	104	h
19	(DC3)	62	>	105	i
20	(DC4)	63	?	106	j
21	(NAK)	64	@	107	k
22	(SYN)	65	A	108	l
23	(ETB)	66	B	109	m
24	(CAN)	67	C	110	n
25	(EM)	68	D	111	o
26	(SUB)	69	E	112	p
27	(ESC)	70	F	113	q
28	(FS)	71	G	114	r
29	(GS)	72	H	115	s
30	(RS)	73	I	116	t
31	(US)	74	J	117	u
32	(SP)	75	K	118	v
33	!	76	L	119	w
34	"	77	M	120	x
35	#	78	N	121	y
36	$	79	O	122	z
37	%	80	P	123	{
38	&	81	Q	124		
39	'	82	R	125	}
40	(	83	S	126	~
41	)	84	T	127	(DEL)
42	*	85	U		

Note: characters in parentheses are ASCII control codes and are not printable.

With this bit of background, we can look in greater detail at how the Word Wrap feature of the system works. As the text is entered, the program keeps count of the bytes/characters being entered on each line, and it also keeps track of each new word. When a word is entered that would make the character count exceed the set line length, the program makes that word appear on the next line of the screen.

What happens internally is that the program inserts one or more special ASCII characters into the text string, between the last word on one line and the first word on the next. The particular characters vary from program to program, but they will most likely be ones with ASCII values either below 32 or, in some programs, above 126. The Return mentioned in Chapter 3 is the most common of these characters, which are called CONTROL CHARACTERS. These characters usually don't appear on the screen, but they are present in the text string nonetheless.

The text-stringing process continues, line by line, with the control characters for each LINE END being automatically inserted in the string according to the Word Wrap rules. When you finally reach the end of the paragraph and so indicate by hitting the Return key, the program inserts one or more different control characters in the text string to mark the PARAGRAPH END. (The ASCII control character for the Paragraph End may or may not appear on the screen; if it doesn't, the program may print another character on the screen to indicate the end of the paragraph.)

This process continues, paragraph by paragraph, as you create your text. When you're finished, you've stored in the computer's memory a string of "printable" ASCII characters (letters, numerals, punctuation marks, and spaces), sprinkled with non-printable ASCII control characters for the Line Ends every 65 characters or so and for the Paragraph Ends where appropriate. On the screen, each line of text (the characters between each of the Line End control characters) is displayed separately.

Reforming

If your margins had been set for 65 characters per line while you created text, the Word Wrap function would have made sure that the text string contained no more than 65 characters between each Line End control character. If you later went back into the text to make revisions, however, you would have added or deleted some characters within the string, and this would have thrown off the character count for the Word Wrap rules. Some lines would now contain far more or fewer characters between Line Ends than the 65 characters designated for each line. On the screen, these discrepancies might appear as lines that trail off the right edge of the display or as gaping holes in the text, as illustrated in Figure 5-1. It's time to Reform.

The word processor has a special command for re-sorting the text string into proper line lengths. A common name for this command is REFORM, the term we'll use in this book. It might also be called REFORMAT or ALIGN. Essentially, the Reform function causes the computer to read through the text string and re-count characters, stripping the Line End characters from their previous positions and inserting new ones so that each line once again contains no more characters than the set margins. The process of stripping and reinserting continues until a Paragraph End character is reached.

This internal process is transparent to you as a writer—all you see is the text shifting on the screen until it is displayed once again as lines of uniform text. Figure 5-2 shows the misaligned text from Figure 5-1 after it has been Reformed.

On most systems, the Reform command operates on just the paragraph at which the cursor is located. This makes sense, since the end of a paragraph signals that the characters-per-line count should start anew. Many programs Reform a paragraph only from the cursor position to the end of the paragraph. On some systems, Reforming is done automatically as soon as each insertion or deletion is made, although manual Reforming is more common.

▶ Reforming is necessary to have your text print correctly. It also helps in checking the result of revisions in the text, for it cleans up the display. If the Reform command operates conveniently and

Fig. 5-1: Paragraph before Reforming

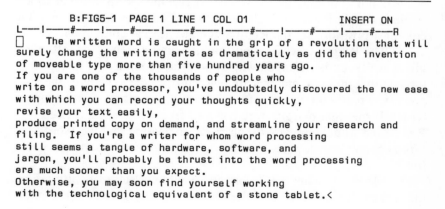

```
        B:FIG5-1   PAGE 1 LINE 1 COL 01              INSERT ON
L---!----#----!----#----!----#----!----#----!----#----!----#---R
☐    The written word is caught in the grip of a revolution that will
surely change the writing arts as dramatically as did the invention
of moveable type more than five hundred years ago.
If you are one of the thousands of people who
write on a word processor, you've undoubtedly discovered the new ease
with which you can record your thoughts quickly,
revise your text easily,
produce printed copy on demand, and streamline your research and
filing.  If you're a writer for whom word processing
still seems a tangle of hardware, software, and
jargon, you'll probably be thrust into the word processing
era much sooner than you expect.
Otherwise, you may soon find yourself working
with the technological equivalent of a stone tablet.<
```

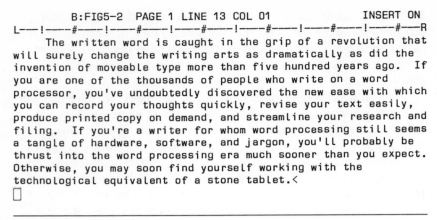

```
L--- ! ----#----- ! ----#----- ! ----#----- ! ----#----- ! ----#----- ! ----#---R
        The written word is caught in the grip of a revolution that
will surely change the writing arts as dramatically as did the
invention of moveable type more than five hundred years ago.  If
you are one of the thousands of people who write on a word
processor, you've undoubtedly discovered the new ease with which
you can record your thoughts quickly, revise your text easily,
produce printed copy on demand, and streamline your research and
filing.  If you're a writer for whom word processing still seems
a tangle of hardware, software, and jargon, you'll probably be
thrust into the word processing era much sooner than you expect.
Otherwise, you may soon find yourself working with the
technological equivalent of a stone tablet.<
☐
```

Fig. 5-2: After Reforming

efficiently on your system, Reform your paragraphs frequently as you make editorial changes.

Margins

We have assumed up to now that the line length was set at 65 characters. This is a standard figure for printing text on an 8½-by-11-inch sheet of paper and, of course, this line length fits comfortably on an 80-column screen. You're not bound by that line length, however.

Most word processors display the current line length on a RULER LINE. On some systems, the Ruler Line is always displayed above the text during writing and editing; on others, it is "called up" on command. Regardless, the Ruler Line will usually indicate both a left and a right SCREEN MARGIN for the entry of text and for the corresponding display on the screen. A common form of Ruler Line is illustrated in Figure 5-3, showing the Left Screen Margin set at the column 1 position and the Right Screen Margin at column 65.

The Right Screen Margin (and in some systems, the left margin as well) can be changed with appropriate commands. Except for the fact that these commands are entered from the keyboard, the process is really no different from adjusting the margins on a typewriter. If the right margin were changed from 65 to 60, a revised Ruler Line would appear on the screen, indicating that the Word Wrap counter was now set to accept no more than 60 characters per line.

Merely revising the Ruler Line would not automatically reform the screen display of the text already entered, however. If you wanted

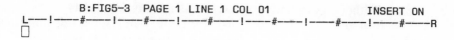

Fig. 5-3: Typical ruler (margins at 1 and 65)

to alter the margin for all the previous text, you would have to go back to the beginning and Reform each paragraph. Just as it did with the Reforming process to adjust for revisions, the computer would read through the text, stripping the old Line Ends and reinserting them according to the new 60-character-per-line count. The process would need to be performed for each paragraph. On the screen, you would see each paragraph redisplayed in the new format.

On many systems, the Left Screen Margin can be adjusted in a similar way. After giving the appropriate command to change the left margin value, you would Reform each paragraph, producing a screen display of the text with greater indentation on the left side. Although you would probably leave the left margin at the leftmost position on the screen most of the time, being able to indent text by changing the margin is especially useful for passages, such as long quotations, that you want to set off visually from the body of the text. In such instances, you could set the left margin several columns in from the edge of the screen, type in the special passage, then reset the margin at its original spot.

On the screen the process of changing the left margin might appear to happen exactly the same way as when you adjust the right margin, but the computer goes through a different process internally. To accomplish what appears on the screen as a left margin shift, the program must actually add an appropriate number of blank spaces to the beginning of each line. These blanks are "printed" to the screen (and, later, on the printer itself), creating the appearance of an indented left margin.

You certainly do not have to understand what's happening inside the computer to write and edit your text, but the way that the program adjusts left and right margins on the screen does affect the operation of the program. Many program manuals recommend that the Left Screen Margin remain at column 1 and the right margin only be adjusted to vary the line length. The immediate reason for this is that the further in from the screen's edge the Left Screen Margin is set, the less room there is for the screen to display each line of text. This is not a detail with which you need to be concerned if you're selecting a system, but once you're writing on one, you should experiment with the margins to find the optimal screen display.

▶ Although formatting the screen display is frequently described in terms of "margins," what is really being set at this point is the length of each line—the difference between the left and right margins on the screen display. Keeping the Left Screen Margin set at column 1 will not limit your ability to specify a wider left margin for the printed page later on. (See Chapter 6 for details.)

Some programs may permit you to specify a line length greater than the width of the screen. In such cases the system might perform HORIZONTAL SCROLLING to let you view each line as it is written (although following this can be very confusing visually). Another common method of displaying extra-width lines is for the screen to show the portion of text that extends beyond the screen's width as the next line of text. (This is another instance of the display's not being an exact preview of what will appear on the printed page.)

Most programs have some way of providing for INDENTATION. One approach is simply to permit the entry of blank spaces at the start of the paragraph (and not to reshuffle them during Reforming). Other programs allow you to specify how many spaces each paragraph is to be indented and automatically perform the indentation during Reforming. Some programs have TABS, like those on a typewriter, which allow for varying indentation. These tab indentations may not survive Reforming, however.

Another feature you may encounter is the MARGIN RELEASE. Like its typewriter counterpart, this function suspends the Word Wrap rules temporarily to permit you to extend text beyond the set margins. Check your manual to see whether the extension will survive subsequent Reforming.

Hyphens and Spaces

In Chapter 3 we noted that you should not try to hyphenate during the entry of text. The reason for this may now be more evident. If a long word were hyphenated at the end of a line, a subsequent Reforming might send both segments onto the same line, treating them as two separate words, with the hyphen still in place. But if the normal Word Wrap rules stay in effect, they might leave a large "hole" at the end of a line if a lengthy word fell there. You might want to hyphenate in some cases to improve the appearance of the text while still permitting Reforming later on.

Many word processors deal with this problem by providing two kinds of hyphens: "hard" and "soft." A HARD HYPHEN is entered by typing the regular hyphen key and is treated just like any other character during Word Wrap and Reforming. If you type 'hyphena-' at the end of a line, hit the Return key and continue with 'tion' on the next line, Reforming the paragraph later might produce 'hyphena-tion' somewhere within your text.

A SOFT HYPHEN is a provisional character. If the word containing it falls at the end of a line, it will be divided at the hyphen and the Soft Hyphen will print. If, on the other hand, Reforming places the word in the middle of a line, the Soft Hyphen will be ignored and the word will be printed as a single entity. This is a very handy feature if you're concerned with the appearance of your text.

There are various methods by which programs deal with the Soft Hyphen. Some programs merely provide it as an additional character to be entered whenever you spot the occasion for doing so. Other programs take a more active role in helping with hyphenation. During Reforming, if a word is encountered that would leave a hole of a certain length at the end of a line, the program pauses and alerts you to the fact, giving you the option to insert a Soft Hyphen or to send the entire word onto the next line. The most sophisticated versions of this "hyphen help" even suggest an appropriate hyphenation point.

▶ The byte value your program assigns to Soft Hyphens will not be the standard ASCII code for a hyphen. If you make use of this feature, you might encounter problems later on if you are transferring your text to another word processing program or to computerized typesetting equipment (discussed in greater detail in Chapter 15).

Some programs provide FIXED SPACES, which can be useful in special applications. For example, if you wanted to place the notation '[Figure 5-]' within your text, Reforming might play havoc with it, as it would treat '[Figure', '5-', and ']' as three separate words. This might place '[Figure 5-' at the end of one line and a lonely ']' at the beginning of the next. By entering the notation as a single "word" containing Fixed Spaces, the program would always treat it as a unit and never send the final bracket as an orphan to start a new line. (If your program doesn't have this feature, use a temporary character such as a '?' instead of a space to avoid severing the bracket from its text.)

Justification

All the text entry discussed so far has been in the format that typographers call "ragged right"; that is, with the right margin being uneven. The alternative is for the text to be JUSTIFIED, with the last word of each line ending flush with the right margin. This is the format in which many professionally typeset books are printed. If your system provides the option of justified text, you can lend an elegant look to your manuscripts and letters.

The program creates justified text, essentially, by adding spaces within lines of text. Assuming a line length of 65 characters, the normal Word Wrap rules might produce a line with 62 characters (if the next word were more than 3 characters in length). To justify the line, the program would add 3 more spaces within the line, making a full 65-character count. This process would be repeated for each line of text that contained less than 65 characters. (On some systems, Justification occurs automatically as part of the Word Wrap function.)

On the screen, the justification would be apparent by a flush right margin. You would also notice extra spaces between some of the words in many of the lines, as Figure 5-4 illustrates. (Compare this to Figure 5-2, which displays the same text ragged right.)

On systems that provide for justified text, it is an option that is invoked with a specific command. If you have created text using the unjustified format and later wish to have it print justified, you would need to Reform each paragraph in your text after turning on the Justification option. (A few w/p programs can print justified text with a special command, even from unjustified text on the screen.)

When is it appropriate to use Justification? As mentioned, it can improve the appearance of notices, reports, newsletters, and other public documents. For personal correspondence, most writers prefer to stick with the ragged right format so that the letter doesn't

Fig. 5-4: Justified text (extra spaces between words)

```
        B:FIG5-4  PAGE 1 LINE 13 COL 01            INSERT ON
L---!----#----!----#----!----#----!----#----!----#----!----#----R
     The  written word is caught in the grip of a revolution that
will  surely change the writing arts as dramatically as  did  the
invention of moveable type more than five hundred years ago.   If
you  are  one  of  the thousands of people who write  on  a  word
processor,  you've undoubtedly discovered the new ease with which
you  can record your thoughts quickly,  revise your text  easily,
produce printed copy on demand,  and streamline your research and
filing.   If you're a writer for whom word processing still seems
a tangle of hardware,  software,  and jargon,  you'll probably be
thrust into the word processing era much sooner than you  expect.
Otherwise,  you  may  soon  find  yourself  working  with  the
technological equivalent of a stone tablet.<
[]
```

look as though it "came from a machine." (This prejudice against computer-assisted writing is likely to disappear as more writers discover the benefits of word processing.)

▶ There are two practical reasons for limiting the use of the Justification option. First, the appearance of extra spaces between words on the screen makes it difficult to proofread text for proper intentional spacing. Also, as has been noted before, encoding the text string with Justification data may make it difficult to transfer the text to other computer applications.

We should mention one other popular feature found on most programs: CENTERING. You type the text for a line, give the appropriate command, and the program automatically centers that line within your set margins. Once you have this handy feature at your disposal, you'll quickly forget what a chore centering used to be on a typewriter.

The Screen Display

Each of the functions described in this chapter—Reforming, setting and changing margins, and Justifying—has involved two processes. Internally, the computer prepares lines of text for printing; externally, the screen displays each of those lines.

Throughout this chapter, we've been anticipating the next one, in which we'll look at the many other variables that can apply to a printed page of text. During the normal Reforming, margin setting, and Justifying processes, the screen does not reflect any of these variables. Many processors do provide ways to view the printing format on the screen, however. At the risk of getting a bit ahead of our discussion (since we haven't yet described just what those variables are), we'll end this chapter with a brief description of these means of ON-SCREEN FORMATTING.

Many word processors provide a special command with a name such as PRINT TO SCREEN. This command causes the computer to display all of the text on the screen, from the beginning, in a way that reflects all the margins, page numbering, and headings that are in effect for printing, as well as where each printed page will end and a new one begin. This Print to Screen function is useful for previewing the printed text, in case minor adjustments must be made before committing the text to paper.

Some programs provide genuine On-Screen Formatting, by displaying some or all of the printing format variables on the screen during the regular process of creating and editing text. With this "what-you-see-is-what-you-get" feature (especially if it displays page breaks), you can anticipate and decide on most aspects of your printed pages.

By now, you should have the irresistible urge to switch on your printer and see some concrete evidence of your writing.

Chapter 6

The Perfect Page

Print Formatting

When writing on a typewriter, you have some control over the appearance of your typewritten pages. You can set the margins, determine how many lines to skip before typing, and listen for the bell to decide when to hit the carriage return. You can do your best to keep track of the end of the page so that you know when to change the paper. In essence, the typewriter requires you to rely on your ears and eyes to keep your pages in the proper format.

The word processor permits you to control the look of your printed pages with a range and precision never before afforded the everyday writer. Presenting your text on the page can become another creative element in your writing. And, once you have issued the appropriate commands to the machine, it will follow all your printing directives automatically, producing a letter-perfect printout.

This chapter describes the many elements that go into formatting a printed page of text. In the computer world, paper printout is often referred to as HARD COPY, as distinguished from the "soft" copy that is visible on the screen. You'll see, however, that there's nothing hard and fast about printing your work; word processing presents you with what might seem like an infinite array of options.

Before exploring the hard-copy landscape, you might want to review Chapter 1, which describes the hardware for printing. In this chapter, we'll assume that you have already selected a dot-matrix or letter-quality printer and connected it to your computer through the appropriate interface, that you have chosen a suitable print element (if you're using a letter-quality printer), and that you have loaded the printer with either continuous-form paper or a single sheet.

From here on, we'll be dealing exclusively with the program commands by which you communicate with the computer and the computer, in turn, communicates with the printer. As with previous chapters, you may not find all of the features we describe present on every word processor. Our guide should help you understand what is available on your system, however, and help to make you the designer of your own "perfect page."

Left and Right Margins

In the previous chapter, we dealt with margins as they appear on the screen while you're writing or editing text. We saw that the on-screen margins produce lines of text, each of a certain length. Now we'll look at how these lines are positioned on the printed page to create the left, right, top, and bottom margins you see in the final product.

In this section, we'll assume that while entering text, you set the Left Screen Margin at column 1 and the Right Screen Margin at column 65, producing lines of text with no preceding blank spaces, each no more than 65 characters in length. We'll also assume for the moment that you're printing on paper 8½ inches wide and that (at 10 characters to the inch) the width of this paper would accommodate a total of 85 characters.

In order to position the lines of text horizontally on the page, you need only to tell the printer how many spaces to skip before printing the first character of each line. This is accomplished by a LEFT PRINT POSITION command, which contains a numerical value. If the value in the command is 1, the printer will start printing at the leftmost print position. If the value is set for 10, the print element will move ten spaces to the right before starting to print the line. The names for this command vary greatly among different systems. You might see references to PRINT COLUMN, PRINT MARGIN, or PAGE OFFSET (and your program might establish 0 instead of 1 as the leftmost position). By whatever name or convention, this command governs the left margin on the printed page.

You won't often find a command for setting the right print margin, because that has already been determined by the line length set at the screen display level. For example (according to our assumptions), if the screen margins had been set at 1 and 65, a Left Print Position value of 10 would produce a right margin on the page the equivalent of 10 characters in width. Figure 6-1 shows the relation of these page-width and margin values.

Fig. 6-1: Page width and left and right margins

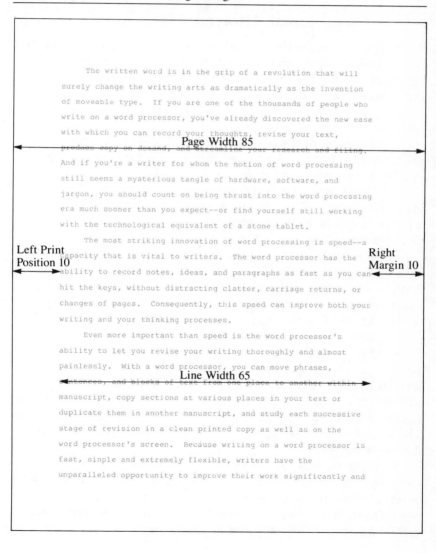

If the Left Print Position were set to 12, the right margin on the page would be eight characters wide (12 + 65 + 8 = 85). If the Left Print Position were kept at 10 but the screen margins had been set to produce lines 70 characters in length, the right margin on the printed page would be only 5 characters wide.

▶ These calculations can get confusing, which is why it's best to keep the Left Screen Margin set at 1 and make all printing margin adjustments with the Left Print Position command, and the Line Length (Right Screen Margin) setting.

Top and Bottom Margins

The margins at the top and bottom of the printed page are controlled entirely by special printer commands. Basically, they instruct the printer to skip lines while in the process of printing the text. For the moment, we'll assume that you're printing on pages that are each 11 inches in length and that the printer has been instructed to print 6 lines per inch.

The length of the page is the first bit of information that the printer has to have in calculating the top and bottom margins. Most systems have a command with a name resembling PAGE LINES or PAGE LENGTH. It takes a numerical value, usually the total number of printed lines that will fit on a page. By our assumptions, 6 lines per inch for 11 inches would produce a Page Lines value of 66, and you would give that command to the printer.

(Most word processing programs have an automatic setting, called a DEFAULT, for the standard page length. If you give no Page Length command, this built-in default will establish the page length. Other defaults usually govern the top and bottom margins. The concept of defaults is discussed further in Chapter 8.)

There is a separate command for setting the top margin on the page and (to preserve our sanity) virtually all systems call it TOP MARGIN. It too takes a numerical value, representing the number of lines to be skipped before starting to print on the page. By our assumption of 6 printed lines to the inch, if you wanted a 1-inch margin at the top of the page, you would enter a Top Margin 6 command. The printer would start printing your text on the seventh line from the top of the page.

There are two general approaches to setting the bottom margin. One of them operates with a command that specifies the number of printed lines per page, with a name something like PRINT LINES, or possibly just LINES. In this method, the bottom page margin is not specified per se; it is determined by subtracting the Top Margin and the Print Lines from the Page Lines. By our assumptions, if you specified a Print Lines value of 54 and a Top Margin value of 6, you would get a bottom margin of an inch (6 lines) as a result. Figure 6-2 illustrates the relation of the top and bottom margins and page length.

Some systems take a more direct approach and provide a BOTTOM MARGIN command that does the arithmetic for you. By this

Fig. 6-2: Page length and top and bottom margins

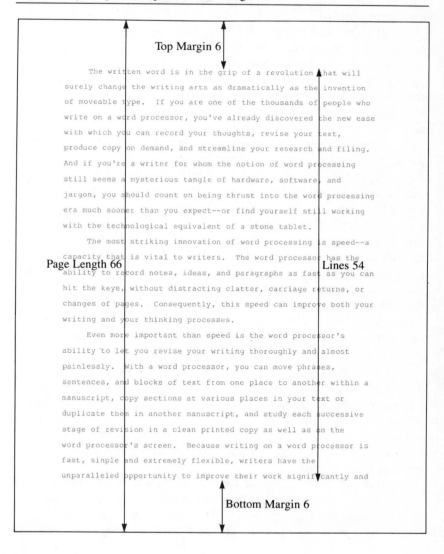

Top Margin 6

The written word is in the grip of a revolution that will surely change the writing arts as dramatically as the invention of moveable type. If you are one of the thousands of people who write on a word processor, you've already discovered the new ease with which you can record your thoughts, revise your text, produce copy on demand, and streamline your research and filing. And if you're a writer for whom the notion of word processing still seems a mysterious tangle of hardware, software, and jargon, you should count on being thrust into the word processing era much sooner than you expect--or find yourself still working with the technological equivalent of a stone tablet.

The most striking innovation of word processing is speed--a capacity that is vital to writers. The word processor has the ability to record notes, ideas, and paragraphs as fast as you can hit the keys, without distracting clatter, carriage returns, or changes of pages. Consequently, this speed can improve both your writing and your thinking processes.

Even more important than speed is the word processor's ability to let you revise your writing thoroughly and almost painlessly. With a word processor, you can move phrases, sentences, and blocks of text from one place to another within a manuscript, copy sections at various places in your text or duplicate them in another manuscript, and study each successive stage of revision in a clean printed copy as well as on the word processor's screen. Because writing on a word processor is fast, simple and extremely flexible, writers have the unparalleled opportunity to improve their work significantly and

Page Length 66   Lines 54

Bottom Margin 6

approach, you would specify a Bottom Margin of 6 to achieve the result in the preceding example.

Page Numbering and Headings

Virtually every word processor has some provision for numbering printed pages automatically. The initial instruction is simply a "yes/no" PAGE NUMBER command—whether or not the system's numbering routine is to operate at all. Beyond that, some systems operate rudimentarily, while others provide sophisticated control of the page-numbering format.

If page numbering is in effect, then you may have a choice of commands to position the numeral on each page. Most systems permit specification of the NUMBERING LINE by entering a Print Line value. Obviously, this value must fall within the lines reserved for the top or bottom margins. Many systems permit specifying the NUMBERING COLUMN at which the numbers will appear on each page, as well.

Some systems have an optional LEFT/RIGHT NUMBERING command, which will print the number for odd-numbered pages at the right side of the page and for even-numbered pages on the left. This can be a useful feature for formatting reports that will later be printed or copied on both sides of the page.

You will often be provided the option of specifying the numerical value at which to START PAGE NUMBERING—useful if you wanted to start numbering a document at page 50, for example. Some systems provide options for specifying NUMBERING INCREMENTS greater than 1, to SUSPEND PAGE NUMBERING for certain pages, or to SUPPRESS NUMBERING ON PAGE ONE. If you have these features available, you can devise ingenious applications for them, but unless you have special formatting requirements you should not select a word processor on the basis of its repertoire of page-numbering options.

Another useful feature found in many w/p programs is the ability to display one or more HEADINGS, such as 'Chapter Six', at the top of each page of a manuscript. The form of the command varies from system to system, but in general it asks for the text of the heading as well as the line on which the heading is to appear. These systems usually permit specifying the column position at which the heading is to be printed.

Many programs provide for FOOTINGS, which are headings that appear somewhere within the bottom margin. If the Footing command permits positioning at any line of the printed page, you can ignore the "head/foot" distinction and format as though you have two headings at your disposal. Some programs allow even more than two headings. The availability of multiple headings can be very useful in formatting documents, or even business letters, as we'll explore further in Chapter 13.

In Figure 6-3, the Top Margin was set at 6; a heading with the text 'Chapter Six: The Perfect Page' was set to print at line 2, column 1; a heading with the text 'page -' was set to print at line 3, column 1; and page numbering was set to print at line 3, column 8.

You're almost ready to have your system transform your text into a multiple-page document, but first you need to give one more command—namely, whether you are using continuous-form paper or will be feeding single sheets into the printer. The command will be in a form such as CONTINUOUS FORM or SHEET FEED, in either case requiring a "yes/no" response.

The Printer Driver

Just as the word processing program contains a set of rules and procedures for dealing with the entry and revision of text, it has a special segment, called the PRINTER DRIVER, which monitors and controls the printer. It would not be incorrect to think of the Printer Driver as a separate subprogram that receives instructions from the main part of the w/p program, processes them, and then sends these processed instructions to the printer. (The actual procedure is a bit more complicated, since the printer itself contains a microprocessor that also interprets commands and manipulates information.)

Fig. 6-3: Heading and page number

```
Chapter Six: The Perfect Page
page - 1
    .


    The written word is in the grip of a revolution that will

surely change the writing arts as dramatically as the invention

of moveable type.  If you are one of the thousands of people who

write on a word processor, you've already discovered the new ease

with which you can record your thoughts, revise your text,

produce copy on demand, and streamline your research and filing.

And if you're a writer for whom the notion of word processing

still seems a mysterious tangle of hardware, software, and

jargon, you should count on being thrust into the word processing

era much sooner than you expect--or find yourself still working

with the technological equivalent of a stone tablet.

    The most striking innovation of word processing is speed--a
```

The Perfect Page

On some systems, the commands we have been describing may be entered directly into the Printer Driver from the keyboard. One way this might work would be that you'd type in the proper command (from the Main Menu) for PRINT FORMATTING. A PRINT FORMAT MENU would then appear on the screen, listing the values of the printing variables currently in effect and allowing you to change them. An example of such a Print Format Menu is shown in Figure 6-4.

Once in the Print Format Menu routine, the cursor would pause after each variable, giving you the option of entering a new variable. (If you made no changes, the original printing format would remain in effect.) When this routine was completed, all the values would be entered in the Printer Driver and printing would be ready to begin.

Another common method of giving commands to the Printer Driver is from within the text. The various commands are entered as though they were lines of text, usually at the beginning of the document. To distinguish the commands from actual text, the commands take a special form, such as having a period or slash mark preceding each one. The generic term for these directives is IMBEDDED COMMANDS, as these instructions are imbedded in the text. An example of imbedded commands at the start of a text file is shown in Figure 6-5.

(Unavoidably, we're having to get just a bit ahead of ourselves. The concept of files will be discussed at great length in the following chapter. Very briefly for now, a TEXT FILE is a sequence of text, plus any imbedded commands that may have been inserted in the text, that has been *saved on a disk* and *given a name*.)

Fig. 6-4: Typical Print Format Menu

```
.===============================================================.
:          <<<   P R I N T   F O R M A T   M E N U   >>>        :
:---------------------------------------------------------------:
:  Page Length        - 66    Page Numbering (y/n)   - Y        :
:  Top Margin         - 6       row:col              - 3:8      :
:  Lines              - 60      starting page #      - 1        :
:  Vertical Spacing   - 8       number p. 1 (y/n)    - Y        :
:  Left Print Position - 10   Justification (y/n)    - N        :
:  Horizontal Spacing - 12    Continuous Forms (y/n) - Y        :
:                                                               :
:  Heading text: "Chapter Six: The Perfect Page"                :
:     row:col           - 2:1                                   :
:  Footing text: "page -"                                       :
:     row:col           - 3:1                                   :
:===============================================================:
```

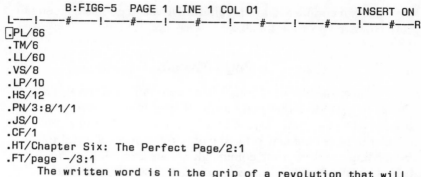

```
L—!—#——!——#——!——#——!——#——!——#——!——#—R
.PL/66
.TM/6
.LL/60
.VS/8
.LP/10
.HS/12
.PN/3:8/1/1
.JS/0
.CF/1
.HT/Chapter Six: The Perfect Page/2:1
.FT/page -/3:1
     The written word is in the grip of a revolution that will
surely change the writing arts as dramatically as the invention
of moveable type.  If you are one of the thousands of people who
write on a word processor, you've already discovered the new ease
with which you can record your thoughts, revise your text,
produce copy on demand, and streamline your research and filing.
```

Fig. 6-5: Imbedded commands at start of file

Now we can look at how the Printer Driver does its job. When the command to PRINT is given, the program first fetches whatever file is to be printed. If the Printer Driver has not already been loaded with the printing commands, the imbedded commands are read into it from the beginning of the text file.

From that point on, the Driver mainly performs a counting routine. It will skip whatever number of lines have been set for the top margin, move over whatever number of spaces have been set for the left margin, and then start printing lines of text. When it has counted 54 lines (or whatever value was set for the number of printed lines per page) it will skip the number of lines set for the bottom margin.

If the Sheet Feed command is in effect, the printer will pause, giving you the opportunity to insert a new sheet of paper before continuing with the printing routine. If the Continuous Form option is in effect, the Driver will keep going, skipping lines for the top margin again, resuming by printing more lines from the text file, and suspending printing to maintain the bottom margin.

Throughout this process, the Driver is keeping track of whatever page numbering and heading commands may be in effect. It will print a page number and/or heading(s) whenever it reaches the specified lines. It also keeps track of how many pages it is printing so that it can increment the page numbering. All you have to do is sit back and be amazed. After your first few printing sessions, you'll have enough confidence in the faithful Driver to go make a cup of coffee or even go walk the dog.

Page Breaks

There may be occasions when you don't want the Printer Driver to perform its normal routine. For example, suppose your text file consists of several chapters, and you want the beginning of each chapter to start on a new printed page. You can accomplish this by imbedding an appropriate command in your text. This feature is called a PAGE BREAK, FORCE PAGE, or NEW PAGE. The instruction resides in your text file at the start of each new chapter, or wherever needed. When the Driver encounters the Page Break command, it skips the number of lines necessary to complete the existing page, resets its counting mechanism, and resumes printing text at the start of a new page.

The page numbering will normally be incremented during a Page Break. If you want the heading to change to reflect the title of the new chapter, you can simply imbed a new Heading command where the text for the new chapter begins. An example of imbedded commands to force a new page and change the heading is shown in Figure 6-6.

Fig. 6-6: Imbedded commands within text (page break and heading change)

```
         B:FIG6-6  PAGE 1 LINE 17 COL 25              INSERT ON
L---!----#-----!----#-----!----#-----!----#-----!----#-----!----#----R
produce copy on demand, and streamline your research and filing.
And if you're a writer for whom the notion of word processing
still seems a mysterious tangle of hardware, software, and
jargon, you should count on being thrust into the word processing
era much sooner than you expect—or find yourself still working
with the technological equivalent of a stone tablet.<
.PB
.PN/3:8/1/1
.HT/Chapter Seven: Housekeeping/2:1
<
<
               Chapter Seven: Housekeeping
<
<
     Many observers have expressed fear that the burgeoning use
of electronic tools such as word processors will severely damage
the literary process.  Just the opposite is true.  Because
writers can record their thoughts easily and then revise their
work extensively, writing has effectively been reborn through the
use of word processing.<
```

Many processors also offer what is termed a CONDITIONAL PAGE BREAK. This feature lets you instruct the Printer Driver, "If, at this point, there are less than *x* lines left to print on the current page, then break to a new page" (where *x* is a value you supply). You imbed this instruction in the text wherever you want it.

Conditional Page Breaks can be used to avoid having fragments of text appear at the bottom of a printed page. For example, suppose your text file consists of several sections, with a section title preceding each one. The normal paging of the document by the Driver might result in a section title appearing on the last line of a page. It would look strange to have the title sitting all alone, with the accompanying text starting the next page. The solution is to imbed a Conditional Page Break instruction just before the section title, with a value of, say, 5 lines. When the Driver encounters the Conditional Page Break command, it will determine whether there are fewer than 5 lines left to print on the current page. If so, it will break to a new page before printing the section title.

Conditional Page Breaks are also used to make sure that tables, charts, or lists aren't broken between two printed pages. If you have a chart consisting of twelve lines that you want to remain intact, you would imbed a command such as '.CP12' just preceding it in your text.

▶ If you anticipate uses for the Conditional Page Break as you are writing, you can avoid unexpected results when you print the text.

Stops, Pauses, and Resets

Inevitably, there will be occasions when the first printout of your text will not be perfect. (Seasoned w/p writers will recognize this as a supreme understatement!) You might discover that you erred in specifying the format or that the automatic paging produced unwanted results, or you may simply spot a typo—or two, or three, or more. Don't panic as the dutiful printer spews more copy. You have several avenues for recovery.

One printer command you should learn by heart is the one to STOP PRINT, which halts the printing immediately. You'll use this frequently to abort the printing routine when you spot a gross error in formatting or, less frequently, a physical problem such as a paper tangle. The convenience and accessibility of the Stop Print command is a salient feature to be considered in the choice of a system.

You'll also have occasion to use the PAUSE PRINT command, which suspends the printing routine temporarily. Printout recommences without dropping any characters or changing format once the RESUME PRINT command is given. This is a very useful command if your telephone sits within earshot of your printer.

Some systems may also provide an IMBEDDED PAUSE feature. As the name implies, this command is placed within the text and will automatically cause the Printer Driver to pause when it is encountered. This feature can be useful if you anticipate having to make some manual operation during printout, such as changing a type font on a letter-quality printer.

What happens if you discover a substantial error on page 23 of your 28-page manuscript? You can go back into the Edit mode and make the correction, but do you then have to reprint the whole document? Many systems anticipate just such situations by allowing you to PRINT FROM A SPECIFIED PAGE. The Driver reads through the document from the beginning, counting pages as usual, and starts printing when the desired page is reached. Since the Driver can "read" much faster than the printer can print, this feature can save you considerable time (and paper).

A related feature enables you to instruct the printer to STOP PRINTING AT A SPECIFIED PAGE. Using this in conjunction with the previous command would let you print only a section of your text file.

Many systems let you PRINT A SINGLE PAGE. This is a very useful feature for correcting a minor error that doesn't alter the number of lines on the page. It avoids the need to print all the way through to the end of the document. Often, this feature (and the one described previously) must be set by calling the text up on the screen and placing the cursor where you want printing to commence.

A related printing feature is PRINT SCREEN CONTENTS. Giving this command will produce a printout of whatever is visible on the screen. (The printout does not continue beyond the last line displayed on the screen.) This is really an editing command, since it doesn't involve the Printer Driver and takes no account of the paging of the document. It's an extremely useful feature for providing quick reference printouts during writing and editing sessions.

Some systems also provide a PRINT MULTIPLE COPIES command. This enables you to specify how many copies of a document you wish printed. When the Driver reaches the end of the text, it resets its page counter, goes back to the beginning of the text, and starts printing again. There really are more efficient ways of making multiple copies, such as locating a copying machine, or using multiple-part printer paper with interleaved carbons.

A few wily program designers have eliminated the excuse that "the computer is tied up because it's printing." On some systems, the program allows both the Printer Driver and the Editor to share the attention of the computer, permitting you to write and edit new material while the printer is running. You can also equip some printers with PRINT BUFFERS (memory storage) that will hold substantial quantities of text, in the range of 8K to 16K (approximately 5 to 10 double-spaced pages). The Driver loads the text into the buffer and the printer carries on from there, freeing the computer for more writing work. (All printers contain a small buffer, usually of not more than 256-byte capacity, for routing the text through the printer's own microprocessor.)

Vertical Spacing

Our examples so far have assumed single-spaced printing (6 lines per inch), but virtually all word processors offer control over the vertical formatting of the printed page. To print DOUBLE-SPACED text, you send an appropriate command to the Driver, either directly or as an imbedded command within the text. The form of this command usually carries a value, such as '.Space1'. This instructs the Driver to skip one line before and after each line of printed text. On many systems, you can specify triple spacing (or more) by stating higher values in the Space command.

If you specify double spacing, do you have to revise the values you specified for the page length or printed lines of text per page? On most systems, the answer is "no"; the clever Driver will adjust its line-counting routine automatically.

If you switch to a different size paper, such as 14-inch length, you will, of course have to specify different Page Length and Print Lines values. At 6 lines to the inch, 14-inch paper would accommodate a total of 84 lines per page. To maintain top and bottom margins of one inch each, you would specify a top margin of 6 lines and a total of 72 printed lines.

You are not necessarily limited to 6 lines per inch, either. Many systems offer the option to print in other LINES/INCH formats. A common one is 4 lines per inch, which produces somewhat wider spacing between lines. If you do have this option and specify 4 lines per inch, you will have to adjust the Lines Per Page and Printed Lines values. (On 11-inch paper, 4 lines per inch produces 44 total lines per page.) Figure 6-7 shows examples of text printed at 6 and 4 lines per inch.

▶ You can and should experiment with these print formatting options. For example, 8 lines per inch printed single-spaced is so tight as to be almost illegible, but 8 lines per inch combined with

```
[This is a sample of printing six lines/inch.]
    The written word is in the grip of a revolution
that will surely change the writing arts as dramati-
cally as the invention of moveable type.  If you are
one of the thousands of people who write on a word
processor, you've already discovered the new ease
with which you can record your thoughts, revise your

[This is a sample of printing four lines/inch.]

And if you're a writer for whom the notion of word

processing still seems a mysterious tangle of hard-

ware, software, and jargon, you should count on

being thrust into the word processing era much

sooner than you expect--or find yourself still
```

Fig. 6-7: Text printed at 6 and 4 lines per vertical inch

double spacing produces a very pleasing and readable vertically condensed format.

    Some systems offer even more control over vertical spacing. If
you are using a letter-quality printer, it might be capable of printing
in VERTICAL MICROSPACING. With this feature, the printer is able to
position vertically on the page in increments of ¼₈ of an inch (a very
fine adjustment). If your word processing program supports the
printer's capability (the two must work together), you can specify
LINE HEIGHT in these microspacing increments. If you specify a line
height of 8 (which is ⁸⁄₄₈), you'll be printing at 6 lines per inch. And
just to make it confusing, if you specify a line height of 6 (⁶⁄₄₈),
you'll be printing at 8 lines per inch. If you specify a line height of
24, the printer will skip 24 of these vertical increments between
lines, and you'll be printing at 2 lines per inch. (Keep your pocket
calculator handy.) This vertical microspacing feature is also used for
various print enhancements, which we'll describe below.

Horizontal Spacing

    The word processor affords a similar range of options in the
horizontal formatting of your printed document. Most typists are
familiar with the typewriter PITCH options of PICA type, which prints
at 10 characters to the inch, and the smaller ELITE type, which prints
at 12 characters per inch.

The choice of these two horizontal pitch formats is available on many word processing systems, again depending on the capabilities of the printer and whether the w/p program supports them. (These extended printer capabilities are most often found on letter-quality printers and less commonly on dot-matrix printers.) On a letter-quality printer, you would change the print font (daisy wheel or thimble) to correspond with the pitch setting instruction given to the printer. In addition, some processor/printer systems offer the option of a super-condensed pitch, called MICRON spacing, which prints at 15 characters per inch.

Most printers that are able to print in very fine vertical increments are also capable of printing with HORIZONTAL MICROSPACING. The horizontal unit is ½₀th of an inch, specified by a CHARACTER WIDTH or HORIZONTAL MOTION INDEX command in microspace units. A character width of '12' (120ths) will produce the standard pica pitch of 10 characters to the inch. A character width of '10' (120ths) results in the elite pitch of 12 characters to the inch. (Whoever designed this topsy-turvy system of specifying pitches and line heights was not considering writers' sanity.)

▶ As with the vertical spacing, you are not confined to the standard pitch values. Experiment. For example, a character width of '9' used with a standard elite type element produces a slightly condensed type that you might find more readable and attractive than the standard setting of '10'. You could create a "spread type" effect by using an elite font and specifying a character width of '11' or '12'. Figure 6-8 shows examples of microspacing.

Some processor/printer systems will also permit PROPORTIONAL SPACING. This feature assigns different character widths to different letters, depending on their typography. For example, an 'M' might take up 12 horizontal units while an 'i' would require only 4 units. The resulting printout keeps all the letters perfectly spaced and produces very professional-looking documents. This feature requires both special printer and program functions, however, as well as a specially designed type element.

There are two methods for representing justified text on a word processor's printer. The simpler method prints each line just as it appears on the screen, with extra spaces between some of the words. The more sophisticated way of justifying the right margin increases the spaces between *characters* in the line very slightly. All of these small increments between characters add up to the number of whole spaces needed to fill out the line.

This second approach is called MICROJUSTIFICATION. With this feature in effect, the Driver automatically adjusts the character width

```
[This is a sample of pica type --

10 characters/inch]

     The written word is in the grip of a

revolution that will surely change the writing

arts as dramatically as the invention

[This is a sample of elite type --

12 characters/inch]

     And if you're a writer for whom the notion of

word processing still seems a mysterious tangle of

hardware, software, and jargon, you should count on
```

Fig. 6-8: Text printed at 10 and 12 characters per horizontal inch

specification for each line so that all the printed lines are of equal width, regardless of the number of characters per line. The resulting document can be very impressive. Occasionally, however, a printed line may have exaggerated spacing.

Systems that offer this printing feature rarely can display text on the screen in a Microjustified form. Instead, they represent the justified text by inserting whole spaces between words.

Print Enhancements

The final group of options consists of various enhancements to the straightforward printing of characters. Probably the most common of these is UNDERLINING. To produce underlined text, the printer must be instructed to print a character, backspace, and then print a line under that character.

Most w/p programs contain an automatic routine for this feature. All you have to do is to insert special control characters before and after the appropriate portion of text while you are writing and editing. (These control characters will appear on the screen but they will not print.) The Printer Driver does the rest. When it encounters the first control character during the printing routine, it will interpret it as an instruction to print-backspace-underline. It will continue doing so for each character until the second control character is reached, and will then resume normal printing.

Figure 6-9 illustrates how two control characters (in this case, the character '^S'—the caret signifies the Control key on the screen) would appear *on the screen* to set off a word for underlining. The control characters would not appear in the printout. Of course, the underline character is also available to you as a standard separate character, such as for printing a signature line, but you'll discover that striking the underline key when the cursor is on a letter that you want to underline will Overtype that letter. So you must use the print control characters to achieve underlined characters.

▶ Be sure to add the control character required to end a print enhancement such as underlining; if you forget, the rest of your text will be underlined.

Some programs offer a STRIKEOVER feature, which works the same as underlining, except that it overprints slashes or hyphens on each character.

To produce accented characters for foreign languages and other special applications, your programs may provide a BACKSPACE or BACK STRIKE command. As with all print enhancements, you insert a special control character in the text. Upon reaching it, the Driver will print the character following it without advancing a space, then print the next character, such as an accent mark, in the same position.

Another print enhancement is DOUBLE STRIKE. This causes the printer to hit the print element twice for each letter. It produces slightly darker letters for emphasized printing, or it can be used to make heavier impressions with carbon forms.

On systems with horizontal microspacing, a true BOLDFACE option may be offered. This prints each character twice, but offsets the second impression by one microspace. The resulting letter will appear darker and slightly wider. Some systems permit you to specify how many microspaces to offset or to do SHADOW PRINTING, which produces several impressions of each character at microspace intervals.

Fig. 6-9: Control character (^S) imbedded in text

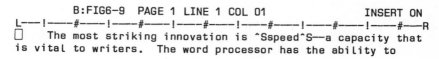

Many word processing printers are capable of doing more than just <u>underlining</u> words. The printer can be instructed to **doublestrike** each character. By making use of microspacing, the printer can produce a **boldface** effect. The printer can print two characters in the same position, such as in <u>étagère</u>. If the printer is also capable of vertical microspacing, it can produce both $_{sub}$scripts and ^{super}scripts.

Fig. 6-10: Sample print enhancements

Vertical microspacing may be used to specify SUBSCRIPTS and SUPERSCRIPTS—characters that are printed slightly below or above the regular line. The subscript and superscript features are implemented with special control characters in the text. The amount of vertical displacement can sometimes be specified in 48th-inch Line Height increments. Figure 6-10 shows examples of these print enhancements.

The last feature we'll describe doesn't affect the appearance of the printed document, but it does make the printing routine more efficient. Many systems let you specify BIDIRECTIONAL printing for your printer. With this option in effect, the Driver prints every other line "backwards," from right to left. The resulting document is indistinguishable from one printed unidirectionally, but printing bidirectionally relieves the print head from having to travel back to the left side of the page for every line. This can reduce wear on the printer and dramatically shorten the time needed to print a document. In the Computer Age, speed is an absolute good.

Chapter 7

Housekeeping

Managing Electronic Files

So far we've seen all the dazzling parts of word processing—writing at top speed on a nearly silent keyboard, moving text around at will, designing and printing pages effortlessly. But this business has its mundane side, too; the work you generate goes into an electronic storage system on disks, and whatever you print becomes a conventional manuscript—so in effect you're managing two sets of files.

As you continue to use a word processing system, you'll develop a sense of how much work you want in printed form and which drafts or letters can be stored only on disk. At first, most writers print almost everything, because they're not terribly confident about disks and they're accustomed to working with paper. But as the screen becomes a more familiar part of the writing process and using disks becomes second nature, most of us discover that printed copies of each draft or revision are no longer crucial.

The problem of managing information is age-old, of course; maintaining a clean desk and a tidy file cabinet is a severe test for any of us. Yet the solution is much the same for electronic files as for paper ones—you've got to get a gimmick. For paper, the gimmicks are for sale, in the form of folders, hanging file holders, and tabs and labels galore. With a word processor, some of the gimmicks are built in and some are up to you.

Disks and Drives

The first built-in gimmick is the disk, which serves as the primary filing cabinet for your work. Although cassette tapes could take the place of disks for word processing, tapes are much slower and more limited in operation, so we will continue to use our imaginary two-disk system for the examples here.

The disk (sometimes called a diskette) is a flat, round object that resembles a 45 rpm record in its jacket (Figure 7-1). Its specially treated surface receives electrical signals and stores them magnetically. The information on a disk is recorded and read in a form that corresponds to the basic units that a computer uses to process all information—the binary 1s and 0s.

Disks are made of flexible plastic, which is coated with a magnetic oxide and protected by a stiff plastic jacket that is never removed. Disks come in two standard sizes—8 inches and 5¼ inches in diameter. (A new 3½-inch disk is used in some systems at present and may also become common.) Information can be stored on one or both sides of the disk, depending on the design of the disk drives. Both sizes of disks are often called "flexible" or "floppy"; the 5¼-inch size has also been called a minifloppy or minidisk.

Figure 7-1 shows the openings in the jacket of a 5¼-inch disk. The disk drive's READ/WRITE HEAD contacts the disk surface through the large oval opening, called the READ/WRITE HOLE. Directly above the read/write hole is the HUB, which on some brands of disks contains a reinforced hub ring to prevent wear or damage at this point of contact with the drive's spindle. The one other hole in the disk's protective cover, the INDEX HOLE, is quite small and serves as a reference point for the drive's read/write head.

There are also several notches at the outer edges of the disk jacket; the two semicircular ones below the read/write hole are used to position the disk correctly in the drive. The single larger notch, on the side of this disk but on the bottom edge of an 8-inch disk, is called the WRITE PROTECT NOTCH. It works differently in the two sizes of disks but has the same purpose: to prevent accidental erasure or writing over of valuable information already stored on a disk. If the notch is covered on the 5¼-inch disk (with one of the paper tabs that come in each box of disks), nothing new can be written on that disk. If the notch is uncovered on an 8-inch disk, the contents are similarly

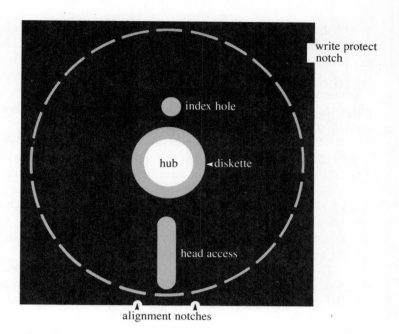

write protect notch

index hole

hub ◄diskette

head access

alignment notches

Fig. 7-1: 5¼-inch disk

protected. (Some computer manufacturers, however, do not build the necessary hardware capability for write-protecting disks into their products. So in some instances, you may not be able to rely on this feature.)

Information is stored on the disk in a pattern of tracks and sectors. Tracks are concentric circles that are numbered consecutively outward from the center of the disk. Sectors are pie-shaped areas of the disk surface that are arranged perpendicularly to the tracks. A specific piece of information is located on the disk by its track and sector numbers, and the index hole is the opening that provides the "home" location for the drive's read/write head to begin its search for a particular file or phrase.

Though all disks use tracks and sectors to store information, there are several types of disks in use. The two major variations in disk storage are the DENSITY with which a disk drive writes data on the disk and the way the tracks and sectors are arranged and used. Eight-inch disks generally do not vary in the number or size of tracks and sectors, but the more common 5¼-inch size may be one of two types.

Each computer or disk drive manufacturer selects a type of disk, and so far the industry has not made any visible progress toward establishing a standard in this area. So the chances of your swapping disks with another writer who has a different system from yours are not promising at the moment. (If you want to transfer data from one type of disk to another, you have at least two options. Chapter 15, "Networking," describes the use of modems and phone lines for this purpose, or you might use one of the commercial services that specialize in converting data from one type of disk to another.)

The two types of minidisks are SOFT-SECTORED and HARD-SEC-TORED. Soft-sectored disks have one hole in the disk surface that lines up with the index hole in the jacket as the disk spins and thus provides one reference point for the location of data. Hard-sectored disks have a number of such holes (usually 10 or 16) and each hole separates two sectors. This system of holes provides a more efficient set of reference points for the drive's read/write head because of the greater number of known locations on the disk.

Disks and disk drives are also designed to store information in different densities; a greater density means that more data is packed into the same amount of space. When disks first came into wide use, only single-density storage was available. Since then, double-density disks have become common, and "quad" or "octi" density is offered with some systems. The more highly condensed formats—quad and octi—commonly use drives that write information on both sides of the disk. This technology is now considered generally reliable, but the greater-capacity disks can wear out more quickly because the read/write heads are working on both sides of the disk simultaneously.

▶ A useful hint in working with disks is to learn the "generic" description (hard- or soft-sectored, number of holes, density, sides used) of your system's disks at the time you begin using the equipment. Then you can purchase new disks without having to memorize the code numbers used by various disk makers for your type of disk.

Storage capacity of the disks in a system is an important point to consider, but sellers often make more of this issue than a writer's situation merits. That is, most writing projects do not require that you have the entire manuscript "on line" at one time. In fact, for purposes of editing, adding new material, or making corrections, you will want to keep the size of individual files relatively small—say, 10 to 15 double-spaced pages. The reasons for limiting file size are essentially speed and safety; these topics are discussed in detail later in this chapter.

If you are using the w/p system for other work in addition to writing, disk capacity could be more critical. For example, if you want to enter and store a mailing list of several thousand names or enter and process financial data, such as accounting records, you may need disks that have a larger capacity than you would need just for writing.

Although amounts of disk storage vary among manufacturers of computers and disk drives, Table 7-1 gives a general idea of these capacities.

As we noted in Chapter 1, one byte represents a single character of information—a letter, symbol, or space. Using the rule of thumb of 6 characters per word, a disk that holds 150,000 bytes could store approximately 25,000 words. If a double-spaced page of text averages 250 words, that disk will hold some 100 pages of manuscript. These estimates may be misleading, however, because many w/p programs automatically create one or two separate BACKUP COPIES or WORK FILES for each file on a disk. Thus, the actual storage capacity of your disks may be only one-half or one-third the ideal estimate—in this example, perhaps 30 to 50 pages per disk. (Disk capacity and its relationship to writing are discussed in more detail later in this chapter.)

▶ If you are evaluating a system, verify the capacity of its disks in units that you are likely to use—words, names and addresses, numbers—before you buy the system, and check the w/p program's use of backup or work files. You could reasonably estimate the capacity by entering a small amount of data, using one of the DOS utilities to report how long it is in bytes, and then projecting this sample against the total bytes available on a disk and the backup procedures of that system.

As noted previously, disks receive information from the computer's memory through a DISK DRIVE. The drive's spindle fits into the round hub at the center of a disk and spins it, as the drive's read/write head moves back and forth over the disk's surface to locate or record data. One or two disk drives usually are integrated into the computer's cabinet in a w/p system, but some manufacturers supply disk drives as separate units.

Whether the drive is mounted vertically or horizontally, the disk will always be inserted in a specific way—that is, with one side

Table 7-1: Disk Storage Capacities

Disk Size	Density		
	Single	Double	Quad
5¼" single sided	100–125K	150–250K	400–500K
5¼" double sided	200–250K	300–500K	800–1000K
8" single sided	300–400K	700–800K	—
8" double sided	600–800K	1400–1600K	—

up and the label or write protect notch in the same position each time. Your system's manual will supply these instructions; if a disk is inserted in any other position, it will not function and may be damaged as the drive tries to make it work.

▶ Choose a reference point that is consistent on all brands of disks you use and always check to be sure that point is in the correct position before inserting the disk. For example, you might use the disk's own label or the one you add to the disk for filing purposes; if that label is facing upward and is at the edge of the disk closest to you as you slide the disk into its slot, verify the label's position each time you insert a disk.

Most drives have an "on" light that indicates that the drive is spinning when it is lit. In some systems with two disk drives, only one of these lights will be on at a time but both drives will be spinning. Whenever either light is on, therefore, you should not open the hinge that covers a disk access slot or try to remove a disk, because this action may damage the moving disk.

Naming Files

By now you've seen many references to files or disk files, but the meaning of this term in computer parlance may not be entirely clear. In short, any information that is stored on a disk is a FILE, whether it's a program or a letter, article, or address list. (To complicate matters slightly, some word processors use the term DOCUMENT instead of file.)

When you begin work on a project or when you first save that work on disk (this file-naming procedure varies from system to system), you assign a FILENAME to each separate part of it, identifying the files with codes and symbols you choose. All of your writing will be TEXT FILES, which store information in the form of ASCII characters. These text files often include elaborate formatting and printing instructions but can only be used or changed by a program, such as the word processor.

In most systems, the disk operating system (DOS) "rules" determine how you name files, if there is a maximum file length (capacity in bytes), and how many files can be stored on one disk. Your w/p program works in conjunction with the DOS, so when you're writing you don't see the DOS performing its routine functions, such as opening files and adding filenames to the Disk Directory.

The DOS also establishes the form and length of filenames, but the w/p program may add further restrictions, as well. The main reason for these limitations is that filenames must be compact enough to fit into the small area of the disk designated for the directory. What these restrictions mean in practice is that you have to be concise in naming files, a frustrating challenge at times but more fun than the Sunday crossword when it goes well.

Most word processors permit no more than 11 characters in a name, and a few allow only 8 or 9. Eleven-character filenames generally are divided into an 8-character main section and a 3-character EXTENSION; the two parts are separated by a period (or "dot" in computer vocabulary), which is not counted as one of the 11 characters. The extension is often used to identify a specific type of file, such as 'BAS' for a program written in the BASIC language.

For writing, though, you needn't use those precious three characters to identify a type of file, because all of your work is text files. And fewer than a dozen characters isn't much room to write a book or article title, its draft number, and a date—or even to note the recipient and date of a letter. Obviously some abbreviations are necessary, and here's where a creative gimmick can keep you organized and also distinguish one file from another instantly. (In Chapter 14 we'll present a detailed strategy for naming and managing files.)

No two files on the same disk may have exactly the same name (although names that differ by only a single character or symbol are all right). If you do use the same name twice, your program probably will warn you with a message to that effect, but if you don't change one of the names, DOS will save the new information and erase the old file with that name.

Generally, you can use any characters, numbers, or symbols in a filename, although some disk operating systems use symbols, such as the asterisk and question mark, as identifiers when listing disk contents or copying files. If your DOS uses such identifiers, you should refrain from including them in filenames so that they don't conflict with the DOS's operations.

Using symbols as part of filenames can help you stick to the character limit for filenames and still provide a clear description of each file's contents. For instance, a letter to Tom Brewster to be printed on the stationery of the company for which you work part-time could have the filename '@^BRWSTR.304'—with '@' signifying a letter, '^' indicating the format for company letterhead, 'BRWSTR' providing a phonetic abbreviation of the recipient's name, and '304' recording the letter's date of March 4th.

As we've noted, a common file-naming convention is an 8-character filename with a 3-character extension. Either part of this type of filename can be shorter than the maximum of 8 and 3 characters, though, but you must use a period to separate the parts. So you could also name your letter '@^TOM.304' and still conform to this particular system. As you can see, the period between parts of the filename is quite helpful, because it visually sets apart the date or other information contained in the extension.

If your system allows fewer than 11 characters for filenames and does not allow extensions, you'll find the symbols even more useful but you'll also have to be resourceful in making meaningful condensations of names and dates. The second example of the letter to Tom Brewster ('@^TOM.304') could work in an 8-character-maximum filename, though you'd have to take out the period to stay within the 8-character limit.

▶ Whatever length of filename your system specifies and however you identify your common types of files, be sure to check the screen carefully after typing the filename and before hitting the Return key. If you've made a typing error in the filename, the computer will accept it and create a file with that incorrect name or warn you that the disk already contains a file by that name. In either case, you'll have to spend some extra time and effort to remedy the mistake; it's much easier to check the screen in advance. This problem is particularly pesky when you want to edit work that's already on the disk—if you mistype the filename, you get a new file (or a different one) instead of the one you wanted.

The typos you are likely to make when naming files illustrate the literal way in which the computer works for you. It does precisely what you ask—so you'll get a file named 'SPIRTS' if your finger hits 'I' instead of 'O'. Somehow it's comforting to know that we're the ones making the mistakes most of the time, and our errors will help us remember this by-now familiar principle of using computer technology: establish your own routines for each procedure in working with the system. You'll find that you can become attuned to this set of tools and that they can increase your productivity and help improve your writing.

One more note about filenames: In almost every word processing system, filenames are displayed on the screen in capital letters (a carry-over from the early days of the Computer Age, when lowercase letters weren't available). Many w/p programs recognize either lowercase or uppercase letters when you type a filename, however, so you may not have to name all of your files with the Shift key engaged.

File Size

As you work with disk files, you'll develop a feel for appropriate size limits, because each word processing program handles files at its own speed. Most writers who now use word processors suggest keeping files relatively small, say, 10 to 15 double-spaced pages. If your system does not display page numbers within the file but measures file size in bytes, you can set an appropriate file limit in bytes. Generally, one page of double-spaced text will occupy about 1,500 bytes, depending on the margins and number of lines per page.

Files longer than 10 or 15 pages can be cumbersome when you're editing. If you try to move around in a large file—say, 20 pages or more—you'll find that searching or saving new work might take too long, because the millisecond speeds you've come to expect from the computer make even a few seconds' wait seem excessive. More important, large files can be dangerous: if that rare-but-possible disk failure occurs after you've edited a long chapter or a program "bug" appears so that you lose some work, you'll have cut your potential losses by keeping files small.

Some word processing programs can't handle large files even if you're willing to wait during searching or saving or take the risk of large losses. These programs have a built-in limit to file length, which may be inconvenient at times but could prevent a greater loss if the power or the disk fails when you're working on a virgin (unsaved) writing project. File length also may be affected by the size of a computer's temporary memory area (RAM), which also holds some or all of the w/p program and thus can only store new information in its unoccupied space. In either of these situations, the program should always display a warning message to alert you that you've reached the file size limit.

▶ Choose a limit to file size, in bytes or pages, and try not to create files that are longer than this limit. If you don't want to divide a chapter or article that is larger than your ordinary maximum, you should take extra precautions against losing data, such as saving text and editing changes more often than usual.

Programs and Filenames

Word processing systems generally employ one of two methods for naming files. With some systems, you can write new text before specifying a filename. You give a command to Edit or Create a file and the program displays a blank screen, ready for you to begin writing. When your text is complete, you give a command to SAVE it on a disk. At that point, the program asks you for a name under which to save what you wrote.

With other systems you must create a text file—and give it a name—before you begin writing. So to compose a letter to a magazine, you would tell the computer that you want to Edit or Create a file. The program would ask by what name you want the file to be identified. You would enter a name, such as 'LETTER.MAG', and the program would indicate that this file had been created and present you with a blank screen so that you can begin writing. After you finish the letter, you would give the Save command and the text of your letter would be written to a disk, under the name previously given.

When you want to edit an existing file, the procedure is much the same with either system. With the first type of program described above, you would instruct the program to RETRIEVE the file called 'LETTER.MAG' and the program would get it from the disk and display it for editing. With the second type of program, you would indicate that you want to Edit and respond with 'LETTER.MAG' when asked for a filename. The program would look for a file of that name on your disk, retrieve it, and display it on the screen. (If it didn't find any file by that name, it would tell you that you were creating a new file.)

The differences between these two file-naming systems are more than just procedural; they reflect the way the word processing program and the computer's memory work with files. The "name-it-later" systems keep all your working text in the computer's memory while you're writing or editing. The "name-it-first" systems don't necessarily do that; they may dip into your disk to load portions of your text into memory and dump portions back to the disk while writing or editing is in progress. The name-it-later method is somewhat like feasting on alphabet soup by bringing a large vat to the table. The name-it-first method sends bowls back and forth into the kitchen until all the soup has been tasted.

Mouth-watering analogies aside, the differences in the two file-naming systems have very real implications for your housekeeping procedures. Because the name-it-later systems must keep the entire text in memory until the edit is complete, the size of any single text file is limited by the memory capacity of the computer. On a 64K system, for example, as much as 45K of the computer's memory might be taken up with the operating system and the word processing program itself. The largest file that you could work with at one time would thus be 19,000 bytes.

The name-it-first systems don't present this limitation. Because they can deal with only portions of a text file, the maximum file size could theoretically be the full storage capacity of the disk (though the program might not work very efficiently with such a huge file.)

The name-it-first systems impose a different limitation, however. Because the disk file being worked on must be identified at the start of the writing or editing session, you usually can't insert a new disk into the drive just prior to giving the final command to Save. This can cause grave problems if the working file becomes so large that there's no room left on the original disk—the dreaded 'Disk Full' situation.

With name-it-later systems, there's usually an easy solution for Disk Full occurrences. All you have to do is insert another disk with more free space and give the Save command again. In fact, you could keep saving the same file from memory onto several disks simply by inserting new disks and giving repeated Save commands.

▶ The distinction between the two file-naming procedures may seem abstract and theoretical, but it's important that you understand the way your particular system works. Your system's file-naming method will determine how you go about allocating space on your text disks and what routines you adopt to make sure that your work is safely preserved. (In Chapters 13 and 14, we'll discuss some specific techniques for dealing with the limitations of both types of system.)

▶ If your program does permit you to change disks, you should always have several disks that are formatted and ready to use. One simple routine for ensuring that your disks are ready is to format all disks in a box whenever you open that box. You can write a symbol, such as 'F', on the disk label to indicate that you've already formatted that disk.

Save Regularly!!!

This rainy-day advice applies in spades to writing with a word processor. It's also easy to forget until the worst happens. As we've mentioned, the writing or editing that you do on the screen is temporary; it does not become permanent until you have transferred it from the computer's memory to a disk. This reality can set the stage for a tragic scenario.

You finish five or six hard-won pages of writing, give the Save command to write the work on the disk, and nothing happens. Or maybe you get a message that says something like 'Disk Full'. In either case you're faced with the prospect of losing all that grueling work, and the contingency measures suggested in your w/p manual may not be able to bail you out.

In most writers' experience, such tragedies happen only once. They have learned a powerful lesson—to save their work often, so that some gremlin of electronic fate won't wipe out more than a few paragraphs. The choice of how often to save is individual, but the standard advice from seasoned computer users is to save every fifteen or twenty minutes. You may not have written much in that length of time, but it's important to develop a routine of storing information permanently on disk, so that the fleck of dust or the household power failure can't jeopardize a whole chapter or article.

▶ Establishing the routine of saving work regularly may just be the most important procedure in using a w/p system, because the transfer of information from the computer's temporary memory to the more permanent disk is one of the few vulnerable points in word processing. The best defense, as they say, is a good offense—and saving your work often, in small chunks, is a strategy of action that can eliminate or at least reduce the chances for disaster.

A good way to acquire the saving habit is by exaggerating at first—perhaps even setting a timer that rings every fifteen or twenty minutes. If you use a quiet timer, such as the "short doze" feature of a clock radio or the alarm provided in some calculators and watches, the timing device won't disturb your work but the alarm will rouse you to give the Save command whenever you hear it. Being slavish about saving may get old in a hurry, but it will serve to ingrain that crucial routine of sending your work to the disk.

▶ One prudent strategy that seems to be a happy medium is to save every time the screen is full of new work. For lightning-fast writers this may be every few minutes, but for most of us most of the time, the two or three paragraphs the screen holds will take at least fifteen minutes to devise. The reason why saving by screenfuls is so useful is not timing, however; it's that if the program or the disk refuses to save the work for some reason, you still have it displayed on the screen. So if all else has failed and you can't use some contingency measure (such as erasing another file to make room on an otherwise full disk) to save that writing, you can copy it manually and retype it when you've diagnosed and corrected the initial problem.

Even if you don't follow this strategy strictly, you'll discover that if the disk won't take your work, whatever is on the screen will stay there until you reboot the system or turn off the machine. The one exception to this rule is that if the electricity goes off (or you accidentally pull the plug), you'll lose the work displayed on the screen as well as the contents of the computer's RAM.

Developing the saving habit is critical, too, so that you do it without thinking—and without interrupting your creative process. There are certainly times in every writer's experience when the words and ideas are flowing so fast that any pause seems to threaten the act of getting it all down. But saving a screenful or a quarter-hour's work, even at such a lightning pace, takes only seconds. (The time for such actions differs among programs and computers, but a typical word processor takes 26 seconds from the Save command to being back at work at the same place you left off in a 10-page file.)

▶ Another very useful time to give the Save command routinely is whenever something interrupts your work. It's a good idea, for example, to save whatever you've done when the phone or doorbell rings, so that if there's a power fluctuation or a helpful child decides to turn off the machine while you're out of the room, the writing will have been safely stored on disk.

The command terms used for saving files vary among word processors. The basic command is usually Save, but the function may yield different results. Some programs allow you several options for storing work on the disk, such as Save and Return to File, Save and Exit to Main Menu, or Save and Exit to Operating System. All these versions of the Save command save the entire file on the disk, so that any minor changes you've made will be saved along with whatever new work was done since the last time you sent work to the disk.

Most programs also have an ABANDON or QUIT command, which allows you to leave a file without saving it. This may seem an aberration among all our cautionary advice about saving work, but abandoning can come in handy when you make a typing error in specifying a filename or if you're editing a file and erase some work that you didn't mean to wipe out. If you haven't done too much other work on that file, you can abandon the current version and begin editing again; the program usually will warn you that you're abandoning an edited file, but the previous version of it will still be intact on the disk.

Backing Up

If saving is the most important routine to establish, backing up your disk files runs a close second. Disks do wear out, get dirty, melt or warp if left in the sun, or simply misbehave sometimes—so you should make backup copies of your electronic manuscripts, just as you would make a copy of an original handwritten or typed draft. Once again, routine is our word for the day—or the chapter— because copying your disk files is a quick and painless process that ought to become a habit.

► An efficient system for backing up your work is to make a duplicate of your current files each time you finish a work session. The precise boundaries of this routine are up to you, of course, but copying work at least once a day is a prudent minimum, and ideally you should make backup copies whenever you'll be away from the system for an hour or more.

This suggestion is based on our own experience and our observations of human nature—if we don't do this mundane task now, we're likely to forget about it or put it off indefinitely. And the easiest time to make copies is when the system is running and your text disk is already in use; then all you have to do is use the DOS or w/p program's copy utility to duplicate the relevant files on a second disk.

► To take full advantage of the protection that backup disks offer, store your duplicate disks in a different location from the working versions of those files. Then if the sun hits a batch of disks or you spill a cup of coffee on them, the backup copies won't be harmed. Some experienced computer users recommend that you make two sets of backup disks, one of which you store in another building altogether.

Many word processors and some operating systems have a built-in backup system, as well. These programs automatically create a BACKUP FILE (and possibly a temporary WORK FILE as well) on your text disk whenever you save additions or revisions in an existing file. Although this effectively halves the storage capacity of the disk, it is a worthwhile protection in the event that you mistakenly erase part or all of a file (which can happen on some systems with one wrong command). The backup file is updated continuously, always containing the most recent version prior to the current one.

In addition to copying your text files, you should duplicate the working copies of your programs for safety and convenience. The w/p program disk is one that you use almost continuously, so it is more vulnerable to wear or dirt than a text disk that is used for a few days and then stored away. The original version of the program—the one you purchase—must never be used as a working disk; you should make copies from it when you begin using the program and thereafter only if your working disks all have some problem.

▶ A wise strategy for backing up program disks is to make three copies of the original (which you store in a really safe, isolated place); one is a current working copy, one is an ordinary backup, and the third is a "rotation" disk that you can exchange for the working copy after a few weeks of use. Text disks that you use constantly should likewise be rotated; for these disks, you might just rotate the backup copy and the working copy and not make a third version. After a few months of heavy use, back up at least one copy of the rotating program and text disks on new disks, and retire the oldest of the first group.

Copying text files and program disks is obviously an integral part of using a w/p system, and it's a chief reason for having two disk drives. You can load the Copying utility into the computer's memory, then insert the text disk and the backup disk and simply copy some files or all of the disk contents from one drive to the other. If you have only one disk drive, you have to copy by loading individual files into the RAM, taking out the first disk, putting in the backup disk, and then copying from the computer memory to the second disk. This process is time-consuming and is limited by the size of your system's RAM (usually 64K or less), so you have no way of copying the contents of a full disk (usually 150K or more) without dividing it into sections.

DOS Utilities

Another file-organization gimmick that comes with your word processor is the utility programs that are part of the disk operating system. As we've noted, two of these programs are used to format blank disks and to list the contents of a disk by filename and, in most systems, by file size in bytes. The other utilities are similar filing tools that can help you make sense of all the work you've stored on disks.

The utility programs that you're likely to use most often are the Disk Directory (sometimes called LIST or CATALOG), Disk Status report, and the Copying utility. In some systems you can use the DOS utilities from within the w/p program; in others you have to "sign out" of the word processor to perform the utility functions. Using the DOS utilities alone is often handy for checking the contents of disks or erasing files before you begin writing. Some of these functions may be duplicated by the word processing program, however, so you can experiment with the DOS or w/p versions and find the procedures that work best for you. Table 7-2 presents a summary of the DOS utilities provided by most systems.

Be Prepared

We're getting perilously close to sounding like a scouting manual here, but slogans such as "save regularly" and "be prepared" are down-to-earth advice for making a w/p system as natural a set of writing tools as paper and pen or typewriter. Our drastic predictions about brownouts, spills, and glitches are simply warnings of what can go wrong; that doesn't mean all of this will happen to you. But some of it undoubtedly will, and the best insurance against the inevitable problems is informed anticipation.

In discussing the importance of saving work on the disk, we've mentioned a 'Disk Full' message. The w/p program sends this message to the screen whenever you've given the Save command but the disk doesn't have sufficient space for that file. If your program allows you to change disks during a work session, you can simply put a formatted disk in the secondary drive and then write the file that's still in the computer's memory on that disk. If your program doesn't permit such disk changes, the w/p manual will probably suggest some alternatives for saving in this situation, such as erasing an unneeded file or one that you're positive has been copied on a backup disk.

▶ To avoid ever seeing that 'Disk Full' sign, check the amount of space available on your text disk—using the Status utility that's part of the DOS—at the start of each work session. If you anticipate writing new material that will take up half the empty space on that disk, begin working with a new text disk instead. You may have to

Table 7-2: Typical DOS Utilities

Probable Name	Purpose
Directory, Catalog, or List	List disk contents
Erase	Erase specified file
Rename	Rename a file
Save	Save designated file on disk
Type	Type contents of file to screen
Status or Check	Show available disk space in bytes
Copy	Copy a file or copy disk contents
Compare	Compare contents of disks or files
Format	Format a blank disk for use
System	Copy essential DOS utilities on disk

copy part of a current file on the new disk, but this is preferable to filling the old one to overflowing.

▶ The most effective way to get out of a tight spot is to know what your system's error messages mean and how your program lets you solve problems. Read the w/p manual's discussion of all error messages and practice using the contingency tactics suggested by the program designers before a real mistake happens. If your DOS has a separate manual, also study the error messages in it, because you may encounter one of those even when you're working within the word processing program.

▶ If you do get the 'Disk Full' signal or some other error message, don't panic. Usually the program will also display another message that tells you how to cancel the Save command that wouldn't work; the whole message might read, for example: 'Disk Full: Press Escape Key'. Remember that the computer will sit patiently for as long as you take to decide what to do next; you needn't press the Escape key immediately just because the screen tells you to. So you can consult the program manual for its description of the error message and its suggestions for how to get out of this tight spot. And when you do finally press the Escape key (or do whatever the screen dictates), in most instances you'll be back where you started, still with a chance of saving the work that's in RAM but not yet on disk.

All these gimmicks and slogans are designed to help you keep your electronic files intact and in order. You may select or adapt them according to your personal work style and the operation of your w/p program. What's most important, though, is that you develop good housekeeping methods and use them consistently; over time, they are certain to make your work easier.

Chapter 8

Personalizing the Program

*Defaults, Commands, and
Program Maps*

Your word processor might be
emblazoned with some computer company's logo and your program
might carry a fanciful name, but once you set up the system and start
writing with it, the word processor becomes your personal writing
tool. Throughout this book, we've encouraged you to experiment
with your system as you learn the ropes, but we've still considered
the computer as the "given"—as a tool that you must learn to handle.

Yet the most revolutionary aspect of this computer technology
is that it is INTERACTIVE—the machine anticipates your needs,
responds to your instructions, and alters its operations accordingly. In
fact, your word processor can be tailor-made to perform in special
ways to suit your tastes. Best of all, you are the tailor.

Now that we've looked at the main elements of a word processing system, we'll consider how the program can be modified, the
ways in which it interacts with you, and finally, how the program's
organization and structure relate to your own writing routines.

Configuration

If your program was written specifically to run on all of your computer's hardware or if you are writing on a dedicated word processor, then you can probably start up the program in its "factory fresh" condition and be off and writing. More likely, though, before you begin using your program for the first time, it will have to be CONFIGURED for your system. This means adding to or altering the program so that it will interact properly with the various components in your system.

You won't need to concern yourself with this procedure if you purchase a word processing program from the dealer who supplied your hardware. The dealer will (and certainly should) make sure that the program is properly configured before you take it away.

If for some reason the dealer's help is not readily available (such as if you purchased a new program by mail), you can usually accomplish the configuration yourself. You should turn to the appropriately labeled section of the program's manual for configuration (called INSTALLATION in some systems) and follow the directions.

With some programs, a configuration routine may be written into the program itself. You give a command to Configure and the program takes you through a series of questions, or prompts. First, it asks you to identify the type of terminal (keyboard and screen) you are using. The prompt might give you options to select on the screen, or you might input a numerical value to represent your terminal, which you would take from a list on the screen or in the manual. The program then uses the information you supply to rewrite itself automatically (called PATCHING in computer terminology). This configuration procedure is necessary for the program to be able to interpret the signals it receives from your keyboard and to send the proper signals to the screen.

Another part of the configuration routine gears your program to work with whatever printer you've chosen for the system. This routine is similar to the terminal configuration. In some instances, however, the program you choose may not be designed to take advantage of all the features built into some printers.

Configuring the program may require that you use your operating system's utilities to modify the program. This will involve locating a particular segment of the program, inputting new or revised specifications, and saving the program in this amended form. Although the notion of dealing with programs at this very primary level may be intimidating if you're not a computer wizard, you shouldn't panic. Just make sure that you're working with a backup copy of your program, go slowly, and follow the directions in the manual. Again, most of the time the dealer will have done all this for you.

Defaults

While configuration is a one-time-only procedure, you will be dealing with the DEFAULTS of your program every time you use it. In the plainest terms, defaults are program variables that the program assumes upon start-up, unless you send alternate instructions to the computer.

We have encountered these variables throughout our discussion so far, particularly in the chapter about printing. Whenever you begin using the program, certain values will be in effect, such as margin settings, spacing, pitch, page numbering, and page length. These are the program's DEFAULT PARAMETERS. In the case of printing, this means that if you give a Print command without specifying any print formatting values at all, the program will print your document according to its default values.

The default parameters apply to every aspect of the program. They determine what margins appear on the screen, whether Justification is in effect, and whether the Insert mode is on. Once you are operating the program, all of these variables may be changed by appropriate commands, as we have seen in many of the examples so far. The defaults only determine how the program "comes up" when you start it and what the parameters will be if you just begin writing and don't specify any variables.

Some of these default parameters may not be as you want them. Suppose, for example, that your program's default for the top margin on a printed page is 6 lines, but you prefer a top margin of 8 lines. You could, of course, give the Top Margin command every time you want to print a document, but what if you preferred larger margins all around? It would be a nuisance to have to respecify a half-dozen values at the beginning of each work session.

For this reason, most programs allow you to alter some or all of the default parameters, so that the program starts off with the values you want. There are several ways to do this. Some programs provide a DEFAULT SPECIFICATION ROUTINE, much like the one for configuring the program, which prompts you for each of the default values. Another method is to give a Set Defaults command, which will reset the parameters at whatever values are in effect at the time the command is given. In either case, the new values are written to the program disk so that the next time the program is loaded it will start with the new parameters in effect. The defaults can be changed again any time by running the specification routine.

An even more flexible approach to setting printing variables is the option of creating DEFAULT FILES or, more properly, FORMAT FILES. Instead of altering your program, you run through a Format Specification routine and then save the values as a separate file on the program disk. You can then put all the parameters into effect by activating the Format File. With this feature, you can store different formats for writing business letters, drafts, manuscripts, and poetry and call them up when needed. (In Chapter 13 we'll explore ways to pre-store formats even if your program doesn't have this Format File feature.)

In most cases, Format Files will contain only the parameters for formatting printed documents. On-screen display variables and editing features are usually alterable only at the primary default routine level. And in many programs, the defaults for some parameters (for example, whether Insert is initially in effect or not) may not be alterable at all. (In almost all instances, however, you can turn these features on and off while using the program.)

▶ The first step in personalizing your program is to check the manual thoroughly to determine the initial values for all defaults. Then consider whether each of these values is best for your writing needs.

▶ Decide how you would like the program to be operating when you start it for each of your work sessions, and set the defaults accordingly.

▶ If your program doesn't permit changing certain default values that you find inconvenient or bothersome, write out the commands for changing them as your own default routine. Keep a list of these default changes posted on or near your terminal so you can set everything just as you want it before you start writing or editing.

Commands

As we've mentioned, you might encounter defaults that determine some of the program's editing or screen formatting commands. A common example is the operation of the Insert command and Insert mode. In many programs, the default is for Insert to be off— when you start the program, Overtype is in effect. You have to give the specific Insert command to insert letters or words.

In some systems, even when Insert is turned on, the mode will revert to the default value (Insert off again) whenever some action is taken, such as moving the cursor, hitting a Return, or Reforming a paragraph. You should carefully check your program for these hidden DEFAULT REVERSIONS so that you can streamline your editing routines.

In this book, we have purposely refrained from describing actual commands or keystroke operations, since no two programs use the same commands. Familiarizing yourself with the commands on your own system is an important aspect of personalizing your word processor, however. Without becoming specific to any one system, we'll discuss a few common forms of word processing commands.

Frequently, commands will make use of the CONTROL KEY. As we noted in Chapter 1, this is a supplemental key, usually located to the side of the standard typewriter-style configuration. When this key is held down and a second, standard key is pressed, it sends a special signal to the computer that the program interprets as a command. In operation, the Control key turns a standard key into a command key, just as the Shift key transforms a lowercase letter to uppercase.

A character that is used in combination with the Control key is called a CONTROL CHARACTER. The screen display often indicates such a control character by showing the standard character preceded by a caret, such as '^S'. Even if imbedded in the text (as a Print Enhancement command, for instance), the control character will not print in the hard-copy document.

Some systems make use of another supplemental key, called ALT (presumably for "alternate," though you'll usually just see references to 'Alt' in a program manual). It operates exactly as the Control key does, transforming standard keys into additional control characters.

Many systems also provide special FUNCTION keys, which implement frequently used commands, such as Insert, Delete, and Print. The dedicated word processors make extensive use of function keys, as do word processing programs that have been written for a specific make and model of microcomputer. Although most hardware and software developers like to brag about how many special function keys they can employ in a system, there is a debate in the word processing community concerning the value of these special keys.

The opposing view reasons that a typist should be able to keep his or her fingers on the main keyboard as much as possible, and so it is more efficient to hit a Control-D to delete a character than to reach off the main keyboard for a separate Delete key.

▶ It seems clear that special function keys make the initiation to word processing a much easier and friendlier process. And for "hunt-and-peck" or "four-finger" typists whose fingers are flying around the keyboard anyway, the existence of special function keys probably helps more than hinders. If, however, you are a proficient typist and are not concerned about the ease with which others will be able to get the hang of your machine, then you should consider the merits of the "fingers-on-the-keyboard" style of programs.

Some systems also provide for PROGRAMMABLE FUNCTION KEYS (also called USER-DEFINED KEYS). As the names imply, these are keys for which the user can specify the input or command that will be sent to the system when they are pressed. The program commonly provides a routine for activating the Programmable Key function. Usually this entails pressing the key to be programmed, then typing the string of characters that this key will send to the computer whenever it's pressed. For example, you could program the '@' key to input a special word or phrase and save yourself many keystrokes—and typos—over the course of a book. (You would certainly be grateful for this function if you were writing a biography of Rachmaninoff.) A programmable key could also be used to enter often-used formatting commands or to call up Format Files.

A term you're likely to encounter in the computer world is TOGGLE KEY. This doesn't refer to any specific key; rather, it indicates a keystroke command that will successively activate and deactivate a function. A common example is our friend the Insert mode, which frequently works by a toggle key. Hit the Insert key once, and Insert mode is turned on; hit the same key again and it is toggled off.

Another favorite computer word is MNEMONIC ("nee-mon-nick"). Derived from the Greek word for memory, a mnemonic command is one for which the letter command reflects the function, such as 'F' for Find and 'R' for Replace. Salespeople and advertisers like to stress that a system makes use of mnemonic commands. In fact, mnemonics do aid considerably in learning and using a program.

Program Maps

We'll look now at various ways in which word processing programs are structured. While this might seem to be merely of theoretical interest, understanding your program's organization is a key to your proficiency as a w/p writer.

One important concept in all computer programs is that of the MENU. As we've noted, a menu is a list of options presented on the screen, often with a prompt asking you to choose an option. An example would be the Command Menu that appears at program start-up, giving you the option to Edit, Print, or manage files (Save,

Delete, Copy, and so forth). Choosing one of the menu items sends you into the portion of the program that accomplishes that task, frequently called a MODE of the program.

Once in a mode, you may be presented with another menu listing other options. These might in turn branch to other menus. Programs that function this way are said to be MENU-DRIVEN. Menus make programs easy to learn, in that they guide the user through all the steps necessary to get the job done. A well-designed menu system will assure that you can't wander off the path and get lost in the woods.

Menu-driven programs and program modes can take various forms. A TREE structure has all its subsidiary modes branching off a main "trunk" mode. To get from one submode to another, you have to return to the main mode. In a CHAIN, the modes are linked in linear fashion. Another model is the RING, in which the modes lead to each other circularly. A fourth possibility is the HUB, with a central mode leading to outlying modes, arranged in a ring. Figure 8-1 shows examples of each of these types of structure, based on a program with four modes.

▶ Although these structuring concepts are abstractions and your program manual is not likely to use them, you will benefit greatly from visualizing your program in this way. It would be worthwhile to try to draw your own PROGRAM MAP and keep it near the system for reference. The modes in your map may not be arranged quite so neatly, but going through this exercise will give you a much better understanding of where you are in the program at all times. In addition, this introduction to program organization concepts can be of help in evaluating a new program or mastering the one with which you're writing now.

Not all programs are organized according to these menu-driven or modal systems. The alternative is what is called a DIRECT COMMAND STRUCTURE. In its purest form, a command-structured program would allow any command to be given from any other point in the program (such as being able to delete one file while editing another).

Both methods of organization have their merits. Menu-driven systems are more "user-friendly," in that they don't require comprehension of the whole program and always give you some course to pursue. Once you have learned your way around a program, however, it can be faster and more convenient to be able to give direct commands. In practice, very few programs are strictly structured one way or the other.

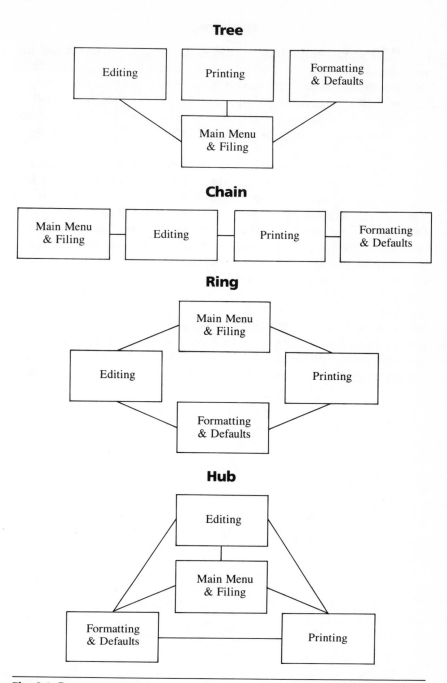

Fig. 8-1: Program structures

Routines

We've raised the subject of routines many times so far, and by now their importance may be placed in perspective. The instructions that a computer follows are merely a series of sequential steps and conditional actions, arranged in a rigid format. The machine is not smart; it is just amazingly fast and wonderfully obedient. The person who wrote the program—and you who make use of it in your writing—are the smart ones.

As you become familiar with the way your system functions and is structured, you'll find that the machine almost teaches you to develop good routines for editing, printing, and file management. Through experience with word processing, you'll become increasingly "in tune" with the way the system goes about its work, and you'll develop personal work routines that complement the system. (All of Part II of this book describes such routines, for a variety of writing applications and situations.)

This tuning in, this habit of mind—which you are likely to develop without even realizing it—will help you become increasingly aware of the kinds of jobs the computer can do for you. As that happens, you will certainly get your money's worth from the equipment and programs you've acquired. You may even discover that these Computer Age writing skills have helped you become a better writer.

Chapter 9

Bells and Whistles

Sophisticated Word Processing

All word processing is divided into three parts. That is, no matter how a w/p program is arranged or what the commands are called, it performs three major functions—editing, printing, and filing. Every program includes some fundamental features in each of these categories, and more sophisticated programs offer a variety of choices for all three functions.

The first eight chapters of this book have introduced the essential word processing features in each category; now we'll get to the fancy stuff. The bells and whistles of writing with a w/p system are like air-conditioning and a tapedeck in a new car—not essential but awfully nice to have. Some of these luxuries are built into one or more of the commercial word processing programs and dedicated w/p systems; others are separate programs or add-on components that you can buy or find listed (in program form) in a book or magazine.

▶ The add-on programs or components won't work with every system, nor will even the most sophisticated program have every one of these features. So if you are considering a program or system—as your initial word processor or to augment what you use now—be sure to read the manual thoroughly and investigate what options and add-ons are compatible with it. And be sure to define your needs carefully and realistically, so that you don't load up on expensive extras that you'll never use.

Extended Editing

Perhaps the most dazzling—and useful—of the word processing options is a DICTIONARY on disk. Such a program is useful because it functions as a first proofreader for all of your work, and it's dazzling because it compares your files with its dictionary at a rate of 5,000 to 10,000 words per minute. Even by computer-speed standards, that's fast—and compared to eyeball speed, it is almost incomprehensible.

The Dictionary or SPELLING CHECKER has become an optional component of many word processing programs, or you can use a stand-alone version if your system doesn't have one built in. Whichever type you use, the procedure is much the same; you use the Dictionary program's control mode to compare a file of your writing with the program's dictionary. Any word that does not conform exactly to a word in the dictionary is marked by the program and shown to you on the screen. You then have the option of letting the word remain as is, correcting it and saving the corrected version, or accepting it as is and adding it to the program's dictionary.

These Dictionary programs vary somewhat in operation, however; some programs will make a list of the unrecognized words and show them to you one at a time for your decision; other versions of a Spelling Checker proceed through the file and highlight the unrecognized words without separating them from your text. In programs that separate the list of words for review, your signal that one needs correction actually puts a special character in that word within your text file; then you use the Search feature of your word processing program to find each occurrence of that character and correct all the marked words.

Another very useful feature of most Dictionary programs is that you can create special dictionaries for individual projects and add or remove words in the basic dictionary. Because words are stored on the disk in highly compressed form, most of these programs have a dictionary of 20,000 to 30,000 words, and some have dictionaries with up to 90,000 words. A few program distributors also offer dictionaries for individual professions, such as law or medicine, as well as foreign-language dictionaries.

The size of a dictionary is sometimes limited by the capacity of a system's disks. Some double-density disks, for example, can't store both the large dictionary and the control program for checking spelling; in this instance, you put the dictionary component in one disk drive and copy your text file onto the disk that holds the control program, check and mark the corrections, then copy the file back to a data disk for use with the word processor. This copying nuisance has been eliminated in newer versions of many Dictionary programs, which further compress the dictionaries or use an alternate short dictionary that fits on the main program disk.

A Dictionary program can help improve your writing in two ways: first, it catches typos and thus lets you concentrate on getting the words down without stopping to consult a dictionary every few minutes. And because the program displays every word it doesn't recognize, you have to look up the pesky words that you chronically misspell, and then correct them in your text—a process that may eventually ingrain the proper spelling of some of those words in your memory. If you didn't have this step-by-step isolation of the words that don't match the computer dictionary, you might just read your text and skip over the words that you commonly get wrong.

Contrary to their name's implication, Dictionary programs do not really contain dictionaries, because no definitions are provided for the words in them. No doubt some enterprising programmer will create a true dictionary on disk, but disk capacity or data compression would have to be greater than current standards to offer a broad selection of words with definitions. One similar type of program is available now for some systems, however—a THESAURUS on disk, which lists synonyms for many common words.

(One alternative for working with programs that require large storage capacity, such as a comprehensive dictionary or thesaurus, is a HARD DISK. This rather expensive hardware option can accommodate several million characters of information, thus providing ample room for programs, reference sources, and files of your work.)

Several other programs that analyze text can contribute to better writing, as well. Some limited GRAMMAR-CHECKING programs have been introduced, although they are necessarily rather inflexible and seem improbable replacements for on-the-spot human judgment and creativity. Such a program may be a good addition to a Spelling Checker, though, because it can catch such non-spelling errors as parentheses or quotation marks that aren't closed.

Some simpler programs report the mechanical details of a chapter or manuscript. Most Dictionary programs also count the words in a file, but independent programs are also available for this purpose. Another useful tool in studying your writing is a WORD-USAGE program, which measures the frequency with which you use words and the length of the words you use. A word frequency and length summary of a piece of writing is the kind of tedious task that you're not likely to attempt by hand, but it can tell you surprising and useful things about your work. And it's the kind of task that is ideally suited to the computer's prowess.

All of these text-examining programs are options or separate components to be added to a word processor. Yet some of the built-in features of many w/p programs can make the writing and editing process faster and easier than relying only on the fundamentals of word processing. For example, some programs have a MARKER SYSTEM that lets you place a marker or control character in the text at a point where you know you'll want to add or change something later. Some programs use numbers or special characters that are displayed on the screen but won't print as part of the file; other programs may have CURSOR MEMORY, which allows you to return the cursor to a previous location.

▶ Whatever type of marker your system uses, you'll be able to take the best advantage of it if you also make a written note of the subject for each marker in the text. Otherwise, you may not remember whether you put a '1' or a '2' at the place where you needed to check a fact, or a '3' or '4' where you want to clean up an awkward passage.

Even if a program doesn't include a marker system, most word processors have some provision for entering COMMENTS in the text that are displayed on the screen but not printed. In fact, this device can serve as a text marker; you could write a comment at each place in the text that needs more work and use the Search command to locate the symbol that identifies the comment. Since comments always begin with the same symbol, however, you'd have to review them sequentially until you find the one desired. (Chapters 11 and 12 provide some additional suggestions for finding specific parts of your text using the standard w/p features.)

One other advanced word processing feature can build a good deal of flexibility into your writing. This is the ability of some programs to WRITE and READ BLOCKS—to copy (or Write) blocks of text to a separate file from the file you're working on, and to Read the contents of other files into the current one. This means that if you're writing an article about the space shuttle and you're seized with a passage for the novel that's been claiming your spare time, you can write down everything for the novel at the moment the inspiration hits, making it a temporary part of your space shuttle file. When this creative storm has passed, you mark the fiction as a block and copy it—often called Writing a Block—to a separate file, without ever having to leave the current file, which would have meant saving and exiting to the Main Menu, establishing a new file for the novel (or entering an existing one), and then recording your sudden thoughts.

Similarly, if you're editing a chapter or article and decide to take out some sections but to keep them for future use, you can mark them as blocks and send them to separate files. (You can then erase them from the current text, but preferably not until you've checked the Disk Directory to verify that they were copied.) Later, when you're working on a chapter where one of these deleted sections will fit, you can simply give the command to Read a File into the current one, then erase the old copy after you're sure you've found the proper home for it.

For many writing projects, putting the manuscript in final form can be almost as big a job as creating it. Some optional or add-on programs can help a lot at this point in your work by setting the form and finding the information for footnotes, tables of contents, and indexes. Generally these add-on components are designed to work with a specific word processing program and use its files to generate the specialized information.

One such program, for example, is a KEY WORD utility. It will search through a completed manuscript (usually a group of files, rather than one file) and compile a list of all chapter titles and major headings, complete with their page numbers. You can then format this listing with the word processor and you have an almost-instant table of contents. This type of program also can usually locate key words that you have marked previously (using symbols that it recognizes but that aren't printed as part of a file) and generate an index, in alphabetical order, with or without a listing of manuscript page numbers.

Similar programs can be used for locating FOOTNOTES, usually by finding the symbol that identifies each reference to a footnote in the text, then designating where the footnote itself should go to be on the same page as its reference. Handling footnotes can be tricky, though, because if you add some text, you may separate the footnote from its reference—so the locating and placing of footnotes should be one of the final steps in completing a manuscript. (Suggestions for generating lists of key words and footnotes by using the basic w/p features are presented in Chapter 14.)

One other highly desirable editing feature is the ability to work with more than one file simultaneously. To date, this capability has been built into very few w/p programs and dedicated systems, but it is a direction that many more programs will take in the future. Specifically, multiple-file editing usually takes place on a SPLIT SCREEN; that is, the top half of the screen contains twelve or more lines of one file, and the bottom half displays a comparable amount of text from another file. Both portions of text can be edited, and you can scroll through one of the displayed files without disturbing the other. Ultimately, the ideal w/p system may include several separate screens, rather like a film-editing setup, so that portions of two or more displayed files could be "spliced" together electronically and the resulting new file displayed on its own screen.

Another ultimate development in w/p programs is the combination of all of the optional features into a single program. This is another likely prospect as computer technology continues its rapid advances; for example, computers with greater internal memory capacities will accommodate larger programs, which could integrate spelling checkers, footnote and index components, and other advanced options into one package. In a few instances, word processors now include such advanced capabilities as generating indexes and tables of contents, as well as numbering footnotes and placing them at the bottom of the appropriate page.

Precision Printing

Just as certain advanced w/p features make for more versatile writing and editing, other options or program enhancements make page formatting and printing a breeze. One of the most useful formatting features is variable settings for TABS in a file. Most programs treat tab stops in the same way typewriters do—you can set them or change them any time as you're writing. More sophisticated word processors also let you manipulate text with the tabs in other ways.

One program, for example, has two possible tab settings for each paragraph—you can specify the amount of indentation for the first line of the paragraph and also indent all the other lines of that paragraph with another command. If you don't put a specific command in the file for either of these tab settings, the program will use its default choices, which provide an indented first line and no indentation for all other lines in the paragraph.

Some programs allow you to override temporarily the established tab settings. For example, if you wanted to add a rather long quotation to your text and distinguish it from your words by indenting all its lines, you could establish one of the tab stops as a temporary left margin, rather than having to reset the actual margin and change it back when you'd finished typing the quote. The tab change can be toggled on and off whenever you need it, without changing the original margin at all.

One other advanced tab feature can be very useful if you have to include columns of numbers or dollar amounts in your writing. This is DECIMAL TABBING, which automatically aligns numbers by the decimal point in a column or table. If you've originally entered the numbers using this tab feature, the vertical alignment of a column of numbers won't be changed if you reformat the text surrounding them.

Another highly useful option or feature of the more comprehensive word processors is a MERGE function. Different programs offer varying versions of this operation, but its main purpose is to print text from one file as part of another. Perhaps the most common form of Merging is a form letter or document, such as a contract, that uses some standard text and some text that's individualized for each occasion. For example, you could send a personalized letter to a group of editors or friends by writing one letter that includes special symbols where the name and address appear, then Merging that letter with another file that contains the names and addresses of the recipients. Each time you print a copy of the letter, the Merge program will select the next name and address on your list.

Merge printing usually lets you enter new information from the keyboard, as well. If you're sending that form letter to a group and want to insert a personal note in each copy, you can put the appropriate symbol in the original letter and the printer will pause and wait for you to add the keyboard input whenever it encounters that symbol. Even if your added note varies in length, the letter will be reformatted as it's printing, so your margins will be the same as in the original version.

In some instances you may not want to write an entire letter to a group, but you would like to address envelopes or mailing labels to the people in your address file. Merge printing can also do this by combining a COMMAND FILE and a text file; the Command File establishes the format for the printed document, and the text file supplies the information. With this kind of built-in flexibility, you can make only one data file of information such as names and addresses and use several different Command Files to print out that information any way you need it. (Specific uses for Command Files and other files for formatting common documents are discussed in Chapter 13.)

Merge printing and Command Files also can be used to print several files in the order you want to use them. Some w/p programs have a LINK function that does this, but if your program doesn't have this feature, you can create a Command File that lists several files. This operation is often called CHAINING files.

Another benefit of some Merge programs is allowing you to change disks in the middle of a printing operation. Many word processors don't provide for this as part of their standard features, but the Merge option often has a signal that notifies the operating system of the change of disks. In most systems, though, you have to know ahead of time at what point you want to change disks and put the Disk Change symbol at the appropriate place in your Command File before beginning the printout.

One additional feature of many w/p programs lets you edit a file at the same time you print one—an operation called SPOOLING. If you're printing the file that you're also working on, the program usually will not let you save the new work in that file until the printing is complete, however. Whether or not the print and edit files are the same, most computers will interrupt the printing momentarily for keyboard activity. If you're entering text, the printer will work a bit more slowly and have a more staccato sound than usual; if you give an editing command, such as moving the cursor to the beginning of the file, the printer will stop for the few seconds that operation takes, then resume when the cursor has reached its destination. Although the printer's choppy sound—or just its regular noise—can be distracting when you're also trying to write or edit your work, simultaneous printing and editing can be very welcome at deadline times. (For linguistic trivia buffs, SPOOL is an acronym for Simultaneous Peripheral Operations On Line.)

Faultless Filing

As you generate more work and thereby gather a library of disk files, some of the word processing bells and whistles can really help manage your work. Whatever the storage capacity of a system's disks, for example, it would be nice to cram more information on each one. Some w/p programs or add-on utilities can CONDENSE text files, providing greater storage capacity on each disk. If the word processor "squeezes" information as part of its regular operation, you won't be aware of the condensed format because all files are stored that way. But if you use a separate program to condense files, you won't be able to work with those files until they are "unsqueezed," a function that is provided automatically by the word processors that routinely squeeze files.

If you use a squeeze program, the name of each condensed file will include a special character to indicate this. When you try to print or edit or simply look at a squeezed file, you'll see only meaningless characters on the screen. Once the file has been unsqueezed, though, you can use it for all normal w/p functions.

▶ Using a separate program to store more information on each disk requires a two-step process: at the beginning you use the program to condense the files, and when you want to work with them again, you use the program to return them to normal length. So you probably shouldn't squeeze files that are still active, and if you fill up a disk with condensed files, you'll have to transfer something off that disk before you can unsqueeze one or more of its files (because the unsqueezed versions always occupy more space). A good routine to avoid 'Disk Full' errors in this situation is to copy the needed file to a disk with plenty of free space and then unsqueeze it for editing.

The directory of each disk will indicate which files are condensed, as well as a lot of other useful information. A few word processing programs provide DETAILED DISK DIRECTORIES that show the filename, the author of that file, a comment about the file, the date it was last revised, and even whether it is protected by a password. These expanded directories can be printed—using part of the program designed for that purpose or a DOS utility—and can serve as a rather complete catalog of your disk files.

Such detailed directories are uncommon features of w/p programs, but several separate CATALOG programs are available to augment the more modest directories of most systems. These programs maintain a master list of all your disks and their directories; this listing can be updated easily by inserting each disk and having the Catalog program check that disk's directory and record any changes. Most Catalog programs also allow you to search the master list for all files with the same or related names and to add comments about individual disks in the list. In this way, you can identify disks with different versions of the same material, such as successive drafts and backup copies, and clearly label disks that shouldn't be revised or erased, such as final drafts and permanent archives. (Chapter 14 presents a cataloging plan for w/p programs that don't have special Catalog options or Detailed Disk Directories.)

▶ Even the simpler built-in directory systems often have mechanisms to group similar files. Certain characters designated by the program or the DOS are WILD CARD characters, which serve to locate or group related files. If you wanted to list all files that have one portion of their names in common, for example, you could specify the part of the name that's identical along with a wild card character and see every filename that contains the desired part. Wild cards are also useful for copying or erasing related files—you can use one command to have the DOS utility copy or erase all files with a common part of their filenames.

Beyond Word Processing

Most word processing systems also can use a variety of other programs—for purposes as diverse as tax preparation, mailing lists, language study, and stock market analysis, not to mention music (the real bells and whistles) and games. (The exception is dedicated word processors, which often have related options such as a Spelling Checker but usually aren't designed to utilize other types of programs.) Like the w/p program, any additional software must be compatible with your system's hardware and DOS, but there are hundreds or even thousands of programs available for the most popular microcomputers, and at least a few dozen for most business-oriented systems.

The largest-selling program for microcomputers is an ELECTRONIC SPREAD SHEET, which does mathematical calculations on the screen in a format like that of a ledger. The broad appeal of this type of program is that you can change any of the variables on the ledger page and recalculate all the other values; in essence, this program lets you ask "What if?" about anything with numbers. Of course the results of your on-screen projections can also be printed on regular paper or on the wider sheets commonly used with large computer systems.

One relatively new feature offered by some software distributors is a group of programs that can work together. For example, the files created by a spread sheet program could be edited and formatted with the word processing program, and a sorting component could compile special lists of information from any of these files. Such compatibility among programs is efficient and useful for most business purposes, or simply for a writer who's handling complicated data such as scientific research or a book about the economy.

An important add-on feature that's available for most systems is COMMUNICATIONS hardware and software, which enable your computer to exchange information with other computers over telephone lines. The exciting possibilities of computer networking are discussed in detail in Chapter 15.

As small-scale computer systems become common in homes as well as offices, the packaged programs are certain to include even more family-oriented offerings. Already computers have found a home in many classrooms, and kids are doing much more with them than shooting aliens. What this may mean to writers who are also parents is that you'll have to compete for computer time, or at least share the wealth. This shouldn't be hard, though; once you've tasted the pleasure and power of working with these amazing tools, you're likely to become something of an evangelist on the subject.

Chapter 10

Care and Feeding

Maintaining the System

Like most other machines, computer systems have been made increasingly reliable and efficient in recent years. As engineers and designers have packed complex circuitry into small boxes and smaller chips, they have also created components that consume relatively little electricity and can run for thousands of hours without a failure. Yet anything can break down at some time, and word processing systems are no exception.

For most of us, dealing with a computer component that won't work is like coping with a car that refuses to start or an air-conditioner that suddenly conks out. Some people will shout and swear a bit; others may calmly inspect the machine's interior and try to diagnose the problem; and many people will just call the repair shop. As with any complicated machinery, however, preventive maintenance can eliminate some of the frustrations and problems you could encounter with this high-tech equipment.

The first consideration in preventive maintenance for your word processor is to give the system a good home. Computers aren't especially temperamental, but they can be sensitive to dirt or smoke or electrical interference—and these are elements that you can eliminate or reduce in their environment. Equally important, if you establish good working routines, you can use your experience to troubleshoot the inevitable glitch and to document it for a technician.

Plugging In

The first thing you have to provide for a w/p system is power, and these components are not the kind you should plug into a couple of extension cords that also supply the portable heater or hair dryer. If possible, the system should not share a circuit with any other appliances, nor should the components be plugged into a conventional extension cord. The interference of other electrical signals and the ups and downs in power when a neighboring appliance is turned on and off may affect the computer's performance, perhaps even causing it to lose some information.

You can take several precautions to avoid this hazard, though. Since most computers, terminals, and printers have three-prong, grounded plugs, you'll need the appropriate outlets or adapters to plug them in. One simple solution to this problem is a POWER STRIP, an inexpensive device that accepts several grounded plugs and contains its own circuit breaker and on-off switch. Although it is not the most sophisticated form of protection for the power supply, a power strip could prevent an electrical overload from reaching the components.

If the wall outlet in your office does not accept three-pronged plugs, you can use an adapter that accepts such a plug and itself has only two prongs and a notch to which you can connect a ground wire. If you know that your wall outlet is grounded, the notch can be connected to the screw of the plastic plate that covers the outlet; if your outlet is not grounded—as is the case in many older buildings—you can connect a covered wire to the notch and attach the other end of the wire to a metal pipe or other wire that leads to the ground outside. You can verify that an outlet or adapter is grounded by using an inexpensive circuit tester. (If you are unfamiliar with electrical wiring, it's wise to consult an electrician for help when installing a w/p system.)

In some residential areas or in older office buildings, the power supply may be unreliable and prey to fluctuations in the flow of electricity. In this situation you may need a LINE FILTER or SURGE PROTECTOR for the computer. These devices are more complex than a power strip and therefore more expensive, but they could prevent damage to the equipment in case of a "power spike," which could occur if heavy appliances (such as an air-conditioner or copying machine) nearby are turned on or if the power fails and then comes back on. In short, a surge protector is usually a wise investment.

All these precautions may imply that the w/p system uses a lot of electricity. In fact, it requires relatively little juice; the reason for grounded plugs and a separate circuit is that the computer processes thousands of electrical signals every second, and any nearby electrical activity could interfere with its work. So there is little risk of short circuits or fires when your system is operating normally, and your electricity bills will not skyrocket because of the system. Even if you use the word processor for forty or fifty hours per week, the cost of electricity for the system should be only a few extra dollars per month.

The Computer Room

Blood banks and data banks have one thing in common—they're always chilly. And although the environment for your word processing system need not be frigid, the temperature of the computer room is an important operating factor. The microcomputer has fewer circuits and generally slower working speeds than large computers, but the same principle applies: all that frantic electrical activity in the machine generates heat, and if the temperature gets too high, the computer may collapse. Even if the circuits keep operating, prolonged overheating or inadequate ventilation will cause the components to wear out prematurely.

For our purposes, a cool operating environment for the computer simply means keeping the sun off it, being sure that the machine's fan (if it has one) has ample room to circulate air, and never covering the vents in the components' cabinets when the system is turned on. Leaving the system on all day should not cause overheating, but if the screen display or a disk begins to behave strangely, you might give the system a rest to see if that solves the problem.

Dust is one of the villains of the computer world. Often the computer is less vulnerable to this problem than are the disks, drives, keyboard, and printer, all of which usually have more exposed parts than the main machine. But a speck of dust on any of the electronic connections or any disk's surface can garble information intermittently or permanently, resulting in lost work and lost time trying to figure out what went wrong.

A healthy environment for the system is also threatened by many writers' traditional props—coffee, tea, or cigarettes. Particles from cigarette smoke, grease from food, or a spilled drink of any kind can be fatal to circuits, disks, and drives.

▶ A prudent rule for working with the word processor is to keep all food, drink, and smoke well away from the equipment. With a minimum of inconvenience, you can probably rearrange your work area to provide a sheltered place for a coffee cup, so that a spill won't destroy any disks or components. Smoking is harder to isolate from the system if you find it necessary while working, but try to direct the smoke away from the equipment and be sure that the room is well ventilated.

A less common hazard in computer rooms is static electricity, which may occur in areas with low humidity. If you get those little shocks after walking to your desk or moving your chair around on the office rug, you may need to cover the floor near your system components with an anti-static mat or spray the vicinity with anti-static spray.

▶ To avoid all of these sources of contamination of the computer room, use plastic covers for each of the system's components whenever the machines are not turned on. If your dealer doesn't sell covers made to fit your equipment, check an office supply store or the advertisements in microcomputer magazines. These covers are available for most common components, and many suppliers will custom make them if you require it.

Disk and Drive Care

Floppy disks are similar to phonograph records in another way besides appearance: a piece of dirt or a fingerprint on either can really garble the message. If anything, disks are more vulnerable to dirt, sunlight, scratches, and general carelessness than are records, because they are flimsier and the information on them is so highly condensed. All this potential for tragedy dictates that disks be handled carefully and stored in a clean, protected package when not in use.

There are several good storage systems available for disks. Some are covered boxes that let you flip through the disks until you find the ones you want to use; others are envelopes that fit into notebooks or file drawers. The system you choose is less important than your fidelity to it; disks should go from the storage container directly to the drive and back again—they must never be left out.

▶ Whatever storage system you use for disks, keep each disk in the paper envelope in which it is supplied. This container covers the holes in the disk jacket through which dirt might penetrate.

Because the information stored on them is written electronically, disks are also prey to the random signals that computers sometimes launch unexpectedly.

▶ To avoid ambient data on a disk, always turn on the computer and wait until the disk drive's light goes off before inserting a disk. When you are finished working, take out the disk before turning off the computer. If you turn the machine on or off with a disk in the drive, information still in the machine's memory may be sent to the disk and scramble its contents.

Disks are also sensitive to static electricity and magnetic fields. They should not be stored or handled near electric motors, magnets, or even the telephone, which gives off a magnetic charge when it rings and thus can damage the data on a disk. (The telephone should also be kept away from the disk drives, for the same reason.)

When labeling disks—always a necessary part of your writing routine—use only felt-tipped pens. Ballpoints or pencils have too hard a point and could push the magnetic coating—and its attendant data—off the surface of the disk.

Occasionally you'll get a defective disk, which may result in some loss of work if you don't discover it right away. (This is another reason for saving and backing up your work often—see Chapter 7 for a full discussion.) More often than a true disk failure, though, you may find that the disk is slightly askew in the drive, which makes it behave strangely, giving you information you didn't ask for or not showing anything at all.

▶ If you get odd information from a disk, wait for the disk drive light to go out, then take the disk out and carefully put it back in. This maneuver often corrects such problems, and you may discover that you originally inserted the disk with the wrong side up.

Another source of a disk's odd behavior could be the drive itself. The read/write head can become dirty simply from use, and some disk manufacturers sell kits for cleaning the heads. Before you attempt to clean the read/write heads yourself, though, consult a technician or your dealer; many knowledgeable service people believe that head-cleaning devices can actually damage the drives rather than improve their performance.

Disk drives also can become misaligned from prolonged use or frequent movement of their cabinet. If a drive is not working properly, and the other drive in a two-drive system is all right, alignment may be the problem. Many computer manufacturers and other program distributors offer a disk that tests drives for proper alignment (and checks disks for error-free surfaces at the same time). Computer service centers can realign the drive—or you can buy an instruction kit and disk to do it yourself, though this is tricky. In general, drives should need alignment no more than once a year.

▶ If you insert a disk and get noises that are unusual or louder than the drive's customary whirring and clicking, wait for the light to go out and remove the disk. Check the center hub to see if there is any tear or rippling and if so, put the disk aside. Try a second disk or re-insert the original one if you can't find any flaw in it. If the drive still makes strange noises, it may need alignment or other repair.

As you use different brands of disks in your system, you'll notice that some may make a more obvious whirring sound than others. This is not a problem unless the disk also behaves strangely when accepting commands or storing data.

Troubleshooting

Even though this chapter has been full of preventive measures and potential hazards, the components of a word processing system are patient, forgiving, and amazingly reliable most of the time. But if you do spill a cup of coffee in a disk drive or drop a paper clip into the computer, something is likely to go wrong. And even without such mishaps, you probably will confront a disk failure or program bug at some point in your word processing career. So here are some suggestions that should help you cope with misbehaving technology while keeping your sanity.

▶ First, if you get strange sounds or smells from any component in the system, turn off power to that unit. After a couple weeks of using the word processor, you'll know the difference between truly unusual occurrences and a noisy disk or rattling printer. In any event, turn off and preferably unplug all parts of the system before poking, prodding, or taking the cover off any component. (Inspecting the guts of your machines is not necessarily a good idea, and you may be violating the warranty by doing so. But curiosity often prevails in the human-machine relationship, and you probably can't hurt anything if you just look.)

▶ If you don't already have one, it's a good idea to get a fire extinguisher for your office. In the event of a short circuit that leads to any electrical fire, you'll need the type of extinguisher that uses halon (a nontoxic gas) or carbon dioxide.

▶ If strange things happen on the system's screen, you probably don't need the fire extinguisher, but you may have a bad disk or a program bug. This is when your methodical routines in using the word processor should help you find the problem, by eliminating some possibilities and perhaps suggesting others. If the program's contingency measures don't work and your logical guesses aren't correct, you'll need expert help to get the system working again. This is where a diary comes in handy.

▶ The most useful aid in describing any hardware or software problem is a concise description of the event, time, date, and any relevant circumstances you can think of. Even if you solve a problem or it goes away spontaneously, you should record the information in a diary that you keep with the system at all times. A defective part or connection in a computer often fails intermittently, causing different problems at different times and perhaps ultimately stopping the component from functioning altogether. If you have a record of all the system's glitches or exotic maneuvers, a technician may use it to discover a significant pattern or a specific problem that caused this failure.

▶ If the system or a component just won't turn on, check all the cords and cables. Often a connection between the computer and the terminal or printer can come loose, causing the peripheral device to play dead even though the computer is working.

▶ When you can't discover the source of a problem or a solution that lets you keep working, ask another experienced w/p user for help. This person may have solved a similar problem or may simply have new diagnostic measures to suggest. That kind of second opinion can often forestall "system surgery" and save you valuable time, energy, and dollars.

One More Routine

Here comes one final chorus of "Establish Routines." By now you're way ahead of us, no doubt—so you probably can anticipate our saying that if you establish a sequence of steps for each w/p procedure and methodically follow those steps every time, you reduce the chances of zapping your work by hitting a wrong key or switch.

▶ For maintaining your system and troubleshooting if something goes wrong, these routines are your diagnostic tools. The computer and its components function in set patterns that are controlled by the programs loaded into them and the commands you enter from the keyboard. If you always turn on the machines, load your disks, work with the word processing program, turn off the equipment, and put the program and text disks away in exactly the same fashion, you'll have a mental checklist to go over when the unexpected happens.

End of sermon—intermission.

Part II

Style

Chapter 11

Fingertip Thinking

Writing Styles and Strategies

Ideally, the writing process is a direct path from the mind to the page. And for this purpose, word processing may be the best game in town. Never mind that the page isn't printed by the w/p system as it is being written; that's often an advantage. The important feature of w/p writing is that it is immediate—that it is, quite literally, fingertip thinking.

So far, no invention—electronic, mechanical, or otherwise—can match the powers of the human brain. But for writing, a word processor comes as close as any machine: the speed of recording letters, words, and pages is limited only by the speed and accuracy of a writer's fingers on the keys. So if you're reasonably agile on the keyboard, you can probably keep up with your brain most of the time.

Of course there are other stages in the writing process—most notably editing—and we'll discuss those at length in the chapters that follow. But the first stage has to be producing some text, whether it is a fractured assemblage of phrases or a coherent sequence of paragraphs. With the help of a word processor, you can make something polished and professional out of either one.

In this chapter, the suggestions and many of the tips could apply to writing with any set of tools. We've presented most of these thoughts in the context of w/p writing, however, so that you can adapt them to your own system, whether it's a fixture in your office or still a contemplated acquisition.

Before getting into styles and strategies, though, we'd like to offer a second bit of advice—a corollary to the suggestion to "Be curious—be fearless" at the beginning of this book. This new advice pertains to the way you go about the work of writing; it is: Be daring—be critical. Because you have such powerful tools at your command with word processing, you can take risks and try writing experiments that might be too tedious or time-consuming with a typewriter or pen and paper, and you can edit all that daring work with just a few keystrokes if the experiments go awry. So don't be timid; attempt miracles, and you're likely to find that occasionally they happen.

Writing Without Barriers

There are two kinds of barriers on that direct path from the mind to the page. The first is physical—the interference of a typewriter's noise and its tendency to seize up if the keys are struck too quickly, as well as the human body's limits in getting the words down in writing, whether on a keyboard or with a pen or pencil. As we've pointed out several times in this book, a word processor very nearly eliminates those physical barriers.

The second wall we writers run up against is psychological, and it's usually trickier than stuck keys or writer's cramp. At times we all must struggle with temptation or lethargy, and having the latest in word processing technology will not automatically drive these wolves away from the door. Yet this set of electronic tools can lessen the psychological burdens by making it easy to write and even easier to edit.

In short, because you know that you can write down unrelated thoughts and put them in order later or begin a sentence three different ways and wait to choose one until you edit the completed draft, you're free to compose and experiment as comfortably and endlessly as you wish. Computer myths to the contrary, the blank screen is somehow friendlier than the blank sheet of paper. Maybe this is because you can fill up the screen faster or because you never have to replace it with another page, or maybe it's because the words appear on the screen as if by magic. When you think about it, the electronic wizardry that puts letters on the screen is a study in miniature of what writing truly is—a mystery that you can participate in and even control.

Styles of Writing

Perhaps the simplest way to pursue this mystery is by writing from the hip, so to speak. This is what we call the Sprint—writing as quickly as possible, without worrying about smooth phrasing or dangling participles or optimal choice of vocabulary. As you put your thoughts into written form rapidly, you are generating a manuscript in much the same way that an artist makes a sketch; the important thing is to get the ideas down in quick, fluid strokes, and you can come back later to polish the rough edges and fill in the details.

▶ Sprint writing is often the most expedient way to create a draft or to get beyond a block. Because word processing gives you extensive tools for editing, you can forget about the organization of your chapter or the appropriateness of your characters' dialogue and give all your energy to discovering ideas and recording them swiftly.

When you write at a Sprint pace, you may find that the speed itself is thrilling and that it sparks new ideas to challenge your mind—and your fingers. In rare instances this combination of pace and concept can achieve a union of mind and machine, so that your thoughts seem to appear on the screen almost as you become aware of them. The prose that comes out of such a session may be far from perfect, but the experience is exhilarating and instructive.

Most writers Sprint some of the time, but few of us can sustain this pace indefinitely. The more likely scenario is a few paragraphs or pages of Sprinting, preceded and followed by the slower, more methodical approach to writing we call (mainly to keep the analogy going) the Stride.

This style of working is deliberate, and it is often aided by a plan, such as an outline or a page of notes. Speed is the obvious difference between Stride writing and Sprinting, but these two styles also usually diverge in tone and editorial quality. That is, because you are proceeding slowly, choosing the right word and the appropriate sentence structure as you go, the finished draft of a Stride piece is likely to require less revision and a good deal less cutting than one written in a Sprint.

These two approaches to writing share a common goal—to create a draft manuscript. Whether you're able to write this initial text at a fast clip, more slowly, or at a varying pace, you've generated a fistful of pages that are ready to be edited. (Rarely, if ever, are drafts complete and perfect; all writing can benefit from your own careful editing and additional scrutiny by another experienced editor.) When you're writing a draft, you may do some minor editing as you go along, but it's wise to stick to the primary objective of completing a given chapter or section of text and make editing a separate stage in the creative process.

At certain times still another style of writing is appropriate. This is what we call Reworking-in-Progress, because it combines the stages of creating draft text and editing that work. (We were tempted to call this style the Foxtrot, to suggest that this writing style is like a dance that moves back and forth and sideways and still gets you somewhere, but we concluded that our pedal analogy had gone far enough.) Predictably, this write-and-edit method is usually quite slow, and for most writers it's an acquired skill.

▶ Reworking-in-Progress may be the most efficient way to write short pieces or to meet a regular schedule, such as producing a weekly column. In these situations, a looming deadline can make separate draft-edit-revise stages too risky; you may finish the draft on time and be tempted—or compelled—to hand in unedited work because you can't get an extension, or you may take time to edit and tarnish your credibility by being late. So the most propitious use of a tight writing schedule could be to polish as you work, drafting a sentence or paragraph and then editing it—honing the phrases, weighing each word, and writing transitions that make the parts flow together.

Of course all of these writing styles are general themes, subject to much individual variation. Most writers develop a personal way of working, which may combine elements of each writing style or may be a fairly pure version of one style. The most important consideration is not that you use one style or another, but that you find the approach that works best for you.

▶ Discovering the most effective writing style is one task for which word processing seems tailor-made. Even if you are comfortable with the work style you've developed, try some experiments with Sprint, Stride, and Reworking-in-Progress when you're not laboring against a deadline. Besides introducing alternative writing styles that could come in handy if the old reliable method deserts you someday, this foray into the unfamiliar may lead to a more efficient way of writing—and it will certainly give you the full tour of word processing.

W/P Features and Writing Styles

Like each writer, each word processing program goes about its work in a slightly different way. We can't anticipate all of these variations, but we've tried to cover the most common versions of each feature in the context of our three writing styles. As you'll note, our discussion here applies only to word processing features, such as inserting text, that have a direct bearing on one or more of the approaches to creating initial drafts. Features that are primarily useful for editing text are discussed in detail in Chapter 12.

Inserting text is probably the most variable w/p feature involved in writing drafts. In fact, the ease or difficulty with which you can insert a word or several sentences into the text will affect your writing efficiency and perhaps even determine the writing style you choose. Consequently, you will be able to make the best use of your w/p system (or any you are contemplating) if you become familiar with the way it handles the insertion of letters, words, and longer sections of text.

For Sprint writing, you'll want a clean slate, so the ability to insert characters or words is not especially important. When you're trying to direct your thoughts to your fingertips as quickly as possible, you needn't be concerned with typos or word choice—the entire focus of your attention is on what you're thinking and writing, rather than how well it is expressed.

For Stride writing or Reworking-in-Progress, however, inserting short or long portions of text can be important. In both of these writing styles, working with the Insert feature on is preferable if your word processor handles this task smoothly. Unfortunately, all w/p programs do not make inserting text a simple matter.

Many word processors insert text by accepting whatever is typed at the cursor position and moving over all text following the cursor. So if you want to add an 'r' to 'gatitude', you would simply place the cursor in the correct spot and hit the 'r', and 'atitude' would step aside. This method works particularly well for short insertions, such as a letter, word, or phrase, but it may be slow or distracting if you want to add several lines or more to the text. Depending on how quickly your system pushes the existing text over and down as you're adding new text, you may find that the program pauses frequently to make these adjustments, giving you a message on the screen that says 'WAIT', or something similar. In addition, you may be distracted by the constant movement of all the text beside and below the words you're inserting.

▶ To avoid these problems, you can give yourself a partially clean slate by inserting several Returns (or blank lines) at the point where you plan to add new text. You can insert just one empty line, which is very helpful in letting you see the new phrases without having them run into the existing text, or you can add enough Returns to send the old text off the screen altogether. When you've finished the insertion, of course, you'll have to delete those blank lines to close up the text.

Some w/p programs automatically insert several blank lines when you turn on the Insert feature. This is desirable for adding long passages, but it can be bothersome if you only want to insert a letter or word. You have to be sure to position the cursor at the correct spot before you turn on Insert, and you won't see the finished results of your addition until you turn Insert off and the blank space is closed up (again, automatically). So with this type of program you may need to turn Insert on and off several times if you miscalculate the location of a change or if you subsequently decide to add something more.

Another group of word processing features can affect production of a draft or a piece that you edit in progress. These are the formatting and printing commands, which are primarily concerned with the printed manuscript but may also determine some aspects of the on-screen appearance of your work. The form of these commands varies among systems, but most programs allow you to imbed some or all of the format and print directives in the electronic files that contain your writing.

Because writing the draft and editing it are separate stages in both Sprint and Stride styles, you can probably ignore most of the formatting and printing commands when writing in either of these styles. The simplest way to write drafts is probably to use the default format and print settings that are automatically in effect when you begin writing. If you customarily change one or more of the defaults, you may want to override those default settings by entering the appropriate imbedded commands at the beginning of your file.

For the most part, however, you don't have to worry about the final format for the manuscript, because you will be editing and very likely Reforming much of the text as you revise it. Also, when you have completed the editing stage, you may find that you have to change the page margins or the type size in order to make the manuscript meet an editor's specifications for length.

Unlike draft writing, the Reworking-in-Progress style aims to avoid a separate editing stage. For this approach, you may want to make most of your formatting decisions when you're ready to start writing. You can then put all the necessary imbedded commands at the beginning of the file and—unless you change your mind—you'll be ready to print the finished product without further ado.

When you're writing in any of the three basic styles, you may want to go back and read from the beginning of your work to see what ground you've covered so far. Often, however, you won't want to read the entire piece; you may read a few paragraphs, get your bearings, and then go to the end of the draft to resume writing. Two fundamental cursor movement commands do this easily; they are usually called Cursor to Beginning of File and Cursor to End of File, or something similar.

The various other features that govern cursor movement are likewise helpful as you're writing, particularly in the Reworking-in-Progress style. For example, if you think of a better word or spot a typo on the top right corner of the screen and the cursor is at the bottom left, you can move the cursor to the top, then to the right side, make your change, then move the cursor back to the left and to its original position with a few deft keystrokes.

Scrolling is also useful for editing as you write; for example, if you want to go back a few paragraphs and edit the text you've just written, you can scroll by screenfuls until you find the passages to be revised. Similarly, if you know a specific word that you want to change but don't know its location, you can use the Search features to find and replace it, although you'll encounter every instance of that word in your text if you've used it more than once.

▶ All of the word processing features that allow you to move around in the text—in essence, to shuffle your electronic pages—are conveniences that let you review your work and possibly change it. These features are most appropriate to editing the drafts you have already written, however. With the exception of the Reworking-in-Progress style, you will probably be more successful at creating a draft if you concentrate on keeping the writing going, rather than on making changes in the text you've already generated. In short, unless you are unusually skilled at first-draft-perfect writing (and few of us are), your work will benefit most from going through separate drafting and editing stages.

▶ One more reminder about using a crucial word processing routine: Be sure to save your work often, no matter which writing style you use. When the creative juices are flowing and you're getting the words onto the screen in a steady stream, be sure to pause long enough to save the work every fifteen to twenty minutes, or each time you fill the screen with new text. Even if you're proceeding slowly, perhaps going back over the same page or two to perfect your work, don't let more than a quarter hour pass without saving the text on disk.

Building Confidence

Regardless of how experienced and productive we writers are, there will be times when we just can't find the right words—or any words at all. Those are the moments when we seriously wonder whether we'll ever have another thought or fashion another sentence, though a few hours later we can usually look back and laugh at our temporary panic. Somehow we manage to finish the assignment or meet the deadline, even if we spend almost as much time worrying as we do writing.

There are strategies to avoid some of that worry, however, and to bolster our confidence that the right words will indeed materialize. And at least some of these measures are ideally suited to writing with a word processor.

For example, you can keep all the drafts, partial paragraphs, and false starts you make on a project and easily integrate some of that work into a later version by using the program's Block Move features. If the writing is going slowly and you are trying one phrase and then another to find the words that seem right, you can work with the Insert feature turned on and keep all of your attempts on the screen until you decide which phrases to use and which to erase.

► The Insert feature is especially useful for sentences that you start over two or three times; if you have one opening phrase and want to try another, you can simply move the cursor back to the beginning of the sentence and write the new introductory phrase in front of the old one. If you want some blank space around the new words to distinguish them from the text already on the screen, you can hit the space bar several times or insert a Return before typing the new phrase, so that you can easily read and judge your latest attempt.

► In some instances the screen's 24 lines are not a large enough window on your text. For example, if you have a number of drafts and sections of text that you've saved but can't decide how to knit together, try printing out each individual piece of text on a separate page. Then you can read the pages and shuffle them until you determine the proper content and order of the sections. Once you've made this decision, you can go back to the electronic files and use the word processor's cut-and-paste abilities to create the manuscript. (You may still want to keep the unused bits of text in a separate file, in case you have an opportunity to include them in some other part of your work.)

One of the chief advantages of w/p writing is that you can have clean printed pages as often as you wish. This can be a real psychological boost, particularly if you've been struggling with a project. You can print out the work you've done so far, and just seeing the finished, professional-looking pages could be the catalyst you need to complete the job. At the very least, you'll probably be surprised at how much you've accomplished.

Similarly, there's a real difference between working with these tidy pages and the old typewriter products that have strikeovers and words inserted between lines and notes in the margin. Even though you're likely to make the same kinds of changes in your electronic pages, you can do that work on the screen and always have clean copy for the next editing stage. This opportunity to read your work straight through, without the visual interruption of handwritten insertions or messy corrections, can be a significant contribution to both your confidence and your ability to assess and improve your writing.

Clearing the Hurdles

As one observer has noted, writing is always easy, except for three times: when you're getting started, when you've got to keep going, and when you're trying to finish. In fact, writing is hard work, and it is prey to the same hazards as any job—at times your energy lags, your insight fails, and you'd rather be doing anything else. These moments are inevitable in a writer's life; the first step in conquering them is to realize that such lapses are natural, temporary, and universal. Then you can meet them head on without shaking the confidence that you've developed through your writing achievements.

The strategies that follow are useful for getting over the temporary hurdles that crop up in your work. Not all of these ideas will appeal to every writer, nor are these methods limited to w/p writing. Like the basic styles of writing, however, we've presented these suggestions in the context of word processing whenever appropriate.

▶ Writing generates ideas. One strategy for getting started is definitely enhanced by the word processor's speed and relative quiet. If you are staring at the blank screen and can't think of a way to begin an article or section of text, simply put down whatever comes into your mind (a process that goes faster with the w/p keyboard than with any other writing instrument). One of your random thoughts will very likely be the opening you need, and even if these jottings aren't "keepers," the process of writing will generate new ideas. When you see these new thoughts on the screen, they will trigger still more connections in your mind, and chances are you'll find that you are writing the piece as you continue to think with the keys.

Of course these random thoughts should be somehow related to the assigned topic, but keeping your mind as free and open to ideas as possible is preferable to stewing over the subject (and therefore staring at the screen instead of writing). By using this technique, you can keep assembling thoughts until you work around to the topic at hand, even if it's by way of a long and windy road of prose. And if the place where your on-screen thinking intersects with the assigned topic doesn't happen to be the beginning of the piece, don't worry—just keep that writing rhythm alive and come back later to knock off an introduction.

▶ The beginning is not always the best start. This is another strategy for getting past what many writers find most difficult—fashioning those first few words that will grab readers and crystallize the topic. If you have trouble finding those opening lines, skip them and begin with a part of the subject that is concrete and familiar. What often happens when you explain the key concepts and details of your topic is that a beginning image or analogy pops into your mind as you're writing or reading this latter part of the work. Granted, sometimes you have a great title or opening line that dictates how the rest of the article will proceed, but more often the beginning can just as easily take its cue from the main body of your text.

Of course the word processor can make writing the introduction when you're halfway through the piece an easy procedure. When the right opening words occur to you, even as you're working on another section of the text, you can get them down quickly, mark them as a block, and transfer this new writing to the beginning of your text. You then can return to the place where you left off or continue to expand the opening section that you've just moved to its intended location.

▶ An outline can be a sight for sore eyes. Even with the versatile editing features of a word processor, which let you bring a file of notes to the screen quickly and easily, a written copy of your outline or list of topics is invaluable. For example, you may already keep a paper holder (one of those metal or plastic triangular gadgets that display pages to be typed) near your keyboard; this is a logical place to put a page of notes or a printout of the outline you've created as an electronic file. In addition to providing an alternative to looking at the screen constantly (thereby helping to avoid possible eyestrain or headache from too much screen exposure), the printed notes can be a stimulant for your mind.

Another useful tactic is to keep some notepaper near the keyboard—index cards, perhaps, or larger sheets—so that you can scribble a phrase or idea that you want to use later. This suggestion may sound vaguely subversive in a book about word processing, but there are times when it's bothersome to interrupt the work on screen to make a note, mark it as a block, and send it to another file. Besides, that note has to be retrieved to act as a reminder when you're working on the later section of text, so on some occasions a stash of notes that fit neatly on some part of your keyboard or monitor can be a source of quick inspiration.

▶ The screen can take a role in your mind's dialogue. Writing is quite often a product of the internal conversations that writers hear. If these sorts of split-personality dialogues are characteristic of your work at times, take advantage of the quick keyboard and let the silent screen play a role. For example, you might consult your notes and find a reference that you don't understand; your on-screen conversation might go like this: "Why did I put 'Roosevelt connection' in my notes? Was it Teddy or FDR or maybe Eleanor?" Then search your mental library for everything you know about the Roosevelts, and write it down. You can do this speedily with the processor, and you'll have a page or two of notes to pore over, instead of just a series of thoughts that flashed through your brain and disappeared.

By asking your internal questions on the screen, you're recording them for future reference and triggering more ideas by virtue of seeing your thoughts in writing. In addition, this technique could be ideal for getting the characters in a story to come alive. Once you give them some tentative dialogue on the screen, they may take over your mind—and possibly your fingertips—and do most of the work from then on.

▶ A letter is worth a thousand words. Sometimes you know everything you want to say, you have a detailed outline, and the piece seems as if it should write itself—but it doesn't. That's when the letter-writing technique can save you: assemble your notes, study the outline, and put everything you know about the subject in a letter to a friend. Depending on how "real" you want to make this process, you could write an actual letter, complete with salutation, small talk, and some explanation of what you're doing. When you're finished, you could use the various Delete and Search functions to remove the personal comments, or you could even print the complete letter and send it to the intended recipient.

The letter-writing strategy is quite valuable for several kinds of writing projects. One of the most difficult types of writing is an "attitude" piece, in which you discuss your views on some pithy topic. Quite often you also discover what you believe about that subject—and the world in general—as you write. But finding a confident, expressive voice for this kind of writing is usually the hardest part of the job, and that's precisely the direct way you're likely to speak in a letter to someone you know.

Another excellent forum for the letter-writing strategy is an assignment that requires you to explain complex, technical information in layperson's language. For example, if you're writing an article about heart surgery for a general-interest magazine, you have to define medical terms, discuss anatomy, and present the causes and consequences with even-handed precision and without confusion or condescension. The problem of finding the right tone for this article might be readily solved if you choose a person whom you know and hold that friend or acquaintance in your mind as you write. When this process works well, you're really having a mental conversation with someone familiar, instead of trying to write for an unknown audience and to guess at what they should know and how you should tell it.

Your choice of the person to whom you direct such a letter is important, of course. If you want your article to be chatty and even intimate, pick a close friend as your mental correspondent; if your article should be more formal, choose someone you respect but can speak openly with, such as a professional colleague. Often the best candidates for your mental missives are people to whom you actually do write occasionally, because you've already established this process of conversing with them in your mind.

▶ It's easier to loosen the reins than to tighten them. This may not sound like a writing strategy, but it is; the reins in this example are writers' attitudes toward a particular project or toward writing in general. Sometimes our "mental muscles" become too tight and we get bound up in our work, taking every word and phrase more seriously than the project merits. These are the times when deep breathing helps—both the physical variety and some mental equivalent. To achieve this mental exchange of air, try coaching yourself to care a bit less about this particular job, if only as an experiment. If you can sit back and wing it, your hastily expressed thoughts could make the points you're after, and you can use your command of language and style to polish the work at the editing stage.

This is not to suggest that you should lower your writing standards or become even slightly cynical about your work. Yet if the effort of writing becomes your focus, instead of the expression of ideas, your writing may seem forced and unconnected, and your progress at filling the pages (or simply the screen) may be painfully slow. Oddly enough, this is a time when easing up a bit can make the work go more smoothly, in the same way that relaxing your arm muscles when carrying a heavy suitcase can make the load seem lighter.

One way to loosen up your approach is to rediscover the fun of writing. The vast majority of writers have chosen this pursuit because they enjoy the work; when the pressure is heavy, though, the fun is easy to forget. If you can recall the times when writing gave you a sense of pleasure and accomplishment, you'll be relaxing those mental muscles as you reminisce. You might also reread some of the work you most enjoyed, which could further loosen the writing reins and let you return to the current project with a refreshed spirit.

▶ A trip away from the keyboard can move you ahead in your work. Just as the mental muscles need stretching, so do the bodily ones. It's wise to change positions often when writing, to avoid stiff muscles or headaches, and ideally you should move away from the the keyboard and screen for ten minutes of every hour. Although such frequent breaks may not be practical, you can relax your muscles and stimulate circulation by doing some exercise at regular intervals. For calisthenic purposes, doing some isometrics at your desk and some flexing and stretching movements away from the desk two or three times each workday will help keep your body as limber as your imagination.

▶ Reading other writers' work nourishes your own. One of the most important contributions writers can make to their work is reading. The flow of words and ideas into our minds is vital to a flexibility of style and a breadth of knowledge for all of us. Although reading can't replace "live" contacts, especially good conversation, a major part of our mental nourishment should be in written form— so that we experience the medium that is also our work.

There is really no substitute for the stimulation that reading good writing can provide. It's a rejuvenation of our writing energies, a replenishing of the stores of vocabulary and expression. In short, writers are almost always inspired by reading quality work by our peers, and we are often moved to respond in kind.

Though reading continually is necessary nourishment for all writers, a good book near the word processor can be an antidote for an occasional block or an overdose of technology. If you are stymied by a particular passage or assignment, or your machine is misbehaving, take a break by turning away from the keyboard and screen, preferably putting your feet up, and opening that safety-valve book. A few minutes—or an hour—of reading could be the catalyst for your flow of words, and perhaps also the needed rest period for a balky machine.

▶ When in doubt, change tools. One final strategy to vary the rhythm of your work is to leave the word processor and spend half an hour or more writing the way you used to—with a typewriter or pen and paper. Just the change in writing mechanics could get you over a hurdle in the project, or at least allow you to view the work from a different perspective. And if you make the temporary switch because you've tired of the keyboard and screen, a short stint of labor-intensive writing the old way could send you back to your system with a new appreciation for its power and efficiency.

All of these writing styles and strategies are designed to help you get your thoughts into words quickly and gracefully. You can think of the keyboard as an extension of your fingers and the screen as an endless page or many-chambered notebook. Whatever images you invent for these writing tools (or whatever names you may call them at times), word processing makes it easy for you to write drafts, take chances, say anything you please in every way you like, and—when you're finished—it will reward you with a bulging pile of pages on which to hone your editing skills.

Chapter 12

Fine Tuning

*Editing and Polishing
Your Work*

In the previous chapter, we encouraged you to take advantage of the freedom that w/p writing provides—to be daring with your words. The reason you can take chances when you're writing is that the system is providing you a safety net at the same time. Nothing that you write is fixed indelibly; every word can be changed or eliminated entirely with the push of a key and the wink of phosphor on your screen.

Once you've completed your daring first draft, you can be critical of your writing—more critical, in fact, than you could afford to be when working on a typewriter. There's no longer any need to say, "Let it go—I don't want to retype the whole page." If a lame phrase survives in your final manuscript, the only excuse is that you simply didn't spot it or couldn't think of a better one. (We hereby take full responsibility for any lame phrases that we didn't catch or fix!)

In this chapter, we'll look at how you can fine tune your writing until it reflects exactly your ideas and inspirations, making use of your best-chosen words. Our preoccupation in this chapter, you'll discover, is with editing speed and efficiency. We're not unmindful of the subjective decisions that go into good editing, but we must leave those to your good judgment. What we hope to share are techniques that can make your editing sessions proceed as smoothly and quickly as the revisions come to mind.

Editing on a word processor produces much more powerful results than the "blue pencil" techniques that prevailed prior to the Computer Age, but it also involves new working styles and routines. And to take full advantage of word processing as an editing tool, you need to make these routines second nature. The more you can free yourself from the pure mechanics of making revisions, the better w/p editor you will be.

Screen Versus Hard-Copy Editing

When writers first convert from their typewriters to word processors, they may find it difficult to shake a reliance on paper printouts for all their editing work. Depending on the quality and readability of your screen display, editing the manuscript on paper may make typos easier to spot and awkward phraseology stand out. As we'll discuss shortly, there is no substitute for a rigorous hard-copy edit of your writing. But if you can learn to work on the screen comfortably, you will save yourself much time—and a substantial amount of paper.

The advantage of doing your first edit on the screen is obvious. Here, the cursor is your blue pencil. You're moving it directly within the copy while you're reading and correcting. Your eyes never have to stray from the screen to find a spot that you want to correct. And you only have to make the revision once—on the screen, before printing—rather than twice, as you would on paper, noting it on the page, then making the change in your electronic file.

▶ Try adopting the routine of making the first edit of your writing a once-over reading on the screen. If you're editing a full-length manuscript, you'll weed out many typos, syntax lapses, and repetitious phrases before you proceed to a hard-copy edit, and thereby make that latter process much more effective. If you've screen-edited a memo or short letter, you'll often be able to have the first printout survive as your final draft.

▶ For any important piece of writing, you should plan to do a hard-copy edit as a standard routine as well. The screen displays only a limited portion of your writing. Even with the scrolling commands, it's difficult to get a sense of the flow of your writing when reading on the screen. And there's nothing like the printed page to put the clarity and style of your writing to the acid test.

The way you mark your printed manuscript for editing should be different from your pre-computer style, however. When a manuscript is going to be retyped, you want to incorporate all the changes as integrally as possible. A typist will be reading the entire manuscript word by word; you want each correction to fit neatly within the text. Also, when working with typewriter technology, it's very likely that you'll be using a single version of an edited draft for several weeks or months. You don't have the luxury of getting a clean draft whenever you want it; consequently, you want to fit your corrections into the draft as inconspicuously as possible.

The opposite is true when editing on a word processor. You're probably going to give yourself a fresh printout as soon as you've completed an edit. But you are at one disadvantage—you're going to have to find your corrections on the printed page and then shift your eyes to the screen while you make the correction.

▶ To be sure that you don't miss a correction, make use of bold, graphic copy-editing marks when working on printed drafts. Legibility counts, of course, but neatness merely for its own sake can be a liability rather than an asset. The sole purpose of hard-copy corrections is to make changes easy to spot when going back to make screen corrections. You are not going to have to work with the draft later.

(Actually, your printouts can be useful as a record of how a manuscript took shape. It's probably wise to date and file all your hard-copy drafts on a continuing project if you can spare the storage space.)

The Basic Character Edit

Now we'll get down to the business of making actual revisions. Regardless of whether you are doing a screen edit or working from a marked hard-copy draft, there are two simple methods of making corrections that work reliably and efficiently for almost every editing situation. In fact, they are such useful techniques that we call them the two Basic Edits (no relation to the programming language called BASIC).

▶ The first technique, the Basic Character Edit, involves inserting a character in the text and then deleting one or more characters, if required. This might seem an all-too-obvious technique; the point we're making is that this method is preferred even when making one-for-one character substitutions.

Consider the example in Figure 12-1. There are five errors in the garbled sentence: only one 't' in 'written'; the absence of the word 'the' preceding 'grip'; the transposition of the letters 'lo' in 'revolution'; the total butchering of the word 'dramatic'; and the incorrect 'a' in 'invention'. Assume that you encounter the sentence while proceeding through the text, doing a screen edit. The way to make the first two corrections is obvious—simply insert the required letters.

When you get to 'revloution', however, you have a choice. You could make the correction by Overtyping the correct letters directly in place of the offending 'lo', or you could take what might seem a more roundabout route, inserting the correct 'ol' after the 'v' and then deleting 'lo'. Why is the second approach the faster and better method of making the correction?

Proceed further into the sentence and consider 'drmattic'. Can the correction be made using only Overtyping, or do you have to make use of the Insert feature? The fact that you have to think about this for even a second indicates that you should spare yourself the decision altogether by simply inserting the correct characters and then deleting the incorrect ones.

Even the substitution of the 'e' for the 'a' in 'invantion' is more easily accomplished by inserting the 'e' and then deleting the 'a'— especially since correcting this entire sentence would otherwise require altering your method of correction (turning Insert on and off) four times.

▶ If you adopt the regular habit of making character corrections using Insert and Delete (and forget about Overtyping), you'll be able to concentrate on making the correction rather than deciding which method to use. When you're doing a wholesale edit of a manuscript, those eliminated decision points add up to time saved and greatly improved editing efficiency.

There certainly will be instances in which the Overtype correction is appropriate, such as going back to a page of text to make one spot correction (and we expect that some Overtype aficionados will dismiss our previous suggestion altogether). Over the long haul, however, sticking with the Insert/Delete edit as your standard method

Fig. 12-1: Text prior to Basic Character Edit

```
        B:FIG12-1   PAGE 1 LINE 1 COL 01                INSERT ON
L---!----#----!----#----!----#----!----#----!----#----!----#---R
The writen word is in grip of a revloution as drmattic as the
invantion of moveable type.
```

will probably serve you best. Even if you now edit another way, give this method a try for an editing session or two and see how it compares with the other techniques.

The Basic Word Edit

There would have been a better way of correcting the word 'dramatic' in the previous example: what we call the Basic Word Edit.

▶ The second Basic Edit involves inserting characters in the text *as whole words* and then deleting *whole words*, if possible. Even if there may appear to be a more efficient way to make the correction in terms of keystrokes, the Basic Word Edit will usually get revisions made in less time and with fewer errors. To illustrate, Figure 12-2 contains another version of the sample text.

Your friend 'drmattic' is back to haunt you, and it should be evident by now that the best way to correct it is to insert the entire word 'dramatic' where you want it and then get rid of the "garbage" characters with a single Delete Word keystroke. Yes, there are some salvageable letters in 'drmattic', but you can retype the entire correct word in much less time than it would take you to figure out which letters should stay and which should go.

Now consider a correction of a different order. Suppose you want to revise Figure 12-2 so that the sentence starts, 'The written word is in'. You could insert 'The' at the beginning of the sentence, insert a lowercase 'w' and delete the 'W' in 'Written', then delete the 's' from 'words', and finally insert 'is' and delete 'are'. But how long would it take you to accomplish that, as opposed to typing the phrase 'The written word is'?

Figure 12-3 shows how your screen would look after typing in the entire new phrase. The cursor will be poised right at the 'W' of 'Written'. All you have to do is hit the Delete Word key three times and your edit is completed. (If your system doesn't provide the Delete Word function, you can delete the required number of single characters.)

Fig. 12-2: Text prior to Basic Word Edit

```
        B:FIG12-2  PAGE 1 LINE 1 COL 01              INSERT ON
L---!----#----!----#----!----#----!----#----!----#----!----#---R
Written words are in the grip of a revolution as dramatic as the
invention of moveable type.
```

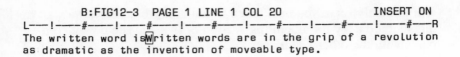

```
L——!——#——!——#——!——#——!——#——!——#——!——#——R
The written word isWritten words are in the grip of a revolution
as dramatic as the invention of moveable type.
```

Fig. 12-3: After insertion of phrase

Making corrections by whole words can be the best method even when it appears that only a single character need be inserted. Consider Figure 12-4. Suppose you wanted to change 'Our' to 'Your'. You're only adding a single character, and it's tempting to insert the capital 'Y' and a lowercase 'o' and then delete the 'O'. But doing it that way, you've got to analyze the correction before you proceed with it, and that takes time. It's much more straightforward to insert 'Your' and delete 'Our', even though it requires a few more key-strokes. Your editorial judgment was, "I want to substitute 'Your' for 'Our'." Let your correction follow the same logic.

▶ We've dwelled on this point because new w/p writers often overlook it. Yes, the word processor provides you with some intricate character-juggling tools. But you don't have to use every one of them in every situation. Frequently, a bit of redundant retyping will get the job done faster and with fewer errors.

Insert Mode

Both of the Basic Edits described above make use of the Insert feature of the word processor. As an editing tool, it's much more ver-satile than Overtyping. For that reason, you should consider the fol-lowing general editing tip.

▶ When editing, keep your system in Insert mode as much as possible, so you are prepared for the Basic Character and Word Edits.

The degree to which you can take advantage of this tip will depend on your system. Some word processors permit you to place the system into Insert mode permanently during an editing session. If your program provides this option, you should take advantage of it. (A few word processors don't even provide a separate Insert "mode"; in these systems, the Insert function is available at all times.) In

Fig. 12-4: Text illustrating choice of editing method

B:FIG12-4   PAGE 1 LINE 1 COL 01   INSERT ON
```
L——!——#——!——#——!——#——!——#——!——#——!——#——R
Our best method for making corrections is to deal in whole words.
```

other systems, the Insert feature may automatically revert to Overtyping after certain operations. It's probably to your advantage to get in the habit of reinstating Insert as you proceed with your edit.

If your processor inserts characters by the "drop-in" method (creating a sizable space in the text for the insertion and then closing it up), you'll have to invoke the Insert function for each correction. Even if that's the case, giving the Insert command should be your automatic initial response for all routine corrections.

Reforming

The "drop-in" systems usually provide automatic Reforming of a paragraph after an Insert correction. On the "squeeze-in" systems, however, you usually have the option of waiting to Reform the paragraph until you give a specific command. (On some systems, particularly dedicated word processors, paragraphs are reformed continually and automatically as editing and writing progresses.)

▶ Depending on your system, it will often be to your advantage not to Reform until you reach the end of a paragraph. This tip is applicable mainly when making corrections from hard copy, when you have to coordinate the corrections on the paper draft with the information on the screen display. If you Reform the paragraph after every correction, the screen display of the paragraph will no longer correspond to your printed draft, and subsequent correction points in that paragraph will be more difficult to find.

▶ If your system provides a command for returning the cursor to its position before the last operation, you can use this feature to streamline the Reforming process. By using the command sequence 'Reform—Cursor to Previous Position', you can Reform and instantly take up editing where you left off.

⌡ ▶ It's a good habit to Reform your entire text file routinely at the end of an editing session. Very often, you'll have failed to Reform the text after one or more corrections, and you'll avoid some too-long or too-short lines if you Reform as a final editing step.

Deleting

As you proceed with an edit, you'll inevitably create extraneous text that gets pushed ahead of your inserted characters and words. It's to your advantage to develop efficient routines for deleting this surplus.

▶ For deleting characters or words within the body of the text, make use of the "verbalizing" technique described in Chapter 3 (quietly reciting each character or word as you hit the appropriate Delete keys). This technique can relieve you from having to coordinate your keystrokes with the shifting letters on the screen. With a bit of practice, this method can produce extremely accurate corrections.

▶ For deleting characters at the end of a line or the end of a paragraph, make the best possible use of your system's Delete to End of Line function. If your system doesn't provide this function, you will often find it useful to insert a temporary blank line or Paragraph End marker (sending the excess text to the next line), delete the unwanted text as one or more whole lines, and then delete the temporary line or marker.

▶ For deleting excess text at the end of a text file, use the Delete to End of File command, if provided. If your system doesn't have this function, make use of the largest incremental Delete function available (such as Delete Paragraph, Line, Sentence, or Word).

Moving the Cursor

As much as 50 percent of your editing time will probably be taken up by simply moving the cursor to the appropriate locations in the text. If you can make use of your system's rapid cursor movement commands, you'll get your editing job done much more quickly.

Often there will be short-cut routes to a spot in your text. Consider, for example, the text in Figure 12-5. The cursor is at the end of 'improve'. What's the best way to go back and make the needed correction in 'ot'? You could move the cursor up one line, then move it to the right by the fastest method (Cursor Right Character, Cursor Right Word, or Cursor to End of Line). But an easier method is Cursor Left Word, which on most systems will "wrap" the cursor back to the end of the previous line.

Similarly, if the cursor was at the word 'and' in Figure 12-5 and you wanted to make a correction in 'Because', it might be fastest to advance the cursor one word to 'extremely' and then move the cursor up one line. The Cursor to Home and Cursor to Bottom of Screen

Fig. 12-5: Text illustrating short-cut cursor movements

```
        B:FIG12-5  PAGE 1 LINE 3 COL 08                    INSERT ON
L---!----#----!----#----!----#----!----#----!----#----!----#----R
Because writing on a word processor is fast, simple, and
extremely flexible, writers have the unparalleled opportunity ot
improve□their work significantly.
```

are also useful commands for moving the cursor quickly. If there are no other alternatives, at least take advantage of moving the cursor by whole word increments.

▶ Moving the cursor a character at a time (even if you have a repeating key function) is almost always the slowest way to get to a spot in your text. Explore the alternatives and make them ready routines.

Searching and Replacing

In Part I, we described in some detail the Search and Replace functions of word processors and considered how they can be used to substitute words or phrases throughout your text. But these features have a utility far beyond changing 'rutabaga' to 'pomegranate'; in fact, some of the best uses of Search and Replace don't involve revisions of the actual text at all.

The Search function can be made to work as a super-mover for the cursor. As was mentioned in the previous chapter, you can search for key words throughout your text. Doing so brings the cursor instantly into position to make any necessary editing revisions.

▶ The Search function can also be used to locate sections within your manuscript, especially if you've used special symbols to designate them. For example, you might start every section heading with a unique symbol such as ' = = Searching and Replacing'. Then if you want to move through your manuscript section by section, you need only search for ' = = ' and the cursor will stop at the beginning of each one. To make this work, you need only plan ahead and use a consistent convention for each level of section headings. (Note that two equal signs are a good choice for the section-heading device. If you had used two hyphens, your search might also have located every instance of a dash.)

▶ When editing a manuscript that will go through several revisions, you'll often want to mark cross-references to other chapters, or make note of style or usage conventions. You can keep these references within the manuscript and mark them with special symbols, such as '[cr]' for cross-references, '[st]' for style notes, and perhaps '<<' and '>>' to enclose notes regarding the development of the manuscript. Later, you can search for these to create a manuscript style sheet, for example, or to purge these symbols just prior to printing the final manuscript.

(Some word processing programs provide a separate Comment feature, which lets you place notes within a file that can be read on the screen but that don't print. If these notes use special symbols, you can search for the symbols that designate them.)

As you develop a system for coding these cross-references, notes, and special symbols, you'll find it useful to maintain a separate written list of section headings and markers so you can refer to it during Search operations.

▶ The Search function also provides an excellent way to check whether style conventions have been followed. For example, to confirm that you've put punctuation in the correct positions inside or outside quotation marks, you could perform a Global Search for double quotes and smoke out any inconsistencies immediately.

▶ The Search function can be used in conjunction with Replace to alter the format of the manuscript. Suppose, for example, that you had indented all paragraph beginnings five spaces and later decided that you wanted a flush-left format. By giving a command to Search for five blank spaces and Replace that with no spaces, you could make your revision instantly throughout the manuscript.

▶ If your system's Search and Replace functions permit specifying non-character entries (such as control characters), you can make sweeping format revisions. For example, you could instruct the program to replace the control character for boldface type with the control character for underlining.

Sometimes a replacement that is technically correct won't work editorially. For example, one author decided that he didn't like the name 'Thompson' for a character in his novel. He was ready to make a global replacement with 'Tompkins' until he realized that possessives in the text would appear as 'Tompkins's'. To avoid this awkward (though correct) structure, he renamed the character 'Wilson'.

As we cautioned in Part I, you must be very careful when instructing the program to make unchecked global replacements. You can never be sure that the Search string you have specified is not hiding in some unforeseen manifestation in your text. No matter how universal a change you intend, your safest method is to proceed through each replacement with manual and visual checks.

Moving and Copying

Whether you're undertaking a complete overhaul of your work or just shifting a single paragraph, the Block Move and Copy features of your system can be invaluable timesavers as well as conceptual aids. As we advised in Part I, you should become adept at using these functions so that you'll never again be tempted to pick up scissors and paste.

▶ Particularly if you wrote your initial draft in the Sprint style, there will probably be sections of text that you want to delete and others that you want to move around. To make these revisions, you could use a combination of hard-copy editing and the system's electronic cut-and-paste abilities. On the printed copy of your draft, mark each section of text that you want to keep intact and pencil in the appropriate heading with it if you hadn't supplied one already. Also mark any stray sections of text that should be moved to one of these major subdivisions of the draft and indicate what text should be deleted.

Then return to the on-screen version of your file and put a special symbol (such as <**> or any other characters that won't be used elsewhere in the text) next to each heading, typing in any new headings in the appropriate spots. Next, transfer the stray bits of text to the subdivisions where they belong, using the Block Move feature.

At this point you should have the major sections of text that you want to keep in your file, but your edited printout may indicate that the order of these sections still must change. Now you can take advantage of the <**> markers you placed with the headings; simply search for the symbol, and when you come to one of the sections that you want to move, mark the whole thing as a block and transfer it to the correct location in the text. Although this process may seem involved, it will probably take you less time to perform these cut-and-paste maneuvers than it has taken you to read this description of it.

▶ If you are simply trying to decide on the best placement of a paragraph, you might find it helpful to Copy it to alternate locations (rather than using the Move function). This procedure will let you read the paragraph in each of the different possible contexts and choose the best one.

▶ Here's an important tip for when you are making cuts in your manuscript. If you are deleting a sizable amount of text (a paragraph or more), the most efficient way to make the cut will usually be to mark the section as a block and then delete it. Don't use the Block Delete function, however. Instead, move the block to the end of your draft (or move it to another file if your system permits). There's no need to destroy this text permanently; often it can be useful later in your work. (In Chapter 14 we'll discuss techniques for moving text among different files.)

Saving

Did you think we could go this far without nagging about saving again? Actually, this work-saving habit can be as crucial when editing as when writing your initial draft. The following tip goes almost without saying:

▶ Before you undertake even a minor edit of your work, be absolutely sure that the original draft has been safely saved to disk.

It's also important to save your work during the course of an editing session—even more frequently than during a writing session. There's nothing more frustrating than somehow crashing your system after a half hour of careful editing. Not only have you lost work, but it can be nearly impossible to determine which revisions had been made prior to the last Save, and so you may end up having to edit from the beginning.

▶ The most prudent course is to save after editing each manuscript section. If you make that your regular habit, you'll never have to guess as to the edited status of your current disk file.

No matter how careful you are, you will, inevitably, unavoidably, zap some of your work and not be able to retrieve it. Perhaps you'll be intending to delete a word and by mistake delete a whole line. Perhaps you'll be energetically cutting and pasting with Block Moves and send a paragraph to electronic purgatory. Or—horror of horrors— perhaps you really will kick the plug out of the socket (don't blame the cat).

▶ As we mentioned in Part I, your first reaction after one of these mishaps (following the appropriate expletive, of course) should be to proceed very slowly and methodically and to consult your manual. Often your work is not lost entirely—merely misplaced. Your system might provide a way of recovering it.

▶ If there's no recovery possible, we have one final important tip for these tragic circumstances: Reconstruct your lost work immediately. Even if it's two o'clock in the morning and this is absolutely the last straw in a haystack of tedium and frustration, don't pack off to bed hoping to deal with the problem in the morning. Although your computer's memory has been wiped clean, your own reliable, human memory is still functioning, and the best time to draw on it is right away. In most cases, you'll be amazed at how quickly you can retrieve those lost phrases. (This tip applies equally to writing and editing.) When you fall off the horse, you've got to get right back on.

Proofreading

This editing tip is a definite survivor from the Blue Pencil Age: Proofread your corrections! We're not talking merely about proofreading the final hard-copy printout before you send out your manuscript. (That habit should have been instilled long before you started working on a word processor.) The situation we're describing is when you discover a typo in your final draft and you go back to your text file to correct it.

▶ Proofread all your on-screen corrections thoroughly. Many times you'll be relying on that last-minute change to put your writing into perfect form. It's easy for an error to creep in at the correcting stage. (The most common is forgetting to delete a word or letter after inserting a correction.)

Previously we suggested that you do an on-screen edit before printing a draft. You'll smoke out even more errors if you make that first on-screen edit a thorough proofreading.

▶ If your system contains a spell-checking program, get in the habit of using it for all your work, just before printing. The creators of these programs promise to make your work virtually letter perfect. Take advantage of their offer.

A Fail-Safe Routine

The final step before printing a finished manuscript (or any work that will represent you as a writer) is to check for unanswered questions in the text, cross-references, and misspelled words. This is what we've called the Fail-safe Routine, which consists of locating all of the symbols you've used to mark special items in the text, such as footnotes, page references, and reminders to yourself to verify or supply some information. Once you've found each symbol, you can resolve the question and delete the symbol from the manuscript. (In a few instances, such as marking key words or page numbers to be added after the copy is set in type, you may want to leave symbols in the manuscript.)

As you've written and edited the drafts of your work, you probably will have marked certain places for checking of facts, adding new information, or reworking a section that could be improved. By the time you've reached this final-draft stage, you'll have resolved most of those questions or problems, but you may have forgotten to delete some of the markers, or you may have overlooked a question or two. If you have kept a written list of the symbols you used in the text, you can use the word processor's Search function to locate each of these places and verify that you answered the question and removed the symbol. If your Search doesn't locate any of these special symbols, of course, it means that your edit has been thorough and is complete.

Similarly, if you have included any cross-references in your text, you ideally should have marked them with a symbol to locate them later. Even if you intend to leave those symbols in the manuscript or if they are special characters that won't print, it's wise to search for each cross-reference and verify that the information it includes is accurate and consistent with your final edit of the text. In some instances, you might have made changes elsewhere in the manuscript, such as reversing the order of two figures, and you may have neglected to make that change in references to them at other points in the text. This is the kind of error that can be difficult to detect in a manuscript, and it's just what a Fail-safe Search can prevent.

Finding any misspelled words that you've overlooked in earlier proofreading is another good part of the Fail-safe Routine. If you use a Spelling Checker, that program will identify the majority of typos and incorrectly spelled words, but at least some of these programs cannot distinguish one-letter words, such as 'I'. Thus, if you typed 'i' instead of 'I', the Spelling Checker would not recognize this as an error and you wouldn't have an opportunity to discover or change it. Similarly, if you typed 'a' when you meant 'at', the spelling program would pass over this because it's a bona fide word, even to programs that can check one-letter words. So you may need to search for some common errors independently.

▶ If you don't have a spell-checking utility and you know that you often misspell certain words or occasionally use the wrong form of a word ('it's' for 'its' or 'there' for 'their') be sure to check each occurrence of those words in your file. And if you are aware that you sometimes transpose letters in a word (such as 'hte' for 'the'), you should check for these mistakes as well. Both of these are simple jobs with the Search feature.

Finally, a good Fail-safe Routine should check the Print Formatting instructions. If your system uses imbedded commands for such printing enhancements as boldface or underlining, you'll prevent possible printing errors if you search for each occurrence of these imbedded commands and make certain that you have inserted the correct characters for each special feature and that you have given commands to both turn on and turn off this feature. This inspection of imbedded printing commands can save you time and frustration at the printing stage, because it's easy to forget to insert the imbedded command that toggles off a feature such as underlining, and if the 'off' command is not in the text, the rest of your manuscript will be printed in underlined form.

If you use a Format File or other set of formatting commands that are not imbedded in the text file, be sure to look at this separate group of commands and verify that they will print your manuscript in the form you want and that you've supplied a command for each formatting variable. Once you've made each of these last-minute inspections, you can print the final manuscript with the knowledge that you've confirmed all the details and answered all the questions.

Perfection

Throughout this chapter, we've explored the techniques you can use to hone, polish, and fine tune your writing until it reflects exactly what you want to say, the best way you can say it. Writers have never before been given the means to revise their work so efficiently and painlessly. Word processing technology has certainly helped many of us to become better writers. For a few writers, though, having a word processor just reinforces the inability to declare a job done.

In some respects, of course, a piece of writing need never be considered complete. The novel will always be there on disk, ready to test a new romantic episode or an alternate conclusion. The research article can always be updated with the latest discovery. Next week, a more elegant phrase might be substituted in the poem. Once you start writing on a word processor, every piece of your writing can be considered a living, changing document.

Deadlines are as much a part of the writing process as inspired prose, however, and we all must declare a halt to certain projects, even if we might have improved them next week or next month. Probably the best solution to this temptation to revise forever is to compromise: keep some projects on the desk (or on a disk that's easy to reach) and give yourself a firm deadline for others. Then you'll have some work that you can constantly improve and some, including assignments that come with deadlines, that impose a measure of discipline. To return to our advice about writing and editing, if you've been as daring as you can be when writing and as critical as possible when editing, your work will reflect well upon you whether you submit it for publication the day it's complete or keep it in a handy file for years.

Chapter 13

Printing It

---

*Producing Elegant
Manuscripts*

We're going to come right out
and say it: Printing is usually the most time-consuming, frustrating,
and error-prone aspect of writing in the Computer Age. Why is that?
Perhaps it's because printing is the only part of the process that deals
with information in tangible, physical form. When an error is made
in writing or editing, it exists as an easily correctable electronic blip.
When an error shows up during printing, it's a permanent one. Since
no self-respecting w/p writer would ever pick up a bottle of "white-
out," the only recourse is to print again.

Yet printing sessions don't have to leave you pulling your hair
and littering your workspace with reams of perforated paper. It can
all come out right—or nearly so—if you plan ahead for some of the
common printing pitfalls. And, while we've stressed the usefulness
of routines for your writing and editing, they're an absolute necessity
when you get to printing your work.

If you've made it this far with us, we know you're not going to
be scared away by these storm warnings. Take some time and care

when it comes to printing your work, and you'll be rewarded with professional-looking documents with a push of a key.

Printer Physics

Before actually printing your work, you should give some thought to integrating your printer into your workspace. Writing on a word processor is distinguished by its relative silence, but w/p printing is not; your printer is likely to create a fair racket while working (especially if it's a letter-quality model). Minimizing the decibel level of your printer's operation will definitely make your work sessions more pleasant.

▶ Place your printer on as solid a surface as possible, and cushion it with a foam pad designed specifically for heavy-duty office equipment. If you'll be using continuous-form paper, make sure that there's a practical location for storing a box of this fan-fold paper where it can feed into the printer during operation, and a flat surface where the printed sheets can pile up without getting wrinkled.

You'll be faced with opposing considerations in locating your printer. Since you'll want to keep its noise intrusion to a minimum, you'll be tempted to place it as far away from your working area as possible. On the other hand, there will be many times when you'll want to put a sheet of paper in the printer and then enter a printing command from the keyboard, so you won't want to put the printer totally out of reach. It's probably best to keep the printer accessible and minimize the noise with sound-absorbing materials.

If you use continuous-form paper, there are two methods for advancing the paper through the printer. Many printers make use of a tractor feed device that guides the punched holes along the edge of the paper through rollers on the tractor, thus keeping the paper from twisting or sliding sideways. The alternative is to rely on the printer's built-in friction feed to move the paper through the printer (much like the friction feed on a typewriter).

The advantage of the tractor feed is that it keeps the paper properly aligned in the printer. The disadvantage of a tractor feed is that it is frequently offered as a rather expensive add-on option to the printer. Many writers who have invested their last treasured dollars on a letter-quality printer may be forced to forego the tractor device—at least until they get paid for the next writing assignment.

▶ Friction feeds can cause problems on longer printing jobs (over ten pages), as the paper tends to skew or shift as the job progresses. You'll minimize this problem if you make sure that the paper supply is aligned as perfectly as possible with its path through the printer.

Paper Position

The key to successful printing is to do the same job the same way—every time. And your first step in this pursuit doesn't involve the programmed aspects of word processing at all. Before you get immersed in your system's array of print formatting options, you need to establish a standard method for inserting paper into and through the printer.

▶ If you are using continuous-form paper, align the paper channel so that the print head will always be in the same starting position relative to the top and left edge of the page. With single sheets, make use of your printer's paper guides to standardize the paper position. (The positioning for continuous forms and single sheets may have to be different if you're using a tractor feed assembly.)

Once you've devised a practical way of loading paper into the printer, stick with that method for all your printing jobs. (We'll touch on exceptions a bit later.) This standardization process is really no different from setting the paper guide on a typewriter, but it's more important, since you're going to be using numerical commands in the w/p program (rather than visual checks) to determine the look of your final copy.

Type Styles

One of the advantages that w/p printing offers is the ability to use many different type styles. If you have a letter-quality printer, you'll be able to choose among various print elements offering a variety of typefaces, but your choices do not end there. You also may have the option of using a justified or unjustified format and of determining the horizontal and vertical spacing for each font and printing application. Deciding on standard type conventions is the next step in developing a detailed printing routine.

▶ Choose a few of the type fonts available for your printer and decide on the vertical and horizontal spacing that you find most appealing for each. You may wish to come up with several typographic conventions, such as a pica font, spaced at 4 lines per inch, for reports, and an elite font, spaced at 6 lines per inch, for correspondence. Some of your type styles may make use of justified text, while others are printed ragged right.

Don't overlook the possibility of adusting the horizontal spacing of a font differently from your program's default spacing. By condensing a font slightly (from 10 microspaces per character to 9 for elite type, for example), you can give a look to your printout that suggests professional typesetting. A slightly expanded font (such as from 10 to 11 microspacing for elite type) might be useful for text that is to print in all uppercase letters. An example of standard, condensed, and expanded type is shown in Figure 13-1.

▶ Create as many different typographic conventions as you think you'll have use for, clearly label and print out samples of each, and then stick with them. You do have an infinite range of options available, but you'll get completely fouled up if you try a new type style every time you write.

Standard Formats

With your type styles established, the next step is to determine a standard page format for each of your anticipated writing applications. Again, you might want to decide on one scheme of top, bottom, left, and right margins for working drafts, another for final manuscripts, and a third to complement your personal stationery.

Fig. 13-1: Elite font printed at 10, 9, and 11 characters per inch

---

```
[These lines are printed with an elite font using
the standard microspacing of 10/120ths.]
     Even more important than speed is the word
processor's ability to let you revise your writing
thoroughly and almost painlessly.  With a word
```

```
[These are printed with the same font using condensed
9/120ths microspacing.]
processor, you can move phrases, sentences, and blocks of
text from one place to another within a manuscript, copy
sections at various places in your text or duplicate them
```

```
[These lines are printed with the same font
using expanded 11/120ths microspacing.]
in another manuscript, and study each succes-
sive stage of revision in a clean printed copy
as well as on the word processor's screen.
```

An aid in designing these page formats is a special text file that we call a Format Matrix. This is one solid page of text, comprised of a series of ruler lines, that indicates where every line and column will print. An example of a Format Matrix is shown in Figure 13-2.

To use the Format Matrix, insert a sheet of paper in your printer according to your paper-insertion routine and print the

Fig. 13-2: Sample Format Matrix

```
 1 /  +---1+0---+---2+0---+---3+0---+---4+0---+---5+0---+---6+0---+---7+0---+--
 2 /  +---1+0---+---2+0---+---3+0---+---4+0---+---5+0---+---6+0---+---7+0---+--
 3 /  +---1+0---+---2+0---+---3+0---+---4+0---+---5+0---+---6+0---+---7+0---+--
 4 /  +---1+0---+---2+0---+---3+0---+---4+0---+---5+0---+---6+0---+---7+0---+--
 5 /  +---1+0---+---2+0---+---3+0---+---4+0---+---5+0---+---6+0---+---7+0---+--
 6 /  +---1+0---+---2+0---+---3+0---+---4+0---+---5+0---+---6+0---+---7+0---+--
 7 /  +---1+0---+---2+0---+---3+0---+---4+0---+---5+0---+---6+0---+---7+0---+--
 8 /  +---1+0---+---2+0---+---3+0---+---4+0---+---5+0---+---6+0---+---7+0---+--
 9 /  +---1+0---+---2+0---+---3+0---+---4+0---+---5+0---+---6+0---+---7+0---+--
10/   +---1+0---+---2+0---+---3+0---+---4+0---+---5+0---+---6+0---+---7+0---+--
11/   +---1+0---+---2+0---+---3+0---+---4+0---+---5+0---+---6+0---+---7+0---+--
12/   +---1+0---+---2+0---+---3+0---+---4+0---+---5+0---+---6+0---+---7+0---+--
13/   +---1+0---+---2+0---+---3+0---+---4+0---+---5+0---+---6+0---+---7+0---+--
14/   +---1+0---+---2+0---+---3+0---+---4+0---+---5+0---+---6+0---+---7+0---+--
15/   +---1+0---+---2+0---+---3+0---+---4+0---+---5+0---+---6+0---+---7+0---+--
16/   +---1+0---+---2+0---+---3+0---+---4+0---+---5+0---+---6+0---+---7+0---+--
17/   +---1+0---+---2+0---+---3+0---+---4+0---+---5+0---+---6+0---+---7+0---+--
18/   +---1+0---+---2+0---+---3+0---+---4+0---+---5+0---+---6+0---+---7+0---+--
19/   +---1+0---+---2+0---+---3+0---+---4+0---+---5+0---+---6+0---+---7+0---+--
20/   +---1+0---+---2+0---+---3+0---+---4+0---+---5+0---+---6+0---+---7+0---+--
21/   +---1+0---+---2+0---+---3+0---+---4+0---+---5+0---+---6+0---+---7+0---+--
22/   +---1+0---+---2+0---+---3+0---+---4+0---+---5+0---+---6+0---+---7+0---+--
23/   +---1+0---+---2+0---+---3+0---+---4+0---+---5+0---+---6+0---+---7+0---+--
24/   +---1+0---+---2+0---+---3+0---+---4+0---+---5+0---+---6+0---+---7+0---+--
25/   +---1+0---+---2+0---+---3+0---+---4+0---+---5+0---+---6+0---+---7+0---+--
26/   +---1+0---+---2+0---+---3+0---+---4+0---+---5+0---+---6+0---+---7+0---+--
27/   +---1+0---+---2+0---+---3+0---+---4+0---+---5+0---+---6+0---+---7+0---+--
28/   +---1+0---+---2+0---+---3+0---+---4+0---+---5+0---+---6+0---+---7+0---+--
29/   +---1+0---+---2+0---+---3+0---+---4+0---+---5+0---+---6+0---+---7+0---+--
30/   +---1+0---+---2+0---+---3+0---+---4+0---+---5+0---+---6+0---+---7+0---+--
31/   +---1+0---+---2+0---+---3+0---+---4+0---+---5+0---+---6+0---+---7+0---+--
32/   +---1+0---+---2+0---+---3+0---+---4+0---+---5+0---+---6+0---+---7+0---+--
33/   +---1+0---+---2+0---+---3+0---+---4+0---+---5+0---+---6+0---+---7+0---+--
34/   +---1+0---+---2+0---+---3+0---+---4+0---+---5+0---+---6+0---+---7+0---+--
35/   +---1+0---+---2+0---+---3+0---+---4+0---+---5+0---+---6+0---+---7+0---+--
36/   +---1+0---+---2+0---+---3+0---+---4+0---+---5+0---+---6+0---+---7+0---+--
37/   +---1+0---+---2+0---+---3+0---+---4+0---+---5+0---+---6+0---+---7+0---+--
38/   +---1+0---+---2+0---+---3+0---+---4+0---+---5+0---+---6+0---+---7+0---+--
39/   +---1+0---+---2+0---+---3+0---+---4+0---+---5+0---+---6+0---+---7+0---+--
40/   +---1+0---+---2+0---+---3+0---+---4+0---+---5+0---+---6+0---+---7+0---+--
41/   +---1+0---+---2+0---+---3+0---+---4+0---+---5+0---+---6+0---+---7+0---+--
42/   +---1+0---+---2+0---+---3+0---+---4+0---+---5+0---+---6+0---+---7+0---+--
43/   +---1+0---+---2+0---+---3+0---+---4+0---+---5+0---+---6+0---+---7+0---+--
44/   +---1+0---+---2+0---+---3+0---+---4+0---+---5+0---+---6+0---+---7+0---+--
45/   +---1+0---+---2+0---+---3+0---+---4+0---+---5+0---+---6+0---+---7+0---+--
46/   +---1+0---+---2+0---+---3+0---+---4+0---+---5+0---+---6+0---+---7+0---+--
47/   +---1+0---+---2+0---+---3+0---+---4+0---+---5+0---+---6+0---+---7+0---+--
48/   +---1+0---+---2+0---+---3+0---+---4+0---+---5+0---+---6+0---+---7+0---+--
49/   +---1+0---+---2+0---+---3+0---+---4+0---+---5+0---+---6+0---+---7+0---+--
50/   +---1+0---+---2+0---+---3+0---+---4+0---+---5+0---+---6+0---+---7+0---+--
51/   +---1+0---+---2+0---+---3+0---+---4+0---+---5+0---+---6+0---+---7+0---+--
52/   +---1+0---+---2+0---+---3+0---+---4+0---+---5+0---+---6+0---+---7+0---+--
53/   +---1+0---+---2+0---+---3+0---+---4+0---+---5+0---+---6+0---+---7+0---+--
54/   +---1+0---+---2+0---+---3+0---+---4+0---+---5+0---+---6+0---+---7+0---+--
55/   +---1+0---+---2+0---+---3+0---+---4+0---+---5+0---+---6+0---+---7+0---+--
56/   +---1+0---+---2+0---+---3+0---+---4+0---+---5+0---+---6+0---+---7+0---+--
57/   +---1+0---+---2+0---+---3+0---+---4+0---+---5+0---+---6+0---+---7+0---+--
58/   +---1+0---+---2+0---+---3+0---+---4+0---+---5+0---+---6+0---+---7+0---+--
59/   +---1+0---+---2+0---+---3+0---+---4+0---+---5+0---+---6+0---+---7+0---+--
60/   +---1+0---+---2+0---+---3+0---+---4+0---+---5+0---+---6+0---+---7+0---+--
61/   +---1+0---+---2+0---+---3+0---+---4+0---+---5+0---+---6+0---+---7+0---+--
62/   +---1+0---+---2+0---+---3+0---+---4+0---+---5+0---+---6+0---+---7+0---+--
63/   +---1+0---+---2+0---+---3+0---+---4+0---+---5+0---+---6+0---+---7+0---+--
64/   +---1+0---+---2+0---+---3+0---+---4+0---+---5+0---+---6+0---+---7+0---+--
65/   +---1+0---+---2+0---+---3+0---+---4+0---+---5+0---+---6+0---+---7+0---+--
66/   +---1+0---+---2+0---+---3+0---+---4+0---+---5+0---+---6+0---+---7+0---+--
```

Matrix. You will then have a printed page indicating how your line/column commands correspond with your standard paper-insertion methods for each type of paper. If you have decided to use different type styles, make sure that you print versions of the Format Matrix for each one, and label them clearly.

Armed with this information, you can specify the page margins precisely for each of your writing applications. Make note of each of these combinations of (a) paper-insertion method (including type of paper); (b) type style (including spacing and justification); and (c) margins (including headings and page-numbering conventions).

The final step is to store these standard format combinations for ready access. There are several methods for recording these standard formats, depending on your system. With some systems, you can store formats as separate files to be used by the program and simply retrieve and use them at the start of a printing session.

► With systems that make use of formatting commands imbedded at the start of each text file, you can create "dummy" files containing only imbedded commands and give them descriptive names such as 'LETRHEAD', 'MNUSCRPT', or 'DRFT-TPL' (draft—triple spaced). Then, to start each writing assignment, you can make a copy of the dummy format, rename it to reflect the current topic, and proceed from there, adding your text to that file.

► Many printers "remember" printing commands once they have been issued by the w/p program. An alternative way to use dummy format files is to leave them completely free of text and "print" them (using the system's regular Print command). This will have the effect of loading the printer with the desired set of formatting options. Once that has been done, any text file subsequently printed will be formatted according to the previously sent commands. In this way, you can leave a text file free of any formatting instructions and print it various ways (such as single- or double-spaced, with wide or narrow margins), depending on the application.

► If your system doesn't provide any practical way of storing format commands for future use, create a list of your various standard formats and keep it posted near your keyboard for easy reference. In some cases, you may have chosen the program's default printing format; if so, be sure to include it on your list.

Does this sound like a lot of trouble just to print a letter to a friend? The point we're making is that all this experimentation should take place before you try to print anything for real. Set aside an afternoon for the sole purpose of working out these format combinations. (And plan on consuming a fair quantity of paper until you get them perfected.) The time you spend will be well worth it in terms of streamlining your work routines; in fact, it's absolutely essential to standardize and store your print formats if you hope to rely on the printer as a labor-saving device.

Page Design

As we noted in Part I, many word processing systems offer print enhancements such as boldface, double-strike characters, and underlining. With the exception of the latter, none of these are available with typewriter-produced copy and so, together with margin and format control, w/p writers are presented with new options and more choices in the presentation of their work. Whether consciously addressed or not, the issue arises: What is the best way to make use of these enhancements?

Although professional graphic design encompasses a far wider range of technologies and skills, the availability of word processing print features does make every writer, in effect, a graphic designer. Bearing in mind a few very basic design principles can be of great help in designing your printed pages.

▶ First, exercise restraint. When you're suddenly provided with a host of enhancement features, your first reaction may be to use them all. Good design keeps to a minimum the number of different typographic and format elements and makes sparing use of embellishments. If you want to use boldface to emphasize words or headings, that's fine. But don't be tempted to use double strike for key words, boldface for *really* key words, and underlined, double-bold, capitalized letters for earth-shattering pronouncements.

▶ Next, be consistent. Just as sound editing requires uniform treatment of syntax and usage, good design must be consistent. Create a style sheet for your manuscript, identifying the different design elements and how each is to be presented. For example, you might determine that major section titles ("A" heads) will be printed in boldface, flush with the left margin; secondary section titles ("B" heads) will be indented and preceded by an asterisk; and key words within the text will be underlined. Keep your style sheet as simple as possible, and make sure that every one of your editorial conventions follows the design scheme. If you find yourself having to make exceptions to the overall style, try to make these exceptions conform rather than create new design elements.

The choice of using justified or ragged right text depends on how formal you want your document to appear. (Even the word "document," much-used in the word processing world, has a rather formal connotation.) Choose either one, but don't be tempted to mix justified and ragged right text. If your pages make use of indentations, be sure that they're used consistently and, once again, don't try to use many different indentation schemes to represent subtle usage distinctions.

These may seem like obvious points for any writer or editor who regularly works with graphic designers or prepares manuscripts for publication. The word processor's powerful print features make every writer a designer and a publisher, however. With this added power goes added responsibility.

► Experiment with the spacing between lines. For working drafts, double- or even triple-spaced text is necessary to provide room for corrections. Single-spaced text is appropriate for business letters. For reports, self-published novels, and other writing designed mainly to be read and used, neither double nor single spacing may be the best format. The "leading," or spacing between lines, is a key element in well-designed printed text. If your system provides vertical microspacing as an option, an intermediate spacing, such as 4 or 5 lines to the inch, may produce the most readable and useful text format.

► A final design tip: Don't be afraid of "white space." The margins around the text are themselves a creative element in the design of a printed page. A manuscript that attempts to cram as much text as possible on the page is neither very readable nor very attractive. Experiment with making your margins wider than you ordinarily would and see whether the appearance of your pages isn't improved.

This might be an appropriate point to note what we foresee as a changing convention in the writing community. Writers have customarily measured the length of their work in word counts or "standard" manuscript pages. These have always been rather slippery concepts since they depend so much on a particular writer's fondness for multisyllabic words or pica type and wide margins.

Recently many w/p writers have begun keeping track of their work in character counts. Many word processing programs and most operating system utilities provide a listing of file sizes in bytes, and the number of bytes in a file is usually an exact measure of the number of characters (although the imbedded commands or control characters may slightly inflate this count). It's natural for a writer to think in terms of a 15K article or a 500K manuscript. It seems just a matter of time before assignment editors and publishing contracts will be using the same terminology. (Typesetters already use the character count as a standard way of measuring files.)

Paging the Manuscript

It's time now to print some actual writing, but the next step is still a preparatory one. Before you push the final button, you want to make sure that everything's set to go, and you should give some consideration to how your text will "page out" when you print it.

You'll recall that the Printer Driver portion of the w/p program is instructed to print a certain number of text lines per page. If your text file consists of a novel or continuous expository material, you can probably just let the page breaks fall where they may. More likely, however, you'll have some section headings in your text that should appear on the same page as the material they describe, or paragraphs or charts that you don't want to be broken between pages. Perhaps the regular page breaks will leave a sentence fragment as a single-line "widow" at the top of a page.

The most common printing mishap (besides simply selecting the wrong format) is producing hard copy that breaks oddly from page to page. When typing a manuscript on a typewriter, you can try to guard against these bad breaks with elaborate "end of page approaching" schemes. Most word processors provide some method of previewing all the page breaks before any printing commences. If you can establish a routine for doing this, you'll rarely have to print a document more than once.

▶ With systems that offer the Conditional Page Break feature, you can imbed certain instructions for page breaks within your text as you're writing. When you type a new section heading, instruct the printer (using a Conditional Page Break command) to start a new page if there are not at least four lines available on the current page. Since the Conditional Page Break commands don't print, they can reside in the text file before every heading, ready to take effect if needed.

The Conditional Page Break feature isn't a practical way to guard against widow paragraph fragments, however. (You would have to see how many lines were in each paragraph and then imbed an appropriate Conditional Page Break command at the beginning of each.) A few w/p programs do ingeniously offer a Discretionary Line feature that will print an extra line at the bottom of a page if it is the last line of a paragraph. With most programs, you have to look through the text and do that manually.

▶ With systems that display page breaks on-screen, spotting paragraph widows is fairly easy. If the system provides for imbedded print formatting commands, you can then add an instruction to specify an extra line of text for that page. (Remember to imbed the standard line count at the start of the next page.)

If your system doesn't provide some way of seeing where the page breaks will fall, your only recourse is to proceed through your text file, keeping track of the line count and anticipating the page breaks accordingly. This can be a real chore, and you may simply decide not to worry about the widows. Before you give up, though, you might try one of the following page preview techniques.

▶ If your system provides a Move the Cursor x Lines command, you could set it for the line count per page and proceed through the text in fairly rapid order.

▶ Another possibility would be to adopt a printing format in which the number of lines per page corresponds to the number of lines that your Scroll Screenful command covers (approximately 23 lines for double-spaced manuscripts and 46 lines for single-spaced). This would produce pages with slightly oversized top and bottom margins, but it might be worth it to be able to preview page breaks simply by scrolling screenfuls.

▶ If none of these techniques are available or appropriate, your recourse will be to print the entire text and later adjust by reprinting selected pages. (Printing single pages is discussed below.) At any rate, you should definitely start out with a page format that gives you some room to squeeze an extra line or two onto a page if you need to make adjustments later.

The way in which you number pages can ultimately cut down on printing time, especially if you're producing a long manuscript or report. It's fairly common in computer-oriented literature to see "sectional" page numbering, that is, '10-3' to indicate the third page of Chapter Ten. Traditionalists may hold out for sequential numbering that proceeds through an entire manuscript, but the fact is that documents are much more easily revised, reworked, and reorganized in the Computer Age. By using a sectional numbering system, you'll be able to revise a portion of your work without having to renumber and reprint the entire document.

▶ Sectional numbering can be produced by placing a heading within the page format that specifies the chapter number or title, such as '10-' to appear on line 2, starting at column 1. Then specify the page number to appear on the same line as the heading and at the appropriate column (in our example, line 2, column 4).

Monitoring the Printer

If you've planned your printing carefully and thoroughly, you should be able to load the paper, give the Print command, and go about other business while the printer churns out your document. We wouldn't recommend being so cavalier as to push the button and actually walk away, however. You should certainly check the start of the printout to make sure that you haven't made some gross formatting blunder.

▶ A more prudent strategy is to wait at least until the printer has started to print page 2 of your document. If the second page shows the proper top margin and page numbering, you can probably count on the entire document's being printed and formatted properly.

If any major problems do crop up immediately, make sure that you know how to bring the printer to a swift halt. There's nothing more nerve-wracking than frantically pushing keys while the printer proceeds to spew quadruple-spaced manuscript.

▶ If you do terminate printing prematurely, you might have to reset some of the formatting parameters, such as the starting page number or the spot where the printer recognizes the start of the "form" (top of page). Some systems will reset automatically; others may require you to specify your file again and start the printing routine from the beginning.

If the first two pages print correctly (and if you have checked your paper and ribbon supply), you can probably go jogging with peace of mind while the tireless printer spits out another draft of your novella-in-progress. It's unlikely that an untended printing session can turn into a Sorcerer's Apprentice nightmare. Most printers will simply stop if something goes technically awry. (Some, however, will not stop if the paper or ribbon runs out.)

▶ If you are printing the final copy of a document, you might put the printing time to good use by running your eyes over the manuscript one last time as it is printed. You'd be surprised how often a typo or misplaced word will manifest itself during the "final" printing.

When you do spot either a textual or minor formatting error during printing, you're probably well advised to make a note of it but to let the printing session proceed. As we'll discuss shortly, there are effective ways of making spot page corrections, and you'll most likely save more time and energy in the long run by printing the rest of the document than by aborting the session.

Spot Corrections

Being able to print or reprint single pages of a document is one of the most useful w/p printing skills. Each system will provide different options for doing this, but you should explore your system's features thoroughly to determine how much control you can exercise when doing these spot printing jobs. We can't anticipate precisely what steps you'll need to take, but we can describe some common reprint situations.

▶ If there is a minor error on a page, such as a misspelled word, you'll first want to figure out the most direct way to make the correction in your text file. Some w/p programs make it easy to do this; on others, you may have to leave the Print mode of your program and return to an Edit mode. Some programs may provide several alternatives for corrections. Whatever method you find most efficient, never make a spot correction in a way that won't save the correction permanently on disk in your text file.

▶ Once you make the correction, you have to be able to specify the page to be reprinted, and make sure that the beginning and end of the text on that page correspond to the originally printed page. On some systems, you can merely instruct the program to print page 3; on others, you might have to bring the text to the screen and manipulate it (using the cursor and scrolling commands) until the first line of text for that page is displayed at the top of the screen.

▶ If you've simply made a spelling correction, you probably won't have altered the number of lines in your text. If you've added or deleted several words, however, your line count at the bottom of the page may not correspond with the previously printed document. In this case, you have to be able to specify a new format for the page to be reprinted—either adding or deleting a line. Once again, you'll have to determine the best way of accomplishing this with your particular program. Finding some way to make spot formatting changes is a very useful printing routine, however. (This is why we recommended earlier that you build some leeway into your standard formats.)

▶ Another common reprint situation is having to change the format slightly to avoid a widow at the top of a page. To do this, you'll usually have to reprint two pages, adding a line to one and deleting a line from the next. Another possibility would be to "squeeze" or "stretch" the lines per page by specifying slightly different vertical spacing for that page (for example, Line Height 8 instead of 9 would fit one or two more lines on a page without an obvious difference in spacing).

Of course, these salvage jobs can eventually become counterproductive. Unless you're in the middle of a very long document, it probably won't be that inconvenient simply to reprint from the correction to the end.

▶ There's one important caveat when making any of these spot changes: Don't leave your text files in a condition that will necessitate your having to make manual reformatting corrections if you ever print the document again. In other words, do what you can to imbed spot formatting corrections or adjustments within your text file.

Linking Files for Printing

A whole range of advanced printing techniques involve printing more than one file with a single Print command. Many word processing programs provide a way of Linking or Chain printing several files sequentially. These files can be on either of the disks in your drives, and if your system allows it, you may also be able to give a signal and then change disks as part of a Linking operation.

One of the best uses for the Linking feature is creating a document out of individual files. This "boilerplate" approach, in which stock paragraphs or sections of text are kept on file and assembled to suit a particular need, is the way many legal documents are created. The technique can also be used for consulting reports, query letters, replies to customer requests, and resumes.

For example, you might prepare a list of articles that you've written and had published and save it as a file entitled 'ARTICLES.LST'. This list could then be linked with a number of other files, as needed. You could link it at the appropriate point in a proposal for a book contract, to evidence your qualifications. Later (after you've received a contract) you could use the same file to link with permission letters during your research. Finally, the same list could be linked with the final manuscript as part of your professional biography.

▶ Beyond making sure that you've instructed the printer to print the files in the proper order, there's nothing particularly difficult about this boilerplate technique, since a single set of printing format commands can often govern the entire printing job. The format can be specified in the first of the linked files, and the files that follow will automatically be printed in the same format.

If your program permits Merging of files during printing, you can assemble boilerplate documents with more sophistication. The Merge feature lets you create a separate Data File containing individual blocks of text data, identified by categories such as name, address, and special interest. A Command File—the one being printed—retrieves text from specified parts of the Data File. The same basic Command File can produce many similar documents, each time merging different sets of text from Data Files. This is how they create those letters informing you that "Yes, *Acme*, the *Corporation* family may be the luckiest people on *General delivery* Street."

Another use of Linking is to print several chapters, each consisting of a separate file, during a single printing session. In this case, you're really not combining text in any involved way—merely ganging several individual printing jobs. You do have to consider the need to change formats, however. This might involve simply making sure that the page numbering resets, if necessary, or actually specifying radically different formats for the different files to be printed.

If your program uses formatting instructions imbedded within the text files, format changes during linked printing should occur automatically. If your program uses a system of formats stored on separate files, these format files may have to be included in the sequence of linked printing instructions.

▶ With some programs, linked printing may be the only way to change formats within a document. For example, if your text included excerpts that you wanted set off by indentations, it might be most practical to create the excerpts as separate files and incorporate them into the text using Link commands, interspersed with format commands specifying alternative left and right margins.

The Electronic Secretary

A common use of the Linking feature that involves both boilerplating and format changes is the creation of a standard business letter. If there are people with whom you correspond regularly, you might want to store their names and addresses as separate text files. Then, depending on the way your system deals with formatting commands, you could use the Link feature to produce your correspondence without having to retype addresses.

▶ If your system uses stored formats on separate files, you could create a file listing the proper format for printing on your stationery and another with the proper margin commands for addressing an envelope. To produce a letter, you would create a new file containing only the text of the letter. The letterhead, envelope, address, and text files could then be linked for printing using commands similar to those in Figure 13-3.

If you included appropriate instructions for pauses, single-sheet-feed commands, and page-numbering resets, you could link many formatting, addressing, and text files and produce all your correspondence for a day during a single printing session.

▶ If your program uses a system of imbedding format commands within text files, you might approach the above job in a slightly different way. As with the previous example, separate files would be created for formatting the letter and the envelope, for the address, and for the text of the letter. The two formatting files would intentionally be left free of any text; the two text files would include no formatting commands. By printing the files in the proper order, as illustrated in Figure 13-4, you should be able to turn out a correctly formatted letter and addressed envelope.

The only difference between these two methods is that the second uses dummy text files (with formatting commands but without text) to send the desired formatting commands to the printer.

Reading about these Linking and formatting commands in the abstract may seem complicated. Depending on your system, however, developing these types of printing routines can turn out to be true timesavers. If you think creatively about the Linking features your system offers, you'll likely be able to accomplish much more than

Fig. 13-3: Linking commands for letter and envelope (stored formats)

```
            B:FIG13-3   PAGE 1 LINE 1 COL 01               INSERT ON
L——!——#——!——#——!——#——!——#——!——#——!——#——R
[.]FORMAT LETTERHD
.PRINT JOHNSON.ADR
.PRINT JOHNSON.LTR
.FORMAT ENVELOPE
.PRINT JOHNSON.ADR
```

Fig. 13-4: Linking commands for letter and envelope (imbedded formats)

```
            B:FIG13-4   PAGE 1 LINE 1 COL 01               INSERT ON
L——!——#——!——#——!——#——!——#——!——#——!——#——R
[.]PRINT LETTERHD
.PRINT JOHNSON.ADR
.PRINT JOHNSON.LTR
.PRINT ENVELOPE
.PRINT JOHNSON.ADR
```

simply printing several jobs at once. (More techniques and routines involving management of files will be discussed extensively in the next chapter.)

Manual Routines

We'll conclude by considering a few aspects of the printing process in which old-fashioned, hand-and-eye-coordinated routines are still the best way to get the job done.

For all the wonders of automatic printing, there will be times when it is too much trouble to calculate and specify a printing format for a one-time application, such as printing a label, filling in a form, or inserting a temporary heading on a previously printed page. In these instances, you'll want to develop a routine for using your printer as—dare we say it?—a typewriter.

▶ Some disk operating systems and word processing programs provide a method for having your printer "echo" whatever character is entered at the keyboard. Once in this mode, you can (if your keyboard and printer are fairly proximate) insert the paper into the printer and proceed to type a character when you want to print a character, hit a space to move a space, and press the return key to move to the next line. Just like the old days! Seriously, this can be a very useful technique.

▶ Another method of accomplishing much the same result is to create a formatting file that specifies "zero" formatting commands; in other words, a format that starts printing with line 1, column 1 and that specifies the maximum column width and page length. You can then create a temporary text file, "formatting" the document solely by the way you create it on the screen, by skipping lines and adding spaces to the text. When you go to print the file, insert the paper so that the print head is aligned exactly at the top left corner of the page.

▶ If your printer provides you with enough horizontal leeway for positioning paper relative to the print element, you can dispense with specifying different left margins for various printing applications and simply mark insertion guides for manuscript paper, letterhead, and envelopes directly on your printer. When you go to print a job, merely insert the paper according to the appropriate guide. This method may not seem like a Computer Age approach, but it might be the most efficient way of dealing with several letterheads requiring slightly different formats.

Finally, we'll share a few tips for working with continuous-form computer paper. When you want to tear off a completed job, hold the edge of the paper taut with one hand, just above the horizontal perforation, and hit the perforation about two inches in from the edge with a quick flick of your finger. This will get the tear at the perforation started nicely. (It's also a rather snappy little move that will surely impress others with your credentials as a bona fide w/p pro.)

Once you've got your job detached, fold the hole-punched edges of the paper in both directions to weaken the vertical perforations and then pull the hole-punched edges down as though you were pulling a zipper. The edges should come off neatly as a unit. (When will some genius figure out what to do with all those strips of hole-punched tailings?)

To separate the pages into individual sheets, place the stack of fan-folded paper on your left (if you're right-handed), with the last page on the top of the stack. Then pull each page over to the right and tear it off, placing each page on top of the torn-off pile in reverse numerical order. (You can check the page numbering as you go.)

Someone has, of course, already invented a machine for doing all this, but you shouldn't deny yourself the satisfaction of letting your fingers run through the tangible results of your electronic efforts.

Chapter 14

Getting Organized

Information and File Management

Up to now, we've emphasized the speed of writing, the ease of editing, and the versatility of print-ing that word processing makes possible. All of these are positive attributes, of course, and they can lead to greatly improved produc-tivity for most writers. And that, in turn, means more information to handle, in the form of electronic files, magnetic disks, and paper printouts. So as your output increases through w/p writing, you may also encounter your own personal version of a Computer Age phe-nomenon—the information explosion.

Managing your notes, drafts, letters, and other writing is a bit more complicated with a word processing system than with paper-only methods, because you have both electronic files and the disks that store them, in addition to printed manuscripts for some or all of your work. With a few good (you guessed it) routines, however, you can keep this deluge of data from overwhelming you. And perhaps the best way to stay ahead of all this information is to start with a good plan.

An Information Overview

One essential step in organizing your work is gaining an overview of the information you have to manage. As you're writing—and as you devise the organizational tools you will use—deciding where to put each file and which ones to print or copy or update will be much easier if you can think of your electronic output as if it were mere paper.

In fact, the flow of information in an office with a w/p system is quite similar to that of a non-computer office, except that the computer and disks serve as the filing cabinet. If you disregard the form of a file—electronic or paper—the overview is the same: the name of a file is a short identifier that fits in a small space (the Disk Directory or the tab on a file folder); each file is a quantity of information that is stored in a file holder (the designated area of a magnetic disk or the traditional file folder); and the file holders are labeled and stored in the appropriate subdivisions of a cabinet or box (disks filled with related files or folders in file drawers, arranged by topic in a suitable container).

When paper and electronic files are mixed, you have the option of storing disks along with printed copies or maintaining separate file areas for each. (Some suggestions for storing disks and printed files appear at the end of this chapter.)

Notes, Ideas, and Research

The first order of a writer's business is not filing, however, but generating the information to organize. Here, too, a series of routines will save you time and enable you to find a draft or a set of notes whenever you need them. The most important consideration is not so much how you label and use the information but that you establish a logical system and stick with it.

One of the more challenging parts of writing from an organizational standpoint is managing the notes that form the basis of an article or book and the random thoughts and ideas about other projects that you write as they occur to you. So you need a method of creating an electronic file for each project that will accommodate long and short bits of data and let you rearrange them at will, as well as a separate catch-all file for other notes. And you also must decide on a way to handle the printed version of your notes, which will be essential for outlining the piece and then writing it.

▶ The most efficient way to work with research notes probably is a combination of electronic and printed files. The word processor is ideal for writing notes and fragments of text; you can be reading a source book or journal and paraphrase relevant portions or copy quotations much more quickly than with pen or typewriter, or you can stare out the window until a thought forms and then key it into the computer quite easily. Yet for most projects, especially books or detailed articles, you will want to print out your notes in manuscript form or on individual cards or pages that you can separate into several piles. The printed pages or cards can then become your reference sources as you write the draft of a chapter or article.

Writers adopt various ways of handling the reference materials they've generated—standard-sized pages are useful if you're also referring to magazine articles or other source materials of the same size; index cards are easy to arrange into separate groupings and rearrange as you work; or you can print a set of notes on continuous-form paper and number the passages in the order you want to use them. Individual cards or pages seem most efficient for the note-taking stage, and some distributors of word processing supplies do sell perforated, continuous-form index cards that can be used in the same way as continuous paper.

▶ If you use the one-note-per-page method, you'll want to establish a printing format so that each note will begin and end on a single piece of paper. (Obviously, if you're using 3-by-5-inch cards, your notes can't be very long and meet this limitation.) The precise instructions for printing one note per page or card vary among w/p programs, but essentially you would establish margins and page length that are consistent with your paper size, then write in the character or command that specifies a new page at the end of each note you write. If you can't imbed a New Page signal with your program, you could end each note with enough Returns to complete the page. If your program doesn't display page breaks, you might also have to count the number of lines that will fit on one card or page and be sure not to exceed this for any one note. Finding the right combination of printing instructions for odd-sized pieces of paper may take some experimentation, but this trial-and-error process will familiarize you with the printing versatility of your w/p system and allow you the flexibility of reshuffling the printed notes as often as you wish.

▶ Whatever your scheme for printing notes, each bit of research or idea you record should be in a standard format. Again, the format can be tailored to each writer's taste, but every note ideally should include the date, the name of the project for which you're writing it, as precise a designation of how you'll use the information as you can supply, and complete data about the source. A typical note might look like the example in Figure 14-1.

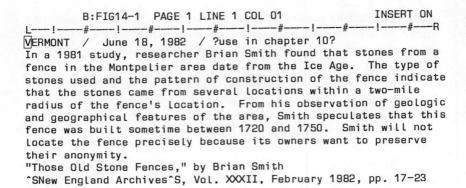

Fig. 14-1: Research note

There are good and bad aspects to the facility with which you can record notes and ideas on the word processor. The good part is that the keyboard-and-screen writing process is so quick and fluid that you're not so tempted to use abbreviations and truncated phrases as when writing by hand or typewriter. This means that some of your notes, like the one in Figure 14-1, could be used verbatim in a finished piece; you have the option of recopying the chosen sections or marking them as blocks and copying them from your file of notes into your text file. (Suggestions for moving blocks of text between files are included under the heading "Transferring Files" later in this chapter.) The negative aspect of this ease of writing is that you may tend to make longer notes than necessary.

Transcribing Recorded Words

Many writers use tape recorders to ensure accurate reproduction of interviews, conferences, and speeches. This is a useful technique, for it frees you to ask questions and to make notes about the speaker or the setting of an event, without having to scribble constantly to be sure of getting down the provocative and revealing quotes. Long after the event or interview, playing the tape will give you a renewed sense of the occasion and even help you remember many visual details, such as the speaker's face and demeanor.

For all their desirable attributes, however, tape recordings must be transcribed. Of course you could hire a service to do this, but another listener isn't likely to recognize the good quotations or decipher a slightly garbled passage as well as you can, so it's usually advisable to transcribe your own tapes. And as you listen, you'll know which parts are irrelevant or when the speaker is launching into a digression, so you can skip over some sections of tape that a hired transcriber would copy (and charge for).

Given the advisability of transcribing your own tapes, doing it with the word processor is far preferable to using a typewriter or writing out the text by hand. The nearly silent keyboard is ideal for this purpose, because you can keep the tape playing and enter quotes at the same time. Chances are that the taped conversation will get ahead of your fingers rather often, but you probably won't have to start and stop the tape nearly so frequently as when you're compensating for the typewriter's noise or the hand's slow motion.

▶ A few gadgets can make the process of transcribing tapes even more efficient. One highly useful aid is an extender that lets you start and stop the tape easily; such accessories are available for most small cassette recorders, in the form of a foot pedal (the least disruptive of your keyboard work) or a hand-held on-off switch. One w/p program even has a built-in command by which you can turn a cassette tape on and off from the keyboard, though only if you have a computer to which the audio cassette recorder can be attached. Another transcription device that many writers find useful is the earphones that stenographers traditionally use; with the combined speed of the electronic keyboard, your increasingly adept fingers, and the sound of the tape directly in your ears, you may find that transcribing tapes is no longer the dreary chore it once was.

Transferring Files

Some of the most useful file management techniques you can develop involve the transfer of information among your disk files. The exact procedures for transferring files vary among w/p systems, and not all systems provide every option, but here are some of the possibilities.

One file transfer feature Writes information from one file to another. Normally, the portion of text to be written is first identified as a block, using the program's standard Block Move or Block Copy feature. Then this block is sent (usually Copied) to another file, the name of which you specify.

▶ With many systems, you have to be careful not to specify a filename that already exists; if you do, that new information will Overwrite (and thereby erase) the contents of the previously existing file. Some systems do give you the option of Appending the block to the end of an existing file, preserving the text already in the file. If you can't Append blocks to a file, you'll have to send each block to its own separate file and combine them (using the Read feature) later.

The corollary to the Write feature is Read, which moves text from another file into the file that you're currently editing. Again, there are several options. Some programs merely request a specification for the file to be Read and then insert that entire file into the current one, usually at the cursor position. Other programs may permit you to specify which portions of the Read file you wish to insert.

▶ The Write and Read features can be used for more than just information transfers. By repeated use of both commands, you can break apart a large file into smaller component files and then reassemble the components into new composite files.

Once you've learned to work with whatever file transfer features your program offers, you should be able to treat all your notes, research, and drafts as flexible, mobile segments of your work, rather than as rigid, static text encased within file boundaries. Making use of these file transfer techniques is essential to advanced word processing routines such as marking and compiling footnotes and indexes.

Footnotes and Bibliography

Many writing projects require footnotes, bibliography, or both. When you're doing such detailed work, the ideal time to write the notes or citations is when you refer to them in the text. Chances are you have the source notes at hand, and by writing the complete footnote or bibliographic information at the draft stage, you won't have to go through the completed manuscript and all of your source notes at a later stage just to tie up these loose ends. More important, perhaps, by writing the note and complete source information as you're citing that source in the text, you avoid the rather significant task of later trying to reconstruct your research because you've misplaced a crucial note card or two—a small tragedy that has happened to most writers.

Some word processors have a built-in or optional component that handles footnotes, and there are some supplemental programs that do this job in conjunction with certain w/p programs. If your system does not have this facility, you can use some of the standard w/p features to mark footnotes in the text and to establish files of the corresponding source information. In most instances, you would not ordinarily reference bibliographic material in the text, but if you write the footnotes and bibliographic citations at the same time, you won't have to retrace your steps when you've finished the draft of your project.

▶ The simplest way to handle footnotes is to use a combination of a symbol and a number at each point in the text where the note is referenced, and to repeat that symbol and number at the beginning of the corresponding note and with the bibliographic citation. (The symbol or number will ultimately be removed from the bibliographic entries, but it's wise to keep track of the sources for all of your citations until you've completed the manuscript, in case something is inadvertently left out or you want to delete a footnote but leave the source in your bibliography.) If you use both symbols and numbers, you can distinguish one note from another and also search your draft text for the unique footnote symbol, which would prevent your turning up every instance of a number alone.

A typical reference in the text and its accompanying footnote and bibliographic citation, then, might resemble the example in Figure 14-2. Even though the numbering of footnotes may change, so long as your text number agrees with the number on its footnote, the order is unimportant in your draft. If you move sections of text around during the editing stage, you can always find the corresponding footnote by searching the footnote file for that symbol-number combination.

It's probably preferable to write the footnotes and citations within the text, as in the example above, and leave them there until the draft is complete. When your text editing is complete, you could then check the order of the footnotes and renumber them if necessary, using the Search feature to locate each occurrence of your special symbol ('&' in our example).

When you're ready to put the manuscript in final form, you have several options. If you're going to place footnotes in a separate reference section, and if your program permits you to Append new data to an existing file, you can simply establish one file for footnotes

Fig. 14-2: Footnote and bibliography references

```
        B:FIG14-2  PAGE 1 LINE 1 COL 01              INSERT ON
L——!——#——!——#——!——#——!——#——!——#——!——#——R
According to Milan,&1 the papyrus could not have supported more

&1.  Lawrence M. Milan, "Ancient Sailors," ^SHistorical
Monographs^S, Vol. 47, No. 3 (July 1979), pp. 77-84.

&1bib.  Milan, Lawrence M.  "Ancient Sailors."  ^SHistorical
Monographs^S 47 (1979):77-84.
```

and another for bibliography and Write the marked blocks to those files each time.

If you can't Write new information to an existing file without erasing the data already there, you could Write each note and citation to its own separate file (which could have the same name as its symbol-number label). When the text is complete, you would then combine all the separate notes and citations into two large files, using the the Read feature of your program.

▶ One way to make certain that the footnote numbers and their text reference numbers agree would be to copy the footnote file at the end of your text, using the Read command. Then you can check each footnote reference in the text and if you change a number, you can immediately search for the second occurrence of its old symbol-number combination (which will be in the footnote file you've appended to the text) and change that as well.

Indexes and Key Words

You can use a similar marking and copying system to identify important terms in a manuscript. If you know that your project will include an index, or even if you think it might, you can save much time and effort by marking the key words as you write or edit the text. For this purpose, using an identifier that is easy to spot on the screen or the printed page is more useful than a modest symbol or number, because you may have to copy each term into a separate file for the index.

As with the marking of footnotes, choose symbols that you won't be likely to include in the regular text, so that when you search for them later you'll locate only the key words. For example, you might mark these terms in one of the ways illustrated in Figure 14-3. All of those terms can be readily noticed in the text, but the identifiers don't take up so much room as to throw off the length of the manuscript. (By putting the symbols only in front of the word or using identical symbols before and after a word, you only have to search once to remove identifiers; if you put different symbols before and after the key word, you have to make two separate searches to find and remove them.)

Fig. 14-3: Key words marked in text

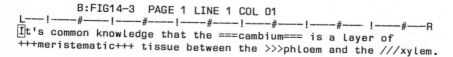

```
        B:FIG14-3   PAGE 1 LINE 1 COL 01
L——!——#——!——#——!——#——!——#——!——#——!——#——R
It's common knowledge that the ===cambium=== is a layer of
+++meristematic+++ tissue between the >>>phloem and the ///xylem.
```

If you have a separate Index program, it will locate each occurrence of the designated key word symbol and compile a separate list of all the marked terms, and probably arrange the list in alphabetical or numerical order. (Such a program could be used to put the footnotes in numerical order as well.)

If you have no Index program, however, the simplest way to compile the list of key words is to work from a printed copy of your finished text. Because you've marked all the terms prominently, you can scan the printout and type each key word into an index file in the processor. Or you could search for each occurrence of the key word symbol in the text, mark the key word as a block, then copy that block to another file.

When you're compiling an index, you usually need the page numbers of key words with the listing. Although the manuscript page numbers will be replaced by book page numbers for conventionally printed books, it will be easier to locate the terms in the book proofs and supply the new page numbers if you've kept a record of their manuscript page numbers in the original version of the index. In addition, an increasing number of Computer Age writing projects are not printed as books, but are reproduced from the computer printouts. In this kind of publication, the manuscript page numbers in the index would be the correct ones for the finished product.

▶ Whatever method you use for marking footnotes, reference numbers, and key words in the text, you'll have to perform a separate operation after you've finished editing to remove the symbols that identify each special item. This final step of putting your manuscript in order is actually quite simple: you can use the Search and Replace feature to find the symbols and, with most w/p programs, to remove the identifiers. (If you didn't include extra spaces when you inserted the symbols, you shouldn't have to worry about deleting any extra spaces during the stripping process.) And if you're really confident that you've used these symbols only around key terms, you could use the Global Search and Replace command to delete all of these identifiers without inspecting each one in the text.

Efficient File Naming

After you've created the various drafts of your writing projects and a number of separate files for research, footnotes, bibliography, and index, you can make good use of an efficient system for naming and identifying files. As we mentioned in Chapter 7, most w/p programs limit the length of filenames, usually allowing only 8 to 11 characters for a name. So you can make the best use of this small range of characters if you establish symbolic identifiers for certain types of files and adopt a standard method of including the date in filenames that require it.

▶ Choose a symbol to identify the common types of text files in your work, such as articles, book chapters, notes, outlines, and letters. Use each symbol—preferably a keyboard character that is seldom used otherwise—as the first letter in a filename, followed by the specific information about that file. Because many word processing programs display the files in alphabetical order (and arrange symbols in the order of their numerical ASCII values) in the Disk Directory, you'll get the added benefit of having all drafts, letters, outlines, and other types of files on a disk grouped together when the directory is displayed on the screen. A sample Disk Directory with the files organized by symbols is shown in Figure 14-4.

A listing of symbols to designate types of files might include these examples:

@ = letter (general)
) = query letter
& = notes for specific project
% = outline for project
# = draft (use with number)
! = final version of manuscript
> = transcript of interview
(= ideas/notes for future projects
< = journal
$ = invoice
~ = format for addressing an envelope
^ = special format for personal stationery or other purpose

The symbols you choose can vary according to the characters on your keyboard and the types of files you use most often. You may want to refrain from using some characters for this filename shorthand, however, if your system's DOS employs them in its utility programs. (You can check your system's manuals to determine if some characters are not permitted in filenames or if some are used as part of DOS operations.)

▶ When you've devised the list of symbols for the kinds of documents you use regularly, be sure to make some reference copies of this list. One logical place to store the electronic version of this listing is on the disk where your word processing program resides; then you'll always have access to it in case you forget a symbol's meaning or want to add a new category. Also make several printed

```
====================================================================
:           <<< C O M M A N D   M E N U  >>>                   :
: R - Retrieve a file    E - Edit a file    F - Format selection :
: S - Save file on disk  P - Print a file   X - eXit to system   :
: Z - delete a file                         H - Help             :
====================================================================
>Please enter your choice:☐

Files on Disk B:

!PVRT.325            >PVRT.315
#PVRT-1.317          @PVRT-OS.325
#PVRT-2.320          @PVRT.201
(PVRT-PA.206         @PVRT.219
(PVRT.401            @PVRT.226
)PVRT-OS.221         @PVRT.430
```

Fig. 14-4: Disk Directory with filenames

copies of the list and keep one near the keyboard (preferably as part of your system diary) and one with each set of working disks.

Many projects go through several stages of letters, drafts, and revisions, and for these files a date as part of the filename can be essential. Certainly you'll save time and trouble by being able to consult the Disk Directory and know which letter or draft is the most recent one, and a quick survey of the dates of files associated with a particular project can tell you how long that work has dragged on or how slowly an editor replies to a query letter. Consequently, if you can fit the month and day into each filename (depending on the number of characters your system permits in each name), always try to include the date. In some instances, too, the year may be useful in a filename.

▶ Dates showing month and day should be presented consistently with three characters. That is, the day of the month should be given two characters even if a single digit would do; this is another of the routines that can avoid confusion at a later time. All month-and-day references can be recorded in only three characters by using the numbers 1 through 9 to represent January through September and the capital letters O, N, and D for October, November, and December. So June 9th would be '609' and December 25th would be 'D25'.

▶ If your system uses filenames that have an extension (usually three characters at the end of the filename, preceded by a period), this concluding part of the filename is the logical place for the date. If the space restrictions of your system do not give you the option of using a period or other character to set off the date from the rest of a filename, you might adopt the routine of always putting the month and day as the last three characters in the name so that you can locate them easily.

▶ If you need to record the year as well, you could assign a symbol at the end of the filename (so that it won't be confused with the numbers for month and day) or simply use the last number of the year (2 for 1982, and so forth) as the last digit of the filename. Adding the year can use up precious space in a filename, however, and in most instances you can plan your use of disks and label the disks and their containers with the year so that you needn't include it in each filename.

Table 14-1 presents some examples of 8- and 11-character filenames and brief explanations of their contents. Note that in each of the two types of filenames, standard abbreviations have been established for the subject of this project ('PVRT' or 'PV') and the publications involved ('PA' and 'OS'). In both types of filenames, the abbreviations occupy the same relative positions, as well. By standardizing filenames in this way, you can make use of the Wild Card feature provided in many disk operating systems, which lets you sort among the files on a disk and display all filenames that contain a

Table 14-1: A Sample File-naming System

Filename		Description
11 characters	**8 characters**	**Description**
@PVRT.201	@PV201	Letter of Feb. 1st to Luciano Pavarotti requesting an interview when he visits here next month
]PVRT-PA.206	]PVPA206	Query letter, Feb. 6th, to *Performing Arts* magazine regarding article on Pavarotti
@PVRT.219	@PV219	Second letter to Pavarotti, Feb. 19th, requesting interview in March
]PVRT-OS.221	]PVOS221	Query letter, Feb. 21st, to *On Stage* magazine regarding article on Pavarotti
@PVRT.226	@PV226	Third letter, Feb. 26th, to Pavarotti at address suggested by editor of *On Stage*
>PVRT.315	>PV315	Transcript of taped interview with Pavarotti
#PVRT-1.317	#PV1-317	First draft of Pavarotti article
#PVRT-2.320	#PV2-320	Second draft of same article
!PVRT.325	!PV325	Final draft of Pavarotti article
@PVRT-OS.325	@PVOS325	Letter to *On Stage* to accompany finished article
[PVRT.401	[PV401	Notes for future article on Pavarotti
@PVRT.430	@PV430	Letter to Pavarotti thanking him for the interview and telling him date of forthcoming article in *On Stage* magazine

common component. For example, you could display a list of all letters you had written to Pavarotti by specifying the letter symbol ('@'), the abbreviation for the subject ('PVRT' or 'PV'), and the Wild Card that designates all occurrences of this combination.

An Annotated Directory

These shorthand file-naming methods will help immensely when you're looking at a Disk Directory to see if that disk contains the file you need or to locate the desired version of an article. Yet sometimes the symbols and abbreviated labels don't tell you enough about each file, and you end up loading and looking at a succession of files with seemingly appropriate names until you find the right one. This is when the wonders of electronic condensation can be discouraging and when the best of filing systems meets its test.

Ah, but there is hope. If you find the limitations of your word processor's filenames oppressive, even with a good system of symbols, you can create one file on each disk that is an Annotated Directory of all the other files on that disk. This is essentially an expanded disk directory, which could include necessary comments about each file, such as the file's length, the amount of time you worked on that version, whether it has been copied on a backup disk, and any other descriptive information that will tell you enough about its contents to avoid having to load and inspect the file itself. (A few w/p programs provide such expanded directories as part of their standard features.)

▶ The Annotated Directory file can be added to each disk and given a universal name, such as 'CONTENT' or 'CONTENTS'. The Contents file would always include the verbatim filename of each file on the disk, along with whatever comments you need about each file. In addition to using this expanded directory to locate a specific version of a project, you can Read this Contents file into whatever file you're currently working on to discover what else is on the disk.

▶ This ability to see the names and descriptions of all files on a disk could be crucial if you give the Save command and are greeted by a 'Disk Full' message on the screen, which could happen in systems that don't allow you to change disks during an editing session. If this were to happen, you could Read the Contents file into the current one, identify a file that you are positive has been backed up on another disk, and erase that duplicate file, thereby creating room on the disk to save your current work. (Although it's good practice—and should be automatic—to check the amount of space available on a disk before beginning work with it, there will be times when you'll have forgotten to check or you've simply written more text than will fit in the available disk space.)

▶ Of course, to take full advantage of the Contents file, you must update it often, changing the comments to reflect whatever new work you've done on the files. It's easy to make this updating a part of your regular routine, though; you can update the Contents at the end of each work session or once a day, at the same time that you make backup copies of the new work you've done.

Updating Files

Just as you need to update a Contents file to maintain its usefulness, you should likewise keep all of your files up to date. Often this is merely a labeling task—changing the draft number of a file after you've done some editing, for example, or renaming a file that you've duplicated. But the text within the file also should be as complete and tidy as possible, and the filename or a comment in the file itself (as well as in the Contents file, if you use that system) should be able to tell its full status.

▶ Many w/p programs include a method of writing comments in a file that appear on the screen but will not print. This feature is particularly useful for adding reminders to yourself at the beginning of each file; you can note the date and time of any revisions and also list whatever tasks remain to be done in connection with that project.

For example, you may have completed all the editing for an article about the timber industry, but you still want to check two of the figures in the text, because they came from a two-year-old book and newer data may have been published since you did the original research for this project. You could use a combination of symbols in the filename to indicate that the article is complete except for this checking, and you could put a full explanation of the details to be confirmed in a non-printing comment at the beginning of the file. The comment might resemble the one in Figure 14-5. When you've confirmed the missing details, you can change the comment and the filename to show that the manuscript is in final form.

▶Updating files and adding comments to them are parts of a good information-handling routine. Another key element in this routine is always leaving files in their best working order. For example, if you make changes or additions in a file, be sure to Reform that part of the text so that it's consistent with the rest of the file. If you haven't Reformed text in which you've made changes, you're likely to discover that the printed version of that file contains lines that go

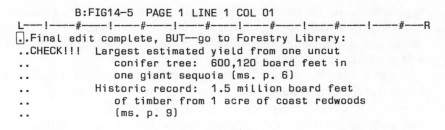

```
      B:FIG14-5  PAGE 1 LINE 1 COL 01
L——!——#——!——#——!——#——!——#——!——#——!——#——R
[.].Final edit complete, BUT—go to Forestry Library:
..CHECK!!!   Largest estimated yield from one uncut
..               conifer tree:  600,120 board feet in
..               one giant sequoia (ms. p. 6)
..           Historic record:  1.5 million board feet
..               of timber from 1 acre of coast redwoods
..               (ms. p. 9)
```

Fig. 14-5: Non-printing comments

beyond the right margin, other lines that stop halfway across the page, and paragraphs that run together or aren't indented.

The formatting instructions in each file also should be identical each time you work on that text. In many instances you'll set special margins for a piece of writing, rather than using the w/p program's default margins. If your system specifies that these instructions be added only once in the file, you needn't worry about them when you revise. But if you must establish some formatting parameters each time you work on a file—and this is true for the right and left margins in many systems—you must remember to set these parameters whenever you start work on that file. (One useful way to remember what formatting instructions you've chosen for a project is to write them in a non-printing comment at the beginning of the file.)

A Program Disk Buffer

The mythical word processing system we established in Part I contains two disk drives so that you can always use one for the program disk and one for a text disk, as well as copy disks and files easily from one drive to another. This ability to transfer files is an important component in managing electronic information. Although there are exceptions (such as a w/p program that is loaded from the disk into the computer's memory at the beginning of each work session, thus freeing that drive for a text disk), a two-drive system is almost always necessary to handle your writing efficiently.

▶ Assuming that your system has two disk drives and that your w/p program disk must stay in one of the drives, here's an arrangement of disks that will allow you maximum flexibility. The program disk always resides in the primary drive (called 'A' or '1' in most systems) and a text disk is used in the secondary drive ('B' or '2'). By devoting one drive exclusively to text and limiting the other to program disks (or occasional text overflow), you've already stream-lined your disk handling procedures, because disks used in the secondary drive will contain only text and disks containing programs will not be used for text.

▶ We just mentioned "occasional text overflow": this usually is text that you wrote but couldn't save because your text disk was already full. If you've kept your program disk relatively empty—so that it contains only the w/p program and the DOS utilities you use regularly while writing—you have a buffer of extra space on the disk in the primary drive. Since the average w/p program and several utilities would occupy no more than 70K on a disk, and the disk capacity in most systems commonly is 150K or more, you'll have perhaps 80K or more of free space to use in a pinch. We'll refer to this extra space on your program disk as the Program Disk Buffer; it is free space that you reserve—not a feature of the word processing program.

You can use the Program Disk Buffer in a number of ways. The most obvious example is making room for the unsaved new writing that you tried to save on the too-full text disk. To be able to save the writing (now in the computer's memory but not yet on disk), you must transfer or erase something from the text disk. Most w/p programs allow you to copy, rename, or erase files and to transfer blocks of text to another file from within the file you're currently editing; that is, you can perform these operations without damaging or erasing any of the text you've just written.

So if you get a 'Disk Full' message, you could cancel the Save command (if the program hasn't done this already) and consult the Disk Directory or Contents file to determine what other file on the text disk you might transfer to the Buffer on the program disk. When you've chosen one that is small enough to fit into the buffer space, you copy that file from the text to the program disk, then erase the file from the text disk. (Most programs also allow you to make certain that the copy has been made by displaying the directory of the program disk.) This should clear enough space on the text disk to accommodate the new writing that wouldn't fit before.

One way to use the Program Disk Buffer without leaving the file you're working on is to mark a large block within that file and copy the block on the program disk. Then you can erase the block from your current file and save the new part of the text. Ultimately, of course, you'll want to make room on a text disk—this one or a new one—for the entire file; then you can transfer the block back into that file from the Buffer.

▶ Marking and copying a block of text from the current file to the Buffer is especially useful if you're editing a long file and you mistakenly erase some text. The parts you erased are still in the original copy of the file, but if you save the version in which you've just made the error, in most cases that new version will replace the original. Yet if you abandon the edit (thereby retaining the original version), you'll lose all the good editing work you've done. In this instance you can mark all the text you've edited as a block (or as several blocks if the sections aren't contiguous) and Write the block to the program disk.

Once you've copied all the portions of the edited file that you want to save, you can abandon the edit and still have your original version, which contains the text you erased by mistake. You'll then have to combine portions of these two files—the block in the Buffer and the old version on the text disk—but this can be done easily by Reading the Buffer file into the original on your text disk (after making sure there's plenty of space available), then erasing the unedited parts of the original file. Having done that, you'll be left with the edited portions, the part you didn't mean to erase, and the remainder of the file to finish editing.

This use of the Program Disk Buffer is prudent and conservative; it avoids erasing anything that you aren't positive you've copied in its latest version. You can always erase a file on the text disk to make room for new writing if you know that you've made a backup copy of that file, but this procedure should be reserved for emergencies—because you may discover that you zapped a file that had not been backed up since you last revised it.

Another emergency possibility for erasing a file is available if your program automatically creates a backup copy of each file on the disk (and this is common to many w/p programs). In some systems you must rename a backup file before you can erase it—another safeguard that should be subverted only in dire circumstances. If you do erase a backup file to make room for new work on the text disk, you should be sure to make a copy of the newly saved file immediately, so that your work is protected if anything goes wrong with the part of the disk where that file resides. You should also know that when you've edited or added to the text file and save the new work, your program might create another backup file automatically—and you may be in the same space bind you were before.

▶ Using the Program Disk Buffer for temporary storage of text files is also helpful for juggling information from one text disk to another. For example, if you get a flash of inspiration about one project while you're working on another, you can write this "hot" text as part of the current file, then mark it as a block and transfer it to the Program Disk Buffer. This is a process you can repeat as often as necessary, so long as the Buffer isn't full. (If the Buffer is full, you can create a separate file on the text disk and later transfer this to another text disk.) The advantage of using the Program Disk Buffer for these fragments of unrelated information is that you can easily transfer them to the text disks where they belong when you've finished work on the current project.

Allocating Disk Space

Depending on the storage capacity of your disks, you may want to be liberal in using them, perhaps even allocating one disk per chapter or article for major projects. Although this may seem to be a waste of disk space, you'll have the advantage of always knowing that each disk contains just one chapter or article, and you may actually fill up a disk with the various drafts of that work. Of course you can consolidate the files when you've finished the article or chapter, as well as when making backup copies of this work, so you won't be devoting too many disks to a project at one time. And when that work is no longer current and becomes part of your permanent archives, you can condense the files by saving only the final drafts of articles or chapters and putting several on each disk.

Another strategy for using disk space, again depending on your system's capacity, is to combine an article or chapter and its research notes and outline on one disk. This is most appropriate for projects that are limited in scope, so that the research is all relevant to just one or two text files, or for work such as short stories or columns that are largely thought pieces and don't have large accompanying files of notes. For longer projects, such as books, it would often be difficult to fit the research and the drafts of chapters on a single disk.

► Whatever method you choose to allocate disk space for various projects, be sure to check the amount of space available on the text disk (and in the Program Disk Buffer if you use one) at the beginning of each writing or editing session. If a disk has little space remaining, start with a new one and transfer any files you need to it; this will save you from a possible 'Disk Full' error and the resulting contingencies to resolve it.

Labeling Disks

Like filenames, the labels on the outside of your disks should be precise and informative. Because each disk is likely to hold several files, the label must accommodate all of the filenames and show some general information about your method of organizing work. Most boxes of new disks contain several small color-coded labels, along with tabs you can use to cover the write-protect notches of disks. Certainly these labels are acceptable, but they lock you into a limited number of colors to designate different types of disks, and they don't hold as much information as the larger black-and-white disk labels available at office supply stores. The larger commercial labels are nearly as wide as the disk itself (they come in two sizes, for 5¼-inch and 8-inch disks), so they can display a good deal more data than the half-sized freebies. Also, if you use a color-coding system, you can change the color markers without sacrificing the label.

▶ As you'd expect us to emphasize, a good routine for labeling disks will save you time and confusion when you're working. For example, when you open a box of new disks, it's a good idea to format all of them at once. You can indicate that a disk has been formatted and is ready to use by putting a symbol, such as 'F', on the tiny manufacturer's seal that is attached to every disk. When you put one of those formatted disks into service, you can write the appropriate information on the label, add color coding if you wish, and attach the label to the disk.

▶ Whenever you write on any disk label that's attached to the disk, use only a soft, felt-tipped pen—never a pencil or ballpoint. The more sharply pointed instruments make an impression in the disk jacket that could reach and damage the disk surface, just as writing with a ballpoint or pencil on the back of a photograph usually leaves a mark on the front of it.

A color-coding system is useful if you are juggling several different kinds of writing projects or several types of files for one big project. For example, you might use one color for the labels of all program disks, another color for correspondence, a third color for invoices and other financial data, and separate colors for each major project. If you divide a book or other large job into subdivisions, such as research notes, chapter outlines, drafts, and final manuscripts, you might also devise a subsidiary color labeling scheme for these related disks.

The least expensive way to implement a color-coding system is by using felt-tipped markers. You might put a wide line of the principal color across the top of each label, making it easily discernible, and a second color elsewhere on the label to identify its subcategory. The label manufacturers also make various color tabs and dots, which can be attached to the labels and easily changed as you recycle disks. The tiny color dots may be the most useful way to designate whether a disk is a backup or main working disk, because you will want to rotate these copies (see Chapter 7 for suggestions about disk rotation) and change this part of the label as you change the disk assignment.

▶ Whatever methods you devise for color coding and disk labeling, be sure to keep an accurate record of that scheme. This is a logical addition to a system diary, and a copy of these instructions should be kept on a handy printout and perhaps on your w/p program disk as well.

Cataloging Disks

As you generate more work—and therefore more disks— you're likely to want a quick reference to the contents of your electronic library. Perhaps the fastest and most elaborate way to keep track of all of your disks' contents is with a special Catalog program, which can generate a listing or update of each disk's files and also compare disk names and even search for specific files in the complete catalog. If you don't have such a program, however, you can still create a catalog with the utilities included in your w/p program and disk operating system.

▶ A disk catalog is one logical extension of the annotated Contents file on each text disk. You can simply print this file for each disk, or even copy all the Contents files onto one combined catalog disk, and make a printout that lists all your work. Using the Contents file has the advantage of containing your comments about each file, in addition to the filenames.

▶ If you haven't established a Contents file on your text disks, there's still a simple way to make a catalog of all the files you've generated. Almost all operating systems, as well as some w/p programs, have a utility that lets you print the contents of the screen. Thus, to make a listing of each disk's files, you could display the Disk Directory on the screen and then print the screen's contents.

▶ Once again, the usefulness of any cataloging method depends upon your faithfulness in updating your filenames or Contents files. So be sure to establish an updating routine—at the end of each workday, for example—during which you tidy up your current files, make backup copies of all new work, update the comments in each file and in the Contents file, change the filenames of any revised work, and revise the appropriate disk labels. You may not need to print out a new catalog listing each day; once a week would probably be adequate for the disks that have changed during that week. This entire updating procedure will take only a few minutes, and it could save you hours of trial-and-error searching through poorly named files on poorly labeled disks.

Protecting Disk Archives

Once you've finished a writing project and it has been published or otherwise given a final disposition, you can assign that work to your permanent archives. In rare instances, you may want to save the drafts as well as the final manuscripts and research for a project, but more often you'll probably erase many of the intermediate versions of the work and save only the raw material and the finished writing. As long as you label the disks well, you can easily combine all the files relating to a project on one or two archive disks. If you have a utility program that squeezes files, this is the ideal use for it— to condense data that you aren't likely to use often, if ever.

Most common w/p systems use disks that contain a write protect notch, which is a small indentation in one part of the disk cover. If this notch is covered in a 5¼-inch disk or uncovered in an 8-inch disk, the information on that disk is protected from accidental erasure or overwriting (unless your computer lacks the hardware to support this, as is the case with some systems). In addition, no new data may be recorded on that disk until the write-protection is removed. As noted previously, small paper tabs are supplied in most boxes of new disks for this purpose.

▶ Using the write protect feature is valuable for all of your archive disks, as well as for program disks that you don't want to change or erase by mistake. If you use the empty space on your w/p program disk as a buffer, though, you won't be able to write protect it. Always keep the write protect feature active on the factory original of program disks that you purchase; in most systems, you can copy the contents of a disk without removing the write protection.

Storing Disks

As we've made clear by now, good routines for organizing information will save you time and protect your work. And few routines are more important than the way you handle and store disks. The magnetic disk surfaces are vulnerable to dirt of all kinds, and these plastic storage units also can be rendered useless by direct sunlight or extremes of temperature. So putting disks away carefully in containers made specifically for them is crucial.

There are several types of disk containers, and any of them is satisfactory so long as you use it consistently. One of the most popular containers is a plastic box that holds up to fifty disks; it has a hinged cover and several dividers to separate the disks into small groups. Several variations of this type of box are made, including less expensive versions with separate covers that are not hinged. These large boxes are excellent for providing easy access to the disks that you use most often.

Another type of plastic container, often called a library box, holds ten disks. A few disk manufacturers supply disks in this type of box, and some versions of the library boxes are made to link together into horizontal or vertical rows, creating a self-contained shelf of disk storage. These smaller boxes are good for keeping all the disks for each project together, and they offer easily portable protection for carrying disks from one office to another.

One other useful disk storage device is a clear plastic page that holds one or two disks. These pages come in several versions; one kind fits into a three-ring notebook; another is attached to a conventional file folder (which can hold the printout of files on the disk); and a third has metal tabs at the top to fit into file drawers made for hanging folders.

▶ The disk storage system you select is largely a matter of personal preference, but the most efficient and safe system would probably be two or more types of containers. For example, you might choose a large covered disk box for current program and text disks; a three-ring notebook with disk pages for backup files; and file folder pages for the original copies of program disks. Each of these groups of disks should be kept in a different area of your office, and you could create an even more secure system by storing additional backup and archival copies in a location away from your office.

A System Diary

In Chapter 10 we suggested that you take careful notes when anything unusual happens with your equipment, so that you will have a complete record that can help diagnose any future problems. Keeping a diary is similarly useful for organizing your work: if you keep a record of the projects you're doing, the symbols and conventions you've developed for naming files and labeling disks, and the locations of all printed and electronic files, you'll have a detailed map of both your w/p system and your work style.

For example, you may be working on several projects simultaneously, and one or more may require that you submit a report of the hours spent on that job (a good thing to know even if you don't have to hand it in to someone). If you keep a notebook or stack of index cards near the keyboard, you can easily note the times you started and stopped work on each project. You might even time your work with a silent timer such as the stopwatch built into some calculators and wristwatches, or with the "real-time" clock that is part of some computer systems.

More important, you may need to consult your key to filenames and abbreviations that you used for various parts of a project. Six months ago, for instance, you may have written three different articles on ladybugs for which you used the same basic research. The one you sent to a gardening magazine has just been accepted, but the editor has asked for more details about the bug's lifespan and a rewrite of the section on pesticides. If you've adequately labeled both your research notes and your final draft of each article, you can go right to the correct disk (or disks) to find the information and make the changes you need. (In this instance, you might want to consult a printed copy of the article for initial revisions and write the new material with the processor.)

The precise contents of a w/p system diary will depend on your methods of identifying files and disks, storing working disks and backup copies, and handling printed manuscripts. The essential ingredients of this document, which should be kept within easy reach of your keyboard, would be similar for every system, however. These should include a list of symbols you use as part of filenames; a key to your labeling system for disks; an up-to-date listing of the directory of the text and program disks you use most frequently; a list of writing assignments and speculative projects and the time spent on each; an explanation of your disk storage procedures; and a record of any odd behavior from your equipment. Ideally, too, the diary should include a chart on which you faithfully record the fact that you've updated all current files and made copies of all working text disks according to some regular schedule.

Although this may sound like a lot of information to generate, all of these procedures become second nature once you've established working routines for them, and they will surely save you time when that request for a rewrite or follow-up article comes in. If you've named files and labeled disks coherently and have a ready reference for those identifiers, you won't have to shuttle five or six disks in and out of the computer, examining the contents of each one, to find the material you need. In short, whatever routines you use to organize your work, you'll have the best control of all your electronically generated information if you map your progress in a system diary.

Chapter 15

Networking

Computer Communications

Writing can be a lonely occupation at times, especially if you've got only a few boxes of electronics for company. Yet those boxes—with help from the telephone—can bring new life to your silent screen and let you swap ideas and work with other w/p writers. That is, with the addition of some relatively inexpensive hardware and software to your system, you can use the phone lines to hook up with other computers and to share their owners' resources as well as your own. In this final chapter, we'll explore some of the ways you can expand your horizons through computer communications.

The possibilities for electronic networking are enormous; the services available now are already impressive. Besides being able to tie your system into a phone line and call another computer, you can connect with large computers that store DATA BASES—huge collections of information on practically any topic—and you can use programs or play games that reside in distant computers, sometimes even copying the software for use on your own system. Collectively these call-up services are known as INFORMATION UTILITIES; several large commercial ventures have begun offering home-oriented data bases, either one-way systems, in which you receive information on your television screen but can't send data, or two-way systems, in which you use a computer or special terminal to communicate with the information service.

Of course you must pay for many of these services: there are always some telephone charges for calls out of your local area, calculated at the same rate you'd pay for conventional calls; and most of the data bases have subscription fees or costs for use of individual files. But there are also at least 300 free BULLETIN BOARDS and message services in the United States and Canada (and some in Europe, Australia, and Asia), and they are yours for the price of the call. Some of these public-spirited networks are in the vanguard of microcomputer use and development, and their messages and operators can be among the most lively companions a solitary writer could wish.

Necessary Hardware

Computer systems send information to other components a short distance away by using cables to carry their signals. For longer hauls, however, special cables are not practical, and the phone lines already in place link all but the most isolated offices and homes. So using the telephone system to transfer computer data is the obvious practical solution for computer networking.

Computers and telephone lines carry signals in different forms, however. The computer works with digital information, a process in which each character is divided into parts and each part is represented by a 0 or 1. Telephone lines carry audio information; they transfer voices and represent numbers or letters as a series of tones or pulses. Thus, to send digital data over phone lines, some means of translation is necessary; this back-and-forth transformation is done by a hardware device called a MODEM. Its slightly bizarre name derives from its functions—the modem "modulates" when translating computer signals to telephone signals, and it "demodulates" when changing signals from phone to computer form (hence, MOdulate-DEModulate).

Modems come in two styles: one has an ACOUSTIC COUPLER, which is basically a cradle into which you put the telephone receiver; the second is a DIRECT-CONNECT modem, which actually replaces the telephone by plugging into the phone outlet. Acoustic modems are less expensive (about $150) but also less accurate, because the connection between computer and telephone relies on actual sound-wave signals jumping back and forth in the cradle where the receiver rests, and any static or other interference might disturb the flow of information. Direct-connect modems cost more (about $300, and possibly much more) but offer greater accuracy in capturing all the data coming from the computer or the phone line; they also can move information at higher speeds than acoustic modems.

The speed of data transfer depends on the distance it travels and the efficiency of the modem. Microcomputers commonly transfer data to and from a terminal over a twelve-foot cable, for example, at a speed of 9600 data bits (approximately 960 characters) per second—far faster than any of us will ever strike the keys. Modems move data at more modest speeds, though still faster than we can blink; the most common rate for phone-line communications is 300 data bits (30 characters) per second (known in computer terminology as 300 BAUD). With more efficient—and expensive—modems, you can send or receive data at 600 or 1200 baud, provided that the phone lines can carry it that fast. (Interference on phone lines can be a problem, even at 300 baud, if the telephone equipment and connections in your area are not operating well.)

The difference between these rates of transfer is obvious; when you type a letter on the keyboard, it appears simultaneously on the screen (at least as far as we can discern), and when you use the DOS's Type utility to display a file's contents on the screen, the text flashes by far faster than you can read it. This is the 960 character-per-second rate (9600 baud) of the terminal; the ordinary modem rate of 30 cps is discernibly slower. If you are sending or receiving a file through a 300 baud modem, the text appears at a pace that is not too rapid for many readers. (In fact, working with text on the screen at 300 baud may be good speed reading practice for those of us who don't yet read that fast.)

Regardless of the type of modem you use, your computer must have one other feature to facilitate networking. This is a SERIAL PORT—the internal electronics and external plug that carry data to the modem. One or two serial ports are often built into a microcomputer, but they may be used for a terminal (if you have one) and a printer (though printers needn't use the serial port to operate—they can use another kind of port, called a PARALLEL PORT). If your system doesn't have a serial port available, you can generally purchase a BOARD or CARD that fits into the computer and contains the needed electronics; a few direct-connect modems even come as boards that are installed in the machine.

Software for Networking

The other prerequisite for computer networking is software to direct the operations. Computers can use different types or brands of modems and the systems won't know the difference, although their transfer speeds must be the same. The programs that control information transfer can assure that the baud rates are alike, but these programs must be compatible for two systems to communicate.

Many commercial programs are available for this purpose; they are usually called COMMUNICATIONS PROGRAMS, and they are always configured to work with a specific disk operating system or brand of computer. Some of this commercial software is able to operate on a number of different systems, and any two computers using that software could connect and transfer information. Systems using different communications programs may still be able to work together, but compatibility is not automatic, and you may need some help to modify a program so that you can "talk" to another type of system.

▶ If you know that you want to use a communications program to exchange data with certain specific systems, ask the distributors of the program if it can be used for that purpose. As a general rule, the more simply the program is designed, the greater its probability of working compatibly with other communications software. Some of the best "plain vanilla" communications programs are available for free or for very little cost from the public bulletin board services or the "users' groups" devoted to particular computers or operating systems. You can often find these folks (as well as bulletin board information) through computer magazines or helpful friends and dealers.

The communications software usually determines the extent of your networking capability. Most commercial or users' group programs have several components, so that you can dial phone numbers; send messages directly to another computer; transfer and receive disk files and save them on disk; and print information at the same time you're receiving it on the screen. Most of the bulletin boards and commercial information services have their own rather sophisticated software, which you begin using as soon as your modem connects your system with theirs, so your own communications program can be rudimentary if you only want to use these services.

In rare instances, you might be able to connect with a distant computer without using any software—or even any computer—on your end. In this situation you must be able to manually dial the phone number for the remote computer and put the phone into the acoustic modem's cradle; when you reach the other computer, you'll be using its software. Although such an arrangement may be cumbersome, this kind of networking is the cheapest way to gain access to a computer, because you'd be using a computer elsewhere without having one yourself. All you need for this purpose is a terminal and a modem, which could cost less than $500, as well as a telephone. (Of course all your work will have to be done and stored on that remote computer, and you could get printouts only by arrangement with people working wherever that computer is. And if that system isn't in your local calling area, you'll still have to pay the phone bills.)

Talking on the Silent Screen

Once you have the hardware and software for networking, you can converse on the screen with another w/p writer. At first this is an almost eerie sensation—you type in a message and it appears on the other person's screen, then he or she types a message to you. You see the incoming message in the same rhythm at which your friend's fingers are hitting the keys, complete with the cursor backing up to wipe out a mistake and the correct letter or word appearing in its place. Like many other aspects of this millisecond universe, talking with a terminal is a bit spooky, but you get used to it.

This screen-to-screen communication also has the virtue of being thoroughly democratic—that is, both participants begin with a kind of absolute equality. And for writers, this strictly egalitarian ground, where all you know about each other is what's on the screen, is the perfect place to practice the art of expressing yourself in words. You could find a group of instant pen pals, and you could even rehearse your fiction by writing it out on another person's screen and seeing how it plays.

Another great feature of networking is that you can participate in elaborate computer conversations and get feedback from all kinds of other people. The public bulletin boards and most commercial networks have message systems that allow you to leave a message for everyone who calls in or for a specific person or group. Some systems also allow you to code messages so that only the person you specify can read them and no one else can read the ones to you. But the real fun of bulletin boards is that we all can eavesdrop!

Two of the most widely used commercial information utilities, CompuServe (located in Columbus, Ohio) and The Source (in McLean, Virginia), have programs that let you enter into conversations as they're happening—not just a matter of reading messages that other people have left previously. This is a sort of on-screen conference call; everyone who is connected to that program can participate in the dialogue, which is handled by mainframe computers that can serve many remote computers at the same time and move information around so fast that the people at their screens don't realize they're waiting in line each time they "speak" from the keyboard.

The contacts you make through such on-screen conversations can be valuable for exchanging ideas and sharing experience. For example, you might point other writers to sources you've found for research and learn about additional avenues of investigation from them. Or several writers might exchange tips on writing query letters or book proposals; by using the bulletin board or electronic mail features of the public networks, you could also trade samples of successful queries and proposals.

Ultimately this kind of networking could develop into an informal support group for many far-flung writers. The group could establish one central phone number (an individual's computer or a public network) where any writer could read or copy a list of members and services, and add his or her name to that list. The central file could include phone numbers to contact other members' computers and the hours that these writers will be available; members' special interests and areas of expertise; and even a catalog of files that writers have donated to the group, such as queries, project proposals, and tips on working with editors and publishers.

Collaborating by Network

Even without a larger association of writers who communicate by computer, networking is ideal for collaboration. If you're working with another w/p writer on a shared project, you can hold conferences on screen and brainstorm together—with the important advantage that all of your conversation becomes part of an electronic file in both of your systems. These on-screen exchanges can lead to the same kind of excitement and synergy that in-person meetings often do, and because the network conversations are written, you'll be exercising your writing muscles (mental and physical) as you think together.

Networking also allows writers to exchange work by sending text files over the phone lines. So you could swap chapters with your collaborator or even send drafts and finished work to an editor or a friend for feedback. These are services still provided by mail carriers, of course, but once you and your collaborator both have the manuscript on your systems' disks, you can insert questions or new material in each other's work and then exchange the edited versions without having to wait for the mail.

Besides saving the time, cost, and bother of mailing text to each other, network collaborating truly provides instant gratification. You can get immediate feedback from your colleague when you want advice on a troublesome chapter or you're excited about your prose in a particular passage of text. More important, perhaps, you can see the project taking shape daily—as you exchange the new writing you've done, make editorial suggestions about each other's previous work, and plan the direction of the chapters to come. This sense of participation and joint effort can help buoy your spirits when the words come slowly or distractions threaten your concentration.

Being able to exchange files can likewise save a great deal of time and expense when researching a collaborative project. You can share information that you've gotten from the public bulletin boards or other public-domain sources of electronic data, thus saving the phone cost and time of duplicating that effort. If you're both doing research and will be using the commercial data bases (whose information is not in the public domain), you and your collaborator can divide up the work; each of you will spend less time and money for your individual research and you're less likely to do the same groundwork without realizing it.

Data-Base Research

Whether you are collaborating or working solo on a project, you could do much of the research for that writing through networking. The general-interest information utilities, such as CompuServe and The Source, contain several current data bases, including the contents of major newspapers, magazines, news wire services, and stock market listings. These services are relatively limited for serious research, however, because their data bases cover only recent material (newspapers for a month or two, usually, and magazines for a year or two) and the data is not completely indexed.

Major research projects will probably require access to more detailed and comprehensive data bases, some of which are available to individual computer users. These larger collections of information are used mainly by libraries, corporations, and government agencies, but writers can establish accounts with at least a few of the services and share in a wealth of technical, historical, and financial data. In addition to offering information from highly detailed and varied sources, the major data bases are thoroughly indexed so that you can search them for specific topics and key words.

The largest and most widely used of the major data-base services is DIALOG Information Service, which is operated by Lockheed and located in Palo Alto, California. This service offers some 130 separate data bases containing at least 50 million individual abstracts or records, and new collections of information are added regularly. There is no fee for opening a DIALOG account; you are charged a varying fee for each individual data base. These charges range from $10 to $300 per hour, though the majority of data bases cost less than $100 per hour. Of course you pay only for the time that you are actually using the service, so 22 minutes on a $90-per-hour data base would cost $33.

Although this may sound expensive, the searching you can do in a few minutes on one of these comprehensive and highly indexed sources would take many hours of library legwork and skullwork, and few libraries are likely to contain all of the publications and other data included in a large data base. In addition, DIALOG maintains two types of on-line order service; one will mail you printed copies of the abstracts or citations listed in the data bases, at a cost that usually ranges from $.10 to $.30 each, or you can use the other to order the complete article that is cited in a data base, at a higher cost—usually a minimum of $8 to $10 for an article that is ten pages or less. Still, most of the things you'd want to order are publications you couldn't find in any neighborhood library, or even on a college campus.

Just a sampling of the data bases available on DIALOG is impressive: all manner of government publications, lists of doctoral dissertations from major universities, newspaper and magazine indexes, foundation and grant listings, numerous social science and political science indexes, all of the major medical and health-related listings, business reports and indexes, environmental and energy information, and numerous scientific and technical data bases. For example, you can tap into the Aquatic Science and Fisheries Abstracts, the Philosopher's Index, the U.S. Public School Directory, the Exceptional Child Education Resources, Standard & Poor's News, the Encyclopedia of Associations, the Meteorological and Geoastrophysical Abstracts, and (dear to the hearts of many writers) the Book Review Index.

From the range of disciplines in even that small sampling of DIALOG data bases, it's easy to see why the service has 50 million records in its computers. (A record always includes either numerical information or a bibliographic citation and usually has an abstract as well.) The question, then, is how to find what you need among those millions of records and the several key words that have been indexed for each. DIALOG publishes guides to the data bases and general information on searching its files, and its staff teaches seminars on the service in major cities. If you plan to begin a research project and want to use DIALOG, it would be wise to read as much about the service as you can and ideally to take the introductory course before trying to use it extensively on your own.

► Once you have some knowledge of a sophisticated data-base service such as DIALOG, you'll want to develop a detailed plan for each search you intend to make. For best results, you should create a special strategy file for each research project, store that file on disk, and have a printout of the strategy next to your terminal before connecting your computer to the service. Then you won't waste time looking up the service's commands or the names of data bases while the phone and data-base charges are adding up.

► You will also be able to make the best use of any commercial data-base service if you are thoroughly familiar with your own computer system and its abilities to communicate via modem and phone lines. Once you're connected to a data base or subscription service that's charging you pennies per second of time that you're using its computers, you want to know what your hardware and software can do and how to efficiently copy information on your printer or to your disk files for later use.

► To save on telephone charges, you may be able to use one of the low-cost alternative phone services to call commercial data bases and public bulletin boards. The description of each information utility or bulletin board usually will contain this information—so you may have to call a service once over the regular phone channels to find out if the long-distance money saver you use will connect with it. In addition, there are several "data line" services that use special phone lines to carry computer information; two of the most widely used are Telenet and Tymnet. These services have local phone numbers in many cities and their per-hour charges are usually lower than long-distance calls or even message-unit charges in many places. You can generally get information about these special data lines from the commercial data-base services.

Words into Type

Many writers have been sending their words directly into type for years. Reporters and editors for most large newspapers do their work on desktop terminals that are linked to a central computer and storage source. The stories are written and filed in the computer, then called up and edited by the editorial staff of the paper. The edited files are then sent back to storage, where they are called by the page makeup department, designed into pages, and sent back to the computer for automatic typesetting in page-ready form.

Now that many writers have personal word processing equipment available, this author-to-editor-to-typesetter chain is becoming commonplace in the magazine and book publishing fields. As a writer, you can complete your story and send it via your modem and the phone lines to your publisher. In many publishing firms, the copy editor works directly within your file using the publisher's word processor and regular editing techniques.

Before the edited manuscript can be sent to the typesetter, some special adjustments must be made. Professional typesetting equipment (which has been computerized for more than a decade) uses its own set of control codes and provides many more formatting options than regular word processors offer. So two conversion steps must be taken: the processor's control codes must be translated into the typesetter's codes, and new codes must be entered to specify the extra typesetting options.

The first of these two steps is accomplished by a TRANSLATION TABLE. This is a separate file, created by the typesetter for the author's specific word processing program, that makes some necessary standard conversions. For example, it is very unlikely that the line length established by the word processing program will be the line length of the printed material. The Translation Table might therefore replace the Returns or Word Wrap signals normally encountered at the end of every line of a word processing file with spaces, so the typesetting equipment can reset its own line length. Other conversions might translate certain w/p characters into typesetting characters, such as converting two consecutive hyphens into the typesetting character known as an "em" dash.

Many typesetters now keep on file standard Translation Tables for the popular word processing programs. Basically, these tables work as subprograms that screen and convert the word processing file as it is received by the typesetter's modem. In many cases, the typesetter can simply receive your file using the Translation Table for your program, although some special adjustment of the table may be necessary to deal with peculiarities in your file or special design considerations.

When a manuscript is sent to a typesetter, it must be encoded with type specifications indicating the typesetting font, point size, leading between lines, margins and indentations, and a host of other variables. With a typewritten manuscript, these codes are normally marked by hand on the manuscript by the graphic designer. With a word processing file, however, these codes can be inserted into the file electronically before it is sent to the typesetter. These TYPESETTING CODES are flagged by special symbols, such as percent signs and dollar signs. The graphic designer or editor can insert them into your text file just as if they were commands recognized by your word processor. When the typesetting equipment reads the codes, it performs the necessary formatting operations. Some typesetting codes are illustrated in Table 15-1, with a portion of encoded manuscript illustrated in Figure 15-1.

The extent to which you need to become familiar with these procedures will depend on the type of writing you do. If you're submitting an article to a magazine, the publisher's editors and designers will probably coordinate the necessary conversions. If you're producing your club's newsletter or a report for your company, you might work directly with the typesetter to create your own custom Translation Table and insert the proper typesetting codes. Regardless of how involved you become, you should keep a few points in mind if you are preparing electronic text that you know is going to be converted for typesetting.

▶ Do not insert soft hyphens between syllables of words in your text, or use a Justified format, even if the final typeset version will be hyphenated and justified. Your w/p format conventions will only have to be stripped away, and there's no need to create extra problems that must be solved in the conversion process. (This does not apply to using hard hyphens in terms that are always hyphenated, such as "well-being.")

▶ Use print enhancements such as boldface and underlining sparingly, if at all. Your processor's codes for these enhancements

Table 15-1: Typical Translation Codes

Code	Typesetting Result
%CN	Chapter start format call
%AA	Section heading format call
%SC	Small caps format call
<CFTRI>	Change font—Times Roman Italic
<CFTR>	Change font—Times Roman
<EP>	End Paragraph/Paragraph Indent
<AF>	Automatic fractions on
<AX>	Automatic fractions off
<MC>	Merge copy
$TR	Triangle Right symbol
$BV	Bullet symbol
$NL	Less Than symbol
$NM	Greater Than symbol
$BN	Open Bracket symbol
$BM	Close Bracket symbol
$AF	Ampersand symbol
$NO	Crosshatch Number symbol
$EQ	Equals symbol
$PL	Plus symbol

```
          B:FIG15-1   PAGE 1 LINE 1 COL 01           INSERT ON
L——!———#———!———#———!———#———!———#———!———#———!———#———R
```
"squeeze-in" type of Insert mode.
%AABlock Moves<MC>We now come to one of the word processor's most
powerful editing tools—the feature that permits you to move
blocks of text from one position to another. Although the
operation of the %SCBLOCK MOVE<MC> function varies widely from
system to system, it invariably involves three steps:
identifying the block, locating the position to which it is to be
moved, and inserting the block at that position.
<EP>To identify the block of text, you insert two %SCBLOCK
MARKERS<MC>, at the beginning and the end of the segment to be
moved. In most systems, you place the cursor at the first
character of the block and give the command to insert a special
character in the displayed text. You then perform a similar
routine after the last character of the block. In some systems,
the marked block may be highlighted on the screen or the block
markers themselves may serve as delimiters. Figure 4—11 shows a
screenful of text in which the last paragraph has been marked as
a block with beginning and end symbols (NLBNM and NLKNM).
<EP>To move the paragraph, you move the cursor to the location in
the text at which you want to insert the marked block (in our
example, to the top of the screen). You give the %SCINSERT
BLOCK<MC> (or %SCMOVE BLOCK<MC>) command, and <CFTRI>Voila!<CFTR>
the text disappears from its former location, appearing at the

---

Fig. 15-1: Encoded manuscript

may be readily converted into type, but unless you're thoroughly
familiar with the typesetter's equipment, you're better advised to flag
special typographic conventions with easily searched-for standard
symbols that can be converted into the proper codes. (And be sure to
keep a list of those symbols.)

▶ Don't use special print commands such as Conditional Page
Breaks and Linking instructions. In general, a file to be typeset
should be as plain and free of embellishments as possible. Of course,
if you have established a regular conversion procedure with a typesetter, you can create your files from the beginning using that typesetter's Translation Table and codes.

The benefit of sending your writing directly to type is, of
course, a considerable savings of time and money. Just as the word
processor eliminates the need for you to retype your manuscript
through several drafts, automatic typesetting avoids having to re-key
the entire job through the typesetting machinery. The streamlining of
the copy editor's and graphic designer's work provides added time-
saving benefits, while the chance of errors creeping in throughout the
writing-editing-designing-typesetting process is reduced to an absolute minimum.

Electronic Publishing

For all its remarkable benefits, automated typesetting still represents using twentieth-century technology to facilitate a process invented in the fifteenth century. The most impressive use of the word processor as a writing tool is true "electronic publishing"—distributing written information in digital form. We are just on the threshold of this new publishing era.

Some experiments in this concept are already under way. Both CompuServe and The Source reserve segments of their network services for authors to transmit their files to the network and place them in public access. The network keeps track of how many people have read (the computer verb is "accessed") each file. On the Source program, authors are paid a royalty of sorts, based on the total access time of their files.

It is inevitable that as more writers (and readers) gain the use of word processors, and as improved methods for transmitting, displaying, and printing text with computers evolve, more public and special-interest networks will emerge to carry written information. And this process will help achieve what all writers want—to have their work published and read.

Epilogue

Writing Reborn

The Computer Age is upon us, and it's here to stay. This technological revolution, like others before it, has changed our daily lives: we do push-button budgeting, banking, and cooking; we watch movies and play games full of electronic sights and sounds; and we cope with a seemingly endless stream of bills, junk mail, and even phone calls that have reached us by computer. As the twentieth century closes, we're likely to feel the impact of computers even more—from two-way televisions, which can record our votes and grocery orders, to "vocal" computers, which can transcribe what we say and even talk back to us.

Most of these fruits of the Computer Age are marvelous and helpful, but a few may be threatening and perhaps awful. Missiles and bombs are programmed to find their targets, and do; unquestioning machines doggedly insist that we owe hundreds or thousands of dollars because somebody put a decimal in the wrong place. But those machines are our inventions and our servants, and we are responsible for their behavior. In other words, we're still in the driver's seat, and it's vital that we remain in control.

That goes for writing in the Computer Age, as well. At times we may think that all this button-pushing and electronic entertainment will hurt writing and publishing and reading. Certainly technology has altered the way we go about these activities, but the bookstores and newsstands are still brimming with printed pages, and the libraries are doing plenty of business.

In fact, writing is central to the use of computers. If you connect with a data-base service, the majority of the information displayed on your television or computer screen will be written— newspaper articles, wire-service bulletins, store catalogs. As these information services grow to include extensive, specialized works, such as doctoral theses or highly technical monographs, you'll go to the library—or call up the library with your computer—and read electronic files on a screen instead of turning pages. But the point is, these files will continue to originate with writers and will be visited by readers.

Both reading and writing are unique experiences for which there are no substitutes; the means of delivery may change, but the experience and responses will not. The Computer Age cannot diminish the universal human desire to communicate with words—to express emotions and describe events through writing and to glimpse other lives and other worlds through reading. Whatever form writing takes—and whatever tools the writer uses—its foundry is always the human mind and imagination.

Some observers have noted, though, that if technological devices such as computers and television become too prominent in our lives, their influence may damage our powers of imagination and thought. Certainly this is a valid concern, to which we should respond by conscientiously engaging our senses and finding ways to express our ideas. As writers, that's what we already do.

Regardless of the increasing availability and decreasing cost of computers as writing instruments, many writers will choose to forgo them. In the coming decade, however, many more—perhaps most— writers will adapt these tools to their styles of working and enjoy the benefits of word processing. We've named the benefits often in these pages: a keyboard that can keep up with the fastest fingers and thought patterns, a collection of powerful features for editing, searching, and copying text, and a set of electronic guidelines for versatile design and automatic printing of pages.

Neither writing nor literacy is threatened by the computer. In addition to the thousands, even millions, of writers who work with word processors, at least as many people will begin writing because they have access to these electronic tools. As microcomputers become commonplace in offices and homes, people will increasingly put their ideas, research, and feelings into words. In a great many instances, these will be the same people who once dictated memos and letters, did business on the phone, or simply refrained from putting their thoughts in writing because they weren't comfortable with the process. But if they use a computer keyboard and screen for other daily tasks, they're sure to discover how easy and natural fingertip thinking can be.

So in one sense, with such a large population of writers out there, we could risk some decline in the quality of writing as the quantity of written information mushrooms. As always, though, committed writers—whether long-time professionals or recent initiates—will be the guardians of literacy and language. There is no reason to suppose that, with the ease of recording thoughts and the power of editing them that word processing offers, working writers are going to let their product suffer.

Quite the opposite is likely. Because writers can fashion so many combinations of words and express thoughts in so many ways, then edit and revise, study printed pages and edit more, the clear prospect is that word processing will enhance the craft of writing. Indeed, even people who seldom wrote before they had computers will probably become better writers as they gain experience in using words to convey their thoughts.

There is one other risk in computer writing, however. This is the potential for homogenization of language and style, which may result from "advanced" word processing options such as vocabulary and grammar-checking programs (similar to the spelling-checking programs so widely used today). Once again, writers must be the guardians of style and usage, and we must be rigorous in expanding the boundaries of our territory—going beyond the limits of the words in a thesaurus-on-disk, not subscribing to every constraint of a grammar-checking program, knowing the broader rules for building structures with words and occasionally breaking those rules on purpose to achieve a literary innovation or a desired impact of language and form.

As writers sustain the literary traditions into the Computer Age, we are likely to have more outlets for our work and a greater variety of readers. The commercial information services will need a constant supply of new material to offer subscribers, in much the same way as the cable television networks do now. In some instances, too, we will be able to enjoy instant publication—on the computer networks and bulletin boards that are free to everyone, and perhaps even as freelance contributors to the electronic newspapers and magazines that are certain to develop.

Yet this electronic future does not spell the death of printed pages. Just as computer technology has made writing faster and more efficient, similar advances will translate electronic files into books or manuscripts many times faster than printers can operate at present. Extremely fast laser printers are currently used in high-budget, high-volume offices, and their low-budget equivalents are not far off. Within a few years, readers should be able to walk into an "information store," order copies of the latest books in specialized disciplines or reprints of popular articles from out-of-print magazines, and have these works printed while they wait.

Although the video displays for electronic files have been vastly improved and made easily portable, most of us will continue to find that a printed page or manuscript offers the fastest, most accessible, and most permanent way to consume information. Even if wristwatch- or passport-sized computers become as common as personal tape-and-headphone units, we will demand a means of transforming the screen's image into printed words, numbers, and pictures that we can pass around or file away.

What all of this coming technology promises is that all writers can do their work more artfully and more productively than ever before. And from that plethora of pages will come a rebirth of writing—new skills, new literary styles, and new sources of communication. Many of those developments are still on the horizon, but their harbinger is here in word processing.

This technology has already lived up to its promise. What word processing has given us, finally, is the chance to do our best—to risk telling our stories and naming our visions with all the power and precision that words can carry. What more could a writer ask?

Appendix

A Biased Guide to Word Processors

For this appendix, we have singled out a number of features and functions that we believe are especially valuable for efficient, powerful writing. These are not all of the word processing features available, nor do we intend this guide to stand alone in representing our explanation of word processing. In other words, the choices that follow are personal and by no means exhaustive. They should be weighed together with the detailed discussions of all major w/p equipment and features in Chapters 1 through 15.

We've been moderate in making judgments about word processing systems in this book, and for a significant reason. We have yet to see the "perfect" w/p system, and doubt that we will find one that would suit all writers, whose needs, styles, and points of view differ widely.

We also believe that, within certain limits, working on a word processor—almost any word processor—gives every writer a valuable new perspective on his or her craft and unprecedented freedom and power in creating text and shaping words. Any writer who has the opportunity to work on a w/p system should take full advantage of it, exploring the system's capabilities to the fullest without feeling stymied by its particular limitations.

Nevertheless, it's natural that we should be asked what our "mythical, universal" word processor would be like if we could specify its features, and what we would consider important if we were shopping for a new system. So, with the caveat that this ideal system does not exist—and the encouragement to be curious and fearless with your own system—we offer the following biased guide.

Hardware

The commonplace advice given to prospective computer purchasers is: Choose the software first and then choose the hardware to run it. This may be a sound recommendation for those with primarily computing needs, such as payroll, accounting, or inventory control. For writers choosing word processors, however, we offer the opposite (and perhaps radical) view: Evaluate the keyboard and screen first and then choose the best available software. For all the intricacies of w/p program features and functions, the inescapable fact is that a word processor is a tool, and a tool that doesn't fit the hand (and please the eye) will not serve you well.

As writers, we seem to be very particular about our writing implements. We've all treasured a certain pen or pencil, a brand of yellow pad, a "creative" chair, or a twenty-year-old, trusty typewriter. Perhaps these preferences reflect our attempt to find the most direct path from mind to page. Or perhaps these are merely self-indulgent obsessions to comfort us in the struggle to squeeze our thoughts into concrete form. Regardless, if you're about to give up your traditional favored writing tool, you should replace it with a worthy successor.

The qualities of the ideal keyboard will be determined by your personal taste; you should not compromise in the selection of a keyboard that is pleasant and responsive to your touch. If the keyboard layout is slightly different from the typewriter keyboard you're used to, you'll probably make an adjustment fairly easily; however, make sure that frequently used characters (such as the apostrophe, whose position varies on computer keyboards) are conveniently accessible.

The attributes of the screen display are also largely a matter of taste. The great debate concerning the virtues of white, green, and amber screens is left for you to resolve (though we personally find green screens the most eye-pleasing). The resolution of the characters on the display is critical, however. They should look like solid, fully formed letters—not a collection of dots—and be easy to read even when the screen is full of text.

Now our biases come into full expression: We emphatically recommend that the keyboard be detachable from the rest of the system hardware (that is, connected to the system by a cable). You want the maximum flexibility in positioning the keyboard at a comfortable typing angle, and it is unlikely that you'll be able to accomplish this if you have to accommodate a cabinet containing a video screen, processing unit, and disk drives.

Another reason for keeping the keyboard separate is that the most comfortable viewing distance to the screen is likely to be eighteen inches to two feet or more, and will vary among users. Most terminals combining keyboard and screen place the screen much closer. Furthermore, we believe that the writing experience is much more pleasant if you're not constantly being confronted by a hulking, humming, phosphorescent piece of equipment. (Our preferred position for the screen is slightly to one side of the keyboard, about two feet away.)

We're such minimalists when it comes to w/p hardware that we also prefer the screen to be housed in a separate unit, free of slots for disk drives and processor cabinetry. With this arrangement, you can position and tilt the screen to achieve the best viewing angle and put the rest of the hardware further from your immediate working space.

These ergonomic considerations are as important as any program feature. You are going to be spending many hours with your fingers, eyes, and spine devoted to your system. You should definitely be able to find a word processor with all the program features you need without compromising on the system's physical setup. Don't be tempted to settle for a second-choice keyboard-screen configuration in pursuit of some exotic word-manipulating function; your back is even more important than your prose.

A few words about printers: For final printed copy of important documents, you'll undoubtedly want to use a letter-quality printer. However, a letter-quality printer can cost as much as half to two-thirds of the rest of your system. If you're on a limited budget and still looking for a way to start writing in the Computer Age, you should consider a dot-matrix printer. These are half the cost of the least expensive letter-quality printers, and many dot-matrix models produce quite legible output. (Just make sure that the printed characters have "true descenders" that extend below the printed line.)

If you do rely on a dot-matrix printer for your personal use, you could locate a letter-quality printer compatible with your system that you can use for your final copy. As more writers use word processors, outlets offering the use of letter-quality printers at an hourly rate should proliferate. This is a viable business, comparable to copy services. If you can afford a letter-quality printer (the less expensive ones function quite well, by the way), we'd recommend one.

Regardless of which type of printer you select, be sure that your w/p program specifically supports it. Getting programs to interface successfully with the wide variety of printers available is the most troublesome aspect of word processing. Don't rely on "spec sheets." Demand a demonstration of your system hardware and software actually running together and print some text that you can take away and examine at your leisure.

Be wary also of a printer that is designed to run only with a certain program. You will probably be using the printer for computer functions beyond word processing. We advise choosing a well-known and popular make and model of printer that numerous programs are likely to support.

We think that the least important hardware consideration is the storage capacity of your disk drives. (Disks, as opposed to cassettes, are pretty much a must for serious word processing.) The current minimum standard storage format seems to be single-side, double-density, 5¼-inch disks, which can hold about 160,000 bytes. This is the equivalent of about eighty to one hundred double-spaced typewritten pages, and should be adequate for most conventional writing needs. (Note, however, that some w/p programs automatically create backup files, so that the effective storage capacity is cut in half.)

More disk storage is certainly convenient, particularly if you want to do extensive global searches or link several files for printing. However, we do not recommend that writers choose a system based on mega-storage capability if it necessitates compromising on the essential hardware features such as detachable keyboard and legible monitor. (If you absolutely need the extra storage capacity, you can usually add it as a separate option.)

In some systems, you can likewise expand the internal computer memory at a later time. Whether or not you choose to do this, you should select a system with sufficient memory to work with your w/p program and accommodate files of adequate size at the same time. This usually translates to memory of 64K or more.

Editing

Most of the time you spend with the word processor is going to involve writing and editing, so you should carefully evaluate the editing features when choosing a system. A few features—such as Word Wrap and screen-oriented scrolling and cursor movement—are so important for writing that we would hardly consider a program to be a real word processor without them. (Some programs, usually called text editors, deal with text on a line-by-line basis only and are really not suitable for extensive writing and editing.)

Beyond those elemental features, the most important consideration is how the program inserts text. We've described several of the alternative methods in the body of this book; our personal preference is for an Insert function that squeezes new characters into the text, moving the existing text to the right without creating any holes. More critical than the insertion method is the ability to keep Insert in effect throughout an editing session, rather than having to give a command every time an insertion is to be made. (Our preference is for an on/off toggle command for the Insert function.) Roughly half of your editing work is going to involve inserting text, and you should be able to do this with a minimum of effort and conscious activity.

Much of the rest of your editing time will be spent deleting text. Three Delete functions are especially important: Delete a Character, Delete a Word, and Delete to End of Line. If these three functions work well, you can make any desired correction very efficiently. If these three are difficult to use, all the other exotic Delete possibilities are not going to save you from frustration.

The two other vital editing functions are Block Moves and Search and Replace. With Block Moves, the critical factor is ease of operation. You should be able to mark blocks in a logical fashion and move them by placing the cursor at a new location and giving a single command. (You should also have the option to copy a block as well as move it.)

Take special note of whether there is a limitation on the size of block that can be transferred. (This may be limited by the computer's memory size.) If there is a limitation on the nature of the block that can be moved (such as marking a block only at the beginning or end of a line—not in the middle), this is not a significant inconvenience, since most of the time you will be moving whole paragraphs.

The best way to determine whether a program's Block Move limitations will hinder your work is to test the feature thoroughly before choosing a program. You will get the best idea of how these w/p features coincide with your work style if you evaluate them while editing some of your own writing.

The key consideration for Search and Replace is not so much ease of operation as sophistication in specifying the Search String and options in making replacements. Having the ability to ignore upper- or lowercase letters in the Search String is a very useful feature. Being able to replace either globally or selectively is a must. It's also very useful to be able to locate control characters (such as the symbols used to designate underlining or paragraph ends) with the Search and Replace functions.

Finally, we take a middle-ground stance in the function-key debate. Having special keys assigned to program functions definitely makes it easier to learn a new w/p system. But if you're choosing a program mainly for your personal writing needs, you'll find that you will learn program commands fairly quickly and easily, regardless of whether you have to hit one key or several keys in sequence.

Certain functions are used so often that it can be handy to have special keys reserved for them. Here's our biased list, which essentially summarizes the editing features we've discussed:

- Cursor Movement (all four directions)
- Cursor to Right/Left Word
- Cursor to Top/Bottom of Screen
- Scroll Up/Down Screenful
- Scroll to Beginning/End of File
- Insert Mode
- Delete Character
- Delete Word
- Delete to End of Line
- Reform Paragraph
- Mark Block Beginning/End
- Move/Copy Block
- Search/Replace
- Help Menu
- Cancel Command/Halt Printing

These are the functions that you'll use regularly while writing and editing. Even though most keyboards cannot provide a special key for each of these functions, the keystrokes you use to invoke these commands should be logical, comfortably located on the keyboard, and easy to remember. Most other functions are invoked so infrequently (and so consciously) that it's not inconvenient to require multiple-keystroke commands for them.

Finally, we find it a great convenience to work with a program that displays the formatted text on the screen during the writing and editing process. This feature shows you where pages will end and how lines will be spaced, so that you can see the results of your formatting decisions when you make them originally or revise them later.

Printing

Whatever system you encounter, it will undoubtedly feature a much-detailed array of print-formatting commands. However logical these commands are, they will require some study and experimentation. Perhaps the most desirable program feature for print formatting is the ability to store collections of commands as "canned" formats so that you won't have to figure out the specifications every time you print a letter.

The system should provide you with the ability to specify at least one heading or footing, and preferably two or more. You should be able to designate the position of the page numbers anywhere within the top and bottom margins and to specify the numeral with which numbering will start.

Another collection of vital features provides a way of controlling the paging of the printed output. Forced and Conditional Page Break instructions are necessary to avoid unexpected printing results. A method of previewing the page breaks (either on-screen while editing or as a separate Print to Screen feature) is required to take advantage of the page-break options.

There are many sophisticated printing features that apply more to general computing and office work than to pure writing. If you know that you'll have special needs (such as writing film scripts, producing reports with unusual formats, or dealing with numerical text), you'll naturally want to think through your intended applications and determine whether the w/p system can format and print it. Generally, if you are able to specify varying formats within a document, you'll be able to devise a way to solve almost any printing application.

If you have invested in a letter-quality printer, your w/p program should support its print-enhancement features, such as boldface, underlining, microjustification, and bidirectional printing.

If you are limited in the size of your text files, because of disk capacity, processor memory, or program structure, then the ability to link several files during printing will be a necessary feature.

Evaluating a program's printing capability is very much a "What if?" exercise. The one thing you can count on is making an error during some of your printing jobs. As we have already stressed, the ability to reprint selected pages will be a welcome feature in these instances. We'd hate to have to work on a system that didn't let you recover from your errors with a minimum of effort.

File Management

The mark of a truly elegant word processing system is the flexibility it affords in the storage and manipulation of disk files.

If you are going to be working with a general-purpose computer rather than a dedicated word processor (see our discussion below), be wary of a w/p system that doesn't store text in the standard format of the computer's disk operating system. Aside from the advantage of using your system's DOS utilities to copy, erase, and name files, keeping your files in standard format will make them "transportable" to other computer functions (such as spread sheet and data-base programs) as well as to other computers sharing the same operating system.

Within the w/p program, you want to be able to do two things: break apart one large file into several smaller ones and assemble a new file out of the pieces. Both of these procedures involve Writing blocks of text to different files and Reading files into the current text. These file-manipulation functions aren't likely to seem important when you're evaluating a w/p system for the first time, but they're really crucial once you've established yourself as a w/p writer and have all your work residing in several hundred files on twenty disks or more.

A final factor to consider is whether the system requires you to name files before editing them or whether you can save and name files after you've worked on them. As we mentioned earlier in this book, the two methods of file storage and nomenclature depend on how files being edited are stored in the computer's memory. All things being equal, you have more flexibility if you are able to work on a new file without naming it and if you are able to change disks in the middle of an editing session.

Program Structure

The "shape" of the entire program is another factor that you're not likely to consider when you're evaluating specific features but that can have a significant effect on your work routines.

Examine carefully the default values for all the program functions. More important than these initial defaults is the ability to modify them (preferably in a new configuration of the program) to suit your tastes and needs. Here's our biased list of the functions for which you might want to change the defaults:

- On-screen Margins
- Justification on/off
- Hyphenation on/off
- Insert Mode on/off
- Help/Command Menus on/off
- All Print-formatting Values !!!

Virtually all programs will allow you to override the defaults for these parameters with specific commands; what you want to be able to do is have the program start up with your desired values already in effect.

Another overall consideration is how "mode-intensive" the program is. It's logical for a program to be structured into editing, printing, and file management modes that must be entered to invoke their functions. Any further division of program functions into exclusive segments will force you to keep a road map in your head while you're working. Whatever a program's structure, you should be able to move freely from any program mode to any other.

A menu-oriented command system can aid greatly in both learning a program and keeping track of your place within it. In the Editing mode, a Help Menu that lists the available editing commands is a necessity for a program to be user-friendly. (Just as important for user-friendliness is the ability to turn the Help Menu off.)

In the Printing mode, you should have available a menu or chart that lists all the printing commands in effect and the ability to alter any or all of them.

The File Management mode should display as much information about the disk files as can be incorporated into a screen display. The minimum information necessary to manipulate files includes the file names, dates of creation, and file size in bytes.

Menu routines can become an impediment if you're forced to proceed through lengthy menus just to execute simple commands. The ideal menu structure permits you to leave the menu at any point. It can also be helpful to be able to specify commands directly, without entering menus, especially once you've become proficient with your program. However, we believe that an intelligent grouping of program functions into menus and/or modes is an aid to developing smooth work routines.

Options

How far you should be able to extend a program's functions depends on your writing needs. Making recommendations in this area would be like advising you whether to put a trailer hitch on your car. But there are two program bells and whistles that we feel should be incorporated into any w/p system.

The first extension is a good Spelling Checker. Reviewing a manuscript for misspelled words is such an obvious good use of computing power that it's almost criminal not to have this function available. (This is an important consideration in choosing a w/p program—is a Spelling Checker available for it?)

The major factor in evaluating a good spell-checking utility is the size of its dictionary. Anything less than 20,000 words will leave out some that you consider quite ordinary. Just as important is the ability to add your own special words to the dictionary. Beyond that, the prime consideration should be flexibility: Do you have the option to ignore capitalized words, and to correct a word, leave as is, or add it to the exception dictionary? The best spelling programs permit you to see the words in context and suggest possible correct spellings for misspelled words.

The other option we would recommend is not a program feature per se, but an addition to your w/p system. That is the ability to engage in computer communications via a modem and the phone lines. For this, you'll need a spare serial communications port in your processor unit, a modem (which might be incorporated in the port), and a communications program to send your files through the port. (The communications program could conceivably be incorporated into your word processing program; more likely, it will be a separate program.)

Our reason for recommending the communications option is, once again, that it is too wonderful a computing function not to have at your disposal. Your word processor gives you tremendous power in creating your work and in shaping it. You should not be confined to sharing it with others in hard-copy form. The expansion of computer communications and networking is the next great leap forward in the Computer Age, and you can easily place yourself in this vanguard.

Dedicated Word Processors or Microcomputers?

We'll conclude by taking a firmly biased stance in another debate—whether a writer should invest in a computer dedicated to word processing or whether he or she should acquire a general-purpose microcomputer and equip it with a word processing program.

The proponents of dedicated word processors claim that "micros" just can't match the special function keys, formatting options, and ease of operation that dedicated systems offer. They believe that using a microcomputer for word processing requires writers to learn more about computers than should be necessary just for writing. The dedicated machines are designed to do one job well, they argue, and so don't have to make compromises in w/p functions.

The opposing view is that using a computer only for writing is a waste of computing power and possibilities. There are many functions apart from pure writing, such as data-base management, numerical spread sheet calculation, communications, and—yes—music, art, and games, that are being transformed by the Computer Age just as dramatically as the writing arts. Why decide that writing on a computer is a significant advance, the micro proponents reason, and yet deny yourself the opportunity to experiment in and experience the rest of the computer world?

Before stating our position, we should note that the lines of this debate are eroding. The manufacturers of dedicated machines are now offering them with the option of running standard microcomputer operating systems, precisely so that the broader computer functions can be utilized. At the same time, the authors of word processing programs for micros are expanding the functions of their programs so that they match the dedicated systems virtually feature for feature. The distinction between dedicated machines and micros is likely to be minimized further as new machines and programs are developed.

We have taken our place in the micro camp. (We considered both types of systems and chose to do our writing on microcomputers.) For an individual purchasing a computer for normal writing work, we believe that a microcomputer-based w/p system will function as well—and cost about two-thirds as much—as a dedicated word processor. But our bias is not based purely on a function/cost analysis.

We undertook this book project with a double-barreled enthusiasm—for writing and for a newfound tool, the word processor. As we have used our systems for researching and writing, our enthusiasm for our traditional craft has been renewed. In the process, however, we have happily become computer evangelists. Which is to say that writing with a word processing system has revolutionized both our careers—not only because of the ease and productivity with which we now work, but, perhaps more exciting, because of the new avenues we've begun to explore with the new technology at our disposal.

This book is about writing, for writers. But it describes only one of many journeys possible in the Computer Age. We urge all of you to become full-fledged computer citizens—as writers, poets, artists, musicians, programmers, number-crunchers, networkers, and radical thinkers—charting your own routes along the many paths now visible and the many more not yet imagined.

Bibliography

Our primary reference sources for this book were our own and other writers' experience in working with word processors, as well as the variety of hardware and software that we investigated. (These products are mentioned in the Acknowledgments.) Although there is little published information that focuses on word processing from the writer's perspective, the articles listed below pertain to certain specific aspects of this technology. In addition, we have suggested several books that we believe to be useful resources for all w/p writers, along with the names of selected magazines and information utilities. We offer these resources as starting points for your own explorations into writing, word processing, and computing.

Articles

Holman, Elli. "The Global Link: Data Banks." *Personal Computing*, October 1981, pp. 35–37ff.

Jong, Steven. "Word Processing Software Roundup." *Personal Computing*, January 1981, pp. 26–33.

Kleiner, Art. "Information Detective Stories." *CoEvolution Quarterly*, Winter 1980, pp. 122–127.

Leerburger, Benedict A. "Almost Like Having a Finicky Old-fashioned English Teacher in the Box." *Think*, November/December 1981, pp. 26–30.

Maloney, Eric. "Video Display Terminals." *Kilobaud Microcomputing*, July 1981, pp. 43–59.

Perry, Robin. "A Writer's Guide to Word Processors." *Writer's Digest*, April 1981, pp. 21–30.

Press, Larry. "Getting Started in Personal Computing." *On Computing*, Spring 1981, pp. 8–17.

Rhodes, Cheryl. "The DIALOG Information Retrieval System." *DataCast*, No. 2 (1981), pp. 51–62.

Rowlett, Frank B., Jr. "Rotating Disk-ettes." *Interface Age*, February 1982, pp. 86–87.

Walker, John. "Adequate Backup: Protecting the Data in Your Computer." *Desktop Computing*, October 1981, pp. 16–21.

Woodbury, Bob. "Beyond Gutenburg." *Kilobaud Microcomputing*, May 1981, pp. 93–101.

Books

Derfler, Frank J. *Microcomputer Data Communication Systems*. Englewood Cliffs, N.J.: Prentice-Hall/Spectrum, 1982.

Elbow, Peter. *Writing With Power*. New York: Oxford University Press, 1981.

Follett, Wilson. *Modern American Usage*. New York: Warner Books, 1974, 1977.

Frenzel, Louis E., Jr. *The Howard W. Sams Crash Course in Microcomputers*. Indianapolis: Howard W. Sams, 1980.

Sippl, Charles J. *Microcomputer Dictionary*. 2d edition. Indianapolis: Howard W. Sams, 1981.

Zaks, Rodnay. *Don't! (or How to Care for Your Computer)*. Berkeley, CA: Sybex, 1981.

Magazines

GENERAL-INTEREST PUBLICATIONS

Byte, 70 Main Street, Peterborough, NH 03458; emphasis on hardware and specialized applications.

Creative Computing, P.O. Box 789-M, Morristown, NJ 07960; programming, personal computing emphasis.

Desktop Computing, 80 Pine Street, Peterborough, NH 03458; business and introductory articles.

InfoWorld, 530 Lytton, Palo Alto, CA 94301; weekly newspaper of microcomputers; software reviews.

Interface Age, 16704 Marquardt Avenue, Cerritos, CA 90701; general articles on business and personal computers.

Kilobaud Microcomputing, 80 Pine Street, Peterborough, NH 03458; general, experience-oriented articles; excellent monthly column on networking.

Personal Computing, 50 Essex Street, Rochelle Park, NJ 07662; emphasis on personal use of computers.

Popular Computing, 70 Main Street, Peterborough, NH 03458; general and introductory articles.

SELECTED MAGAZINES FOR SPECIFIC TYPES OF COMPUTERS

Compute!, P.O. Box 5406, Greensboro, NC 27403; for users of Apple, Atari, Commodore, and OSI computers.

DataCast, 345 Swett Avenue, Woodside, CA 94062; for computers using CP/M operating systems, with special emphasis on communications.

80 Micro, 80 Pine Street, Peterborough, NH 03458; for users of TRS-80 computers.

Microsystems, P.O. Box 1192, Mountainside, NJ 07029; for users of CP/M and S-100 computers.

PC, 1528 Irving Street, San Francisco, CA 94122; for users of IBM Personal Computers.

Data-Base Services

DIALOG Information Services, Inc.
3460 Hillview Avenue
Palo Alto, CA 94304
(800) 227-1927 (U.S., except CA)
(800) 982-5838 (CA only)

CompuServe
500 Arlington Centre Boulevard
Columbus, OH 43220
(800) 848-8990
(614) 457-8650 (in Ohio)

The Source
1616 Anderson Road
McLean, VA 22102
(800) 336-3330

Index of Word Processing
and Computing Terms

hot zone, 53
hub (disk), 106
hub (program structure), 128
hyphen, 82

I/O, 30
imbedded command, 94
imbedded pause, 98
indentation, 82
index, 204
index hole, 106
information utility, 220
input, 30
insert line, 69
insert mode, 64
installation, 123
interactive, 122
interface, 30

justified, 83

key commands, 127
key words, 135, 204
keyboard, 32
kilobyte, 30

language, 44
left print position, 88
letter-quality printer, 40
line end, 78
line filter, 143
line height, 100
lines (print), 90
lines/inch, 99
link printing, 138, 192
list (command), 119
load (from disk), 31

machine language, 44
main menu, 48
margin (print), 88-90
margin (screen), 80
margin release, 82
marker system, 134
memory, 30
menu, 45, 127
menu-driven, 128
merge printing, 137

microcomputer, 30
microjustification, 101
micron, 101
microprocessor, 30
microspacing (horizontal), 101
microspacing (vertical), 100
mnemonic, 127
mode, 45, 128
modem, 221
monitor, 36

numbering, 92
numeric keypad, 32

on-screen formatting, 85
output, 30
overtyping, 63

page break, 96
page length, 90
page lines, 90
page numbering, 92
page offset, 88
paragraph end, 78
parallel port, 222
parameter, 124
Pascal, 44
patch, 123
pause print, 97
peripherals, 29
pica, 100
pitch, 100
pixel, 37
place markers, 73
power strip, 143
print buffer, 99
print column, 88
print command, 95, 97–98
print format menu, 94
print formatting, 94
print lines, 90
print margin, 88
print position (left), 88
print to screen, 85
printer driver, 93
program, 28
program disk buffer, 211
program map, 128
program structures, 128
programmable function key, 127

prompt, 45
proportional spacing, 101

quad density, 108
quit, 117

ragged right, 83
RAM, 31
random-access memory, 31
read block, 134
read/write head, 106
read/write hole, 106
reform, 79
reformat, 79
rename, 120
repeat (key), 59
replace, 72
resume print, 98
retrieve, 114
return, 33, 53
reverse video, 37
reworking-in-progress, 154
RGB monitor, 36
ring (program structure), 128
rubout, 64
ruler line, 51, 80

save (to disk), 31, 39, 115
screen formatting, 85
screen margin, 80
scroll, 55
search (and replace), 71
sector, 46
selective replace, 73
serial port, 222
shadow printing, 103
sheet feed, 93
sign-on message, 48
single density, 108
soft hyphen, 83
soft-sectored, 108
software, 28
Source, The, 224
spelling checker, 132
split screen, 136
spooling, 138
spread sheet program, 190

sprint writing, 153
status (utility), 120
status line, 51
stop print, 97
stride writing, 153
strikeover, 103
subscript, 104
superscript, 104
surge protector, 143
system, 22
system (command), 120

tabs, 82, 136
terminal, 32
text file, 94, 110
thesaurus, 133
thimble, 41
toggle key, 127
top margin, 90
track, 46
tractor, 41
translation table, 229
tree (program structure), 128
typesetting codes, 229

underlining, 102
user-defined key, 127
user-friendly, 128
utilities (DOS), 46, 120

vertical microspacing, 100

w/p, 22
wild card, 139
window, 57
word, 53
word edit, 169
word processing, 28
word processor, 28
word wrap, 53
word-usage program, 134
work file, 109, 118
write (to disk), 39
write block, 134
write protect notch, 106

The Electronic History of This Book

Writing in the Computer Age was written on two microcomputer systems and composed by a computer typesetter. Here are the specifics regarding the equipment and programs involved.

Andrew Fluegelman worked on an IBM Personal Computer with a total of 256K of RAM, two 5¼-inch disk drives, and the system's green-and-black monitor, with the PC-DOS (IBM/Microsoft) operating system. His system also included an NEC Spinwriter 5530 printer and a D.C. Hayes Smartmodem for transmission of files at 300 baud.

During the course of preparing the manuscript for this book, he used several word processing programs, including EasyWriter (IBM/Information Unlimited Software), Volkswriter (Lifetree Software), and WordStar (MicroPro International). He wrote a program for converting the EasyWriter and Volkswriter text files into the WordStar text format and a communications program, PC-TALK, for exchanging files.

Jeremy Joan Hewes used a North Star Horizon computer with two 5¼-inch disk drives and 64K of RAM, an IBM 3101 terminal with green-and-black screen, a C. Itoh Starwriter printer, and the D.C. Hayes Smartmodem. Her system uses the CP/M (Digital Research) operating system. She wrote and edited the text for this book with the WordStar word processing program and used SpellGuard (Innovative Software Applications) to check the spelling of the completed text. Her communications program for exchanging files was Micro-TELNET, a CP/M program in the public domain written by Frank J. Wancho.

Individual chapters were written and edited on each of the authors' systems. In some cases, partial drafts of chapters were sent via phone lines from one system to the other for further editing. When all chapters were complete, the IBM PC files were transmitted to the North Star Horizon, where a final composite manuscript was prepared.

The composite manuscript was then transmitted back to the IBM PC system, where special typesetting codes were inserted. After two successful test transmissions, the coded manuscript was transmitted to Design & Type via phone lines at 1200 baud using a Universal Data Systems 212 LP modem. Transmission time for the 600,000 character manuscript, consisting of 18 separate files, was approximately 1½ hours.

Design & Type received the coded manuscript via a Raycal-Vadic 3451 modem, utilizing the communications software on a Computer Composition International CCI 400 input system. Galleys were produced from the coded manuscript files by a Mergenthaler Linotron 202N. The text was composed in Times Roman, with heads in Frutiger 75 and Century Expanded Italic.

The figures depicting sample screens were created as separate WordStar files and printed with the NEC Spinwriter Prestige Renown font, using the IBM PC "PrintScreen" function.

Mechanicals incorporating the galleys and illustrations were produced by hand.

About the Authors

Andrew Fluegelman is founder and owner of The Headlands Press, Inc., an independent book-production firm located in Tiburon, California. He is the editor of *The New Games Book* and author of *More New Games!* (both published by Doubleday/Dolphin and produced by The Headlands Press). Among the other books he has produced are *Sushi* by Mia Detrick (Chronicle/Headlands, 1981), *How to Make and Sell Your Own Record* by Diane Sward Rapaport (Putnam/Headlands, 1978) and *A Traveler's Guide to El Dorado and the Inca Empire* by Lynn Meisch (Penguin/Headlands, 1976). He is also Associate Editor of *PC* magazine, a publication devoted to the IBM Personal Computer, and the author of PC-TALK, a widely used communications program for the IBM PC.

Jeremy Joan Hewes is the author of *Worksteads: Living and Working in the Same Place*, published by Doubleday/Dolphin in association with The Headlands Press (1981); *Redwoods: The World's Largest Trees* (Rand McNally, 1981); and *Build Your Own Playground!* (Houghton Mifflin, 1975); and co-author with E.E. Shev, M.D., of *Good Cops/Bad Cops* (San Francisco Book Company/Stein & Day, 1977). She has been Associate Editor of *PC* magazine since its founding, and she also serves as an editor and consultant for Island Press of Covelo, California. She is producer-writer of the radio series "Inside/Outside" for Island Press. A strong believer in worksteading, she does most of her writing and editing in her home office in San Francisco.